SEQUEL TO DEVIL'S KNOT

DARK SPELL
Surviving The Sentence

✦————————————✦

Mara Leveritt
with Jason Baldwin

BIRD CALL PRESS
LITTLE ROCK

ALSO BY MARA LEVERITT

Devil's Knot
The True Story Of The West Memphis Three

✦━━━━━━━━━━━━━✦

The Boys On The Tracks
Death, Denial, and a Mother's Crusade
to Bring Her Son's Killers to Justice

CONTENTS

BIRD CALL PRESS

For information, contact Mara Leveritt at MaraLeveritt.com
Book Design by PatrickHouston.com

Library of Congress Cataloging-in-Publication Data

Leveritt, Mara.
Dark Spell - Surviving The Sentence / Mara Leveritt.

ISBN – 13: 978-1499175752
ISBN – 10: 1499175752

1. Murder--Arkansas--West Memphis--Investigation Case studies.
2. Judicial Process--Arkansas--West Memphis Case studies.
3. Murder Trial--Arkansas--West Memphis Case studies.
4. Baldwin, Jason. 5. Echols, Damien. 6. Misskelley, Jessie.
7. West Memphis Three--United States--History--20th century.
8. Alford Plea--Arkansas--West Memphis Case studies.

First edition, June, 2014, by Bird Call Press.
Printed in the United States by CreateSpace

To LSB with love

ACKNOWLEDGEMENTS

In memory of Ron Lax, the first supporter
1949 – 2013

I thank my family, the nuclear one that fuels my heart, and the expansive, generous one that has helped me write this book. As I cannot possibly list everyone who has supported me and this project for the past twenty years, I'll take this page simply to thank: Jason Baldwin and Holly Ballard, Christian Hansen and the contributors to Callahan.8k.com, Joe Berlinger, Helen Bennett, Kathy Bakken, Grove Pashley, Burk Sauls, Lisa Fancher, Martin Hill of jivepuppi.com, Laird Williams, Patrick Houston, Stephanie Keet, Mike Poe, Mike Ledford, the family of Booker Worthen, the Central Arkansas Library System, Laman Library, my "DK2" subscribers, the gang at *Arkansas Times*, everyone who granted interviews or helped me get records, and *all* the supporters, attorneys and investigators who helped free the West Memphis Three.

The madness unleashed in West Memphis, Arkansas, in May 1993 ended three young lives and horribly altered three more. Since then, it has touched thousands of other lives—some, like mine, profoundly. I began writing about the murders the summer they occurred, shortly after the teenagers were charged. For a reporter focused not just on "what" but "why," the case became an irritant. Ordinary information was sealed, while key records were released improperly—signaling irregularities to come. When the trials were finally held in 1994, they resembled a dance of phantoms with innuendos more than a rational process. Yet the convictions that resulted were as real as the children's graves.

I wrote *Devil's Knot* to explore the legal underpinnings of verdicts that seemed insupportable. In contrast to the prosecutions, I wanted that book to be as straightforward and emotionally neutral as possible in order to credibly challenge the conclusions of two juries and a state Supreme Court.

Dark Spell is different. First, although Chapters One and Two cover some of the period examined in *Devil's Knot*, including events that preceded and led to the convictions, here these episodes are seen through Jason's eyes, and the book focuses primarily on what followed those convictions. Second, while *Devil's Knot* dealt with all three of the accused, *Dark Spell* is Jason's story. I thank him for letting me relate this painful part of it. Quotes come from letters exchanged while he was in prison, visits with him there, and interviews since his release. Finally, this book makes no attempt at neutrality. While I remain as committed to fact-based reporting as ever, I tell this story plainly as I've come to see it: a tragedy replete with victims and heroes responding to abuses of power.

It is unusual for a reporter to devote so much of her life to a single "story." This case deserves such attention because, in its complexity, it represents so many of the individual problems that plague American courts. A forthcoming book will conclude this Justice Knot Trilogy.[1]

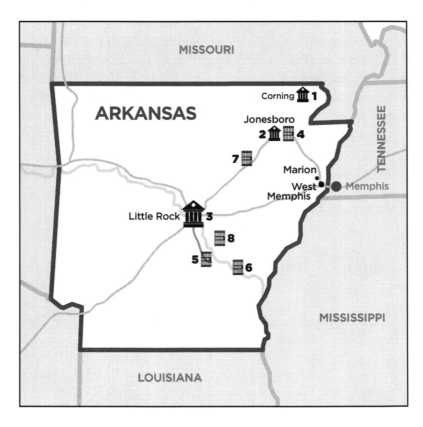

LOCATOR MAP

Jason's World
1 9 7 7 - 2 0 0 7

COURTS

1. Corning District Court
2. Jonesboro District Court
3. Arkansas Supreme Court

JAIL & PRISONS

4. Craighead County Juvenile Detention Center
5. Diagnostic Unit
6. Varner & Supermax
7. Grimes Unit
8. Little Tucker and Tucker Max

"A prosecutor has the responsibility of a minister of justice and not simply that of an advocate. This responsibility carries with it specific obligations to see that the defendant is accorded procedural justice, that guilt is decided upon the basis of sufficient evidence, and that special precautions are taken to prevent and to rectify the conviction of innocent persons."

~ *American Bar Association*

A prosecuting attorney "may prosecute with earnestness and vigor—indeed, he should do so. But, while he may strike hard blows, he is not at liberty to strike foul ones."

~ *Berger v. United States*

"A lawyer should avoid even the appearance of impropriety."

~ *Arkansas Supreme Court, "Rules of Professional Conduct"*

CHAPTER ONE

HOME

April 11, 1977 - June 3, 1993

No child understands the forces that gather before he is born. No one tells children that they've been born into a matrix, especially if it's a dangerous one, in part because some intricacies are too fine even for adults to see. So, like most kids, Jason Baldwin took life at face value. Absorbed in the familiarity of his growing up, he could not imagine the violence at hand, how formally it would come cloaked, or how hard it would try to kill him.

>————————————<

In 1977, the year Jason was born, John A. Fogleman, Chief Justice of the Arkansas Supreme Court, wrote the controversial opinion that declared Arkansas's death penalty to be constitutional.[2] The court's decision was a narrow one, with three of its seven justices dissenting. But Chief Justice Fogleman maintained that Arkansas law provided "adequate safeguards against arbitrary, capricious or freakish imposition of the death penalty."[3]

Jason didn't know that eleven years later, by the summer of 1988, the Chief Justice's nephew, John N. Fogleman, was already serving as a deputy prosecuting attorney in the family's stronghold of eastern Arkansas. Nevertheless, in August of that year, Jason's childhood path would cross that of the up-and-coming young prosecutor.

Jason was about to enter the sixth grade. Prosecutor Fogleman was in his early thirties. The young district attorney had charged a group of trailer park kids, including Jason and his younger brother

Matt, with vandalism. The boys said the cars were junkers, kept in a rusted, overgrown shed with one collapsed wall. To the kids, the shed presented adventure, one of the few places around to play. But the building's owner caught the kids playing there. He claimed the junks were antique autos that the boys had damaged, and he called authorities. Ultimately, that meant Fogleman. The slim, erect prosecutor agreed that the boys had destroyed valuable property. In court, he argued that the lot of them should be sent to reform school.

They weren't. Instead, the court ordered the kids' parents to pay a fine for each child charged—with the understanding that, if they failed to pay, the reform school option would kick in and their children would be taken away. Jason couldn't see well. His vision had been poor since birth, his family too poor to afford glasses. Still, he saw well enough to realize what went on that day in court. He saw that it was all about power. Put simply, the trailer park kids and their families had none, while Fogleman, the scion of a well-established family, wielded it like a prince.

The experience offered Jason an inkling of the adult-world dynamics around him. But he was more focused on school, fishing, his brothers, his cat Charlie, his art—the substantive elements he called "life." Besides, even if someone had been able to explain the malignancies forming around him, Jason would not have believed. A serious but easy-going kid, by the early 1990s, he'd come to love rock music, and though lyrics usually meant little to him, he'd taken to heart the line from one of his favorite band's songs.

"Forever trusting who we are, and nothing else matters..."
~ Metallica

No brave sentiment, however, could protect Jason from the fateful vortex forming around him. Once he was caught in it, five years after the shed incident, he again faced Fogleman in court. This time Jason was sixteen, the prosecutor was planning to run for judge, and Jason, along with two other teenagers, was charged with murdering three children. Only one of the other boys arrested, Damien Echols, had reached the age of eighteen. The third, Jessie Misskelley, Jr. was seventeen. Though Jason and Jessie were still juveniles, Fogleman charged all three as adults, and he announced that he would ask jurors to sentence all three to death.[4] After all, the death penalty was constitutional in Arkansas, even for teenagers—so long as the trials did not rest, as the prosecutor's uncle on the Supreme Court had opined, on anything "arbitrary, capricious or freakish."

Families known as Fogleman (and Fogelman) moved to the area around Memphis, Tennessee, before the Civil War. One branch, the Foglemans, settled on the other side of the Mississippi River, a few miles northwest of Memphis, in the region around the present-day town of Marion, Arkansas.[5] There, a stone marker in front of the Crittenden County Courthouse commemorates the family's role in a monumental historic event that coincided with—and has remained overshadowed by—the assassination of Abraham Lincoln. The marker honors the heroic actions taken by the prosecuting attorney's ancestors in the chaotic days just after Gen. Robert E. Lee's surrender. In the dark of night on April 27, 1865, as President Abraham Lincoln lay dead but not yet buried in Washington, a steamboat overloaded with newly freed prisoners of war exploded in the middle of the Mississippi River, a few miles north of Memphis, Tennessee, and just south of Marion, Arkansas. Only the jubilation over the war's end, followed by the shock of the president's assassination, could have eclipsed news of what still remains America's greatest maritime disaster.

The steamship Sultana was laboring upstream from New Orleans to St. Louis. Built to hold three hundred seventy-five passengers, the boat was packed instead with more than two thousand just-released Union prisoners, three hundred ninety-eight civilians and seventy-five horses. Plowing against a river fast with winter's runoff, the Sultana's engines overheated. While most aboard the boat slept, three of the boat's four boilers exploded, tearing it apart and igniting a blaze that could be seen from Memphis. Passengers were blown into the freezing water, some alive, others instantly dead from scalding steam, fire or shrapnel.[6]

A paper the next day reported: "The river for a mile around was full of floating people; the light of the burning boat shone over a scene such as has never before been witnessed; such as language cannot paint or imagination conceive."[7] An estimated eighteen hundred people perished in the Sultana disaster—almost three hundred more than would die forty-seven years later with the sinking of the Titanic.[8]

Boats from both sides of the river came to help, and almost 500 lives were saved. Men from the Arkansas side, including one named John Fogleman, rescued nearly one hundred of the survivors. That Fogleman and two of his sons lashed together logs that they paddled into the river to raft victims to shore. Thereafter, a newspaper reported: "Mr. Fogleman's residence was converted into a temporary hospital for the sufferers, and every possible care and attention were bestowed on them by Mr. Fogleman and his family."[9]

In the years that followed, the Foglemans of east Arkansas rose to prominence in farming, real estate, politics and law. For generations, the family christened men John. By the end of the twentieth century, when Chief Justice John A. Fogleman was a state Supreme Court justice, his brother Julian Fogleman served as both a deputy prosecuting attorney and Marion's city attorney. John N. Fogleman, Jason's prosecutor, was Julian's son. John N. Fogleman had graduated from law school in Arkansas with honors when Jason was about six. By 1993, when police found three children murdered in the city of West Memphis, a few miles south of Marion, John N. Fogleman had a private law practice and was serving, as had his father, as Marion's city attorney and as a deputy district prosecutor, in addition to holding a seat on the Marion School Board.[10]

Jason's family was almost rootless by comparison. He was born on April 11, 1977, across the river in Memphis to a mother who had earned a high-school equivalency degree and a father who at the time was illiterate. Though Jason's vision suffered from birth, he savored vivid memories, such as sitting on the kitchen floor as a child, scraping cake batter from the sides of a bowl with his finger, while his dad, Charles Baldwin, sat at the table holding Jason's baby brother Matt in his arms. From a later time, he remembered going to the movies—*Beast Master* and *Conan the Barbarian*—with his dad. That was all before his parents divorced when Jason was four.

Jason was five when Gail moved him and Matt across the Mississippi River to Marion, where the three lived just down the road from Gail's mother in her home at Lakeshore Trailer Park. Jason started kindergarten in Marion. But when Gail married another man, Terry Ray Grinnell, the family moved again, back across the river, to a community north of Memphis, where Jason attended first grade. Every Sunday and Wednesday, Gail took him and Matt to a Southern Baptist church. Jason liked the Bible stories in Sunday school and though his mom didn't talk about the Bible at home, Jason felt "she lived it." He believed she instilled in him the "the flavor" of the Bible.

With second grade came a new little brother, named Terry after his dad, and a "nicer" house in Memphis. Jason started another school, his third in as many years, but he didn't mind the changes. Life was an adventure to him. The new house had trees that he and Matt could climb, and they reveled in the freedom of riding their bikes to school. Sometimes, their stepdad took them fishing. Other times, the family would drive back to their former trailer park in Marion to visit Gail's mother. Jason's grandmother owned a regular-sized trailer at Lakeshore, in which she lived. But she also owned a doublewide that fronted the park's namesake lake, and this she rented out. One summer, while Jason was visiting, one of Gail's brothers built a dock on the rental property into the lake. Jason hung around during the construction and got to know Mrs. Littleton, the woman next door. He helped her with various chores, and she brought lemonade to him and the builders.

But home was back in Memphis, and there, life was rough and getting rougher. Terry, Sr., worked maintenance at a motel. He stayed sober during the workweek but drank heavily on the weekends. Gail and her boys suffered living with a weekend drunk. Jason remembered: "He'd be off in the bars, and she'd get us all in the car, going out in the middle of the night, going into bars, checking and looking for him. It happened every weekend. He was responsible at his job, but on weekends, he'd go out to shoot pool. He was good at it. He won our washer and dryer by shooting pool. But he'd also be drinking. Mom would be trying to get him to come home. There'd be arguments. He'd be yelling. It would escalate to violence. I'd have to run out the door to the neighbors to get them to call the cops. And there we were—me and Matt—having school the next day."

At first, only Gail felt Terry's direct violence. "He didn't take it out on us until later on," Jason said. Finally, Gail ended it. Jason was almost at the end of fifth grade when he and Matt came home from school one day to find Gail's mother at their house. Again, they packed. And again, Gail—now with three boys in tow—crossed the river to Marion, to move in with her mother.

In Marion Jason turned eleven and Matt nine. They had few places to play in the trailer park, but the fallen-in building with the old cars was a favorite. "Some of the cars were burnt out, with trees growing up through them," he recalled. "They looked like they'd been there for years. None of them had windows. And the shed had only three walls. It was like a Little Rascals place. All the kids played there all summer." Jason doesn't remember damaging the cars, and Matt doesn't recall Jason "breaking anything," either. However, Matt does remember that he was "jumping from one antique car to another" and that "a lot of us were wrecking the place." Whatever was going on, the fun ended with the appearance of two men demanding to know, "What are you kids doing in here?"

"We told them we were playing," Jason said. "They said, 'Y'all just wait right here.' And we did. Then they went and called the cops. The police took us all to jail. Our parents had to pick us up. The next thing I knew, we needed a public defender." Jason's only memory of the attorney who was assigned to represent him and Matt was that "he just gave us a New Testament and told us everything would be okay."[11]

Jason recalled that he, Matt and the other boys were charged with breaking and entering. The owner of the shed claimed that some of the cars were damaged and that at least one headlight had been shot out. Jason remembers the chill he felt when he heard Fogleman recommend that all of the children be sentenced to two years in reform school. He remembers his even greater shock upon hearing his own attorney agree that "That would probably be for the best." In the end, however, Jason, Matt and the other kids were placed on probation. His mother, now named Gail Grinnell, was ordered to pay a fine of four hundred fifty dollars for each of her two boys.[12]

Nine hundred dollars was a lot for a woman who could never spend more than one hundred dollars for her three children at Christmas. One family had four children who'd been at the shed. These parents would spend years trying to pay off the fines, while their children now all had records.

For Jason, the episode slid into the category of "life's disappointments," where it joined poverty, an absent dad, a fragile mom and a drunken stepdad. But his nature bent towards resilience. On the cusp of adolescence, he envisioned a better life for himself and his family. Unconsciously embracing "the American dream," he looked for what was hopeful and kept his focus on that.

> **"Half of the harm that is done in this world is due to people who want to feel important."**
> ~ *T.S. Eliot*

Whatever they did in that shed, the kids clearly should not have entered. The court held them responsible, and their families suffered the consequences. That, supposedly, was justice. But "justice" has always played favorites, especially with regard to its own. For example, Fogleman, as a young prosecutor, made some mistakes of his own. And though it could be argued that they bore consequences much more severe than whatever damage was done to the cars, and though, like the kids, courts found him at fault, he suffered no penalty.

By the time Fogleman charged Jason, Matt and the other children with vandalism and threatened them with reform school, the Arkansas Supreme Court had already cited Fogleman's improper conduct in orders that reversed two high-profile convictions he'd won. The first concerned Fogleman's prosecution of a fifteen year-old boy from West Memphis. Ronald Ward was in the seventh grade—and had been for three years—when Fogleman took him to trial in 1985 for the fatal stabbing of two elderly sisters and their twelve year-old great-grandnephew. The jury found Ward guilty, and Judge David Burnett, a former prosecutor himself—and the judge who would later officiate at Jason's trial—pronounced Ward's sentence of death.

Ward became the youngest person on death row in the United States, and his sentence drew national attention. In an interview weeks after his trial, Ward, an African-American, claimed that he was innocent. "When they gave me an all-white jury," he told a reporter, "right then I said, this is not going to be a fair trial." Two years later, on Ward's direct appeal in 1987, the Arkansas Supreme Court agreed that Ward's trial had, indeed, been unfair.

In reversing Ward's conviction, the high court noted, "All of the peremptory challenges exercised by the prosecuting attorney—eight in this case—were used to strike black people from the jury." The Supreme Court found that Fogleman's use of the peremptory challenges had violated the Equal Protection Clause of the U.S. Constitution and thus denied Ward a fair trial. The Arkansas Supreme Court wrote that "any prosecutor who uses all of his peremptory challenges to strike black people [from the jury] better have some good reasons." The Court found that some of the reasons Fogleman had offered "were exactly the type of explanations the United States Supreme Court said were unsatisfactory."[13]

Ward was retried before Burnett. This time the jury sentenced him to life in prison.

Fogleman's other early reversal as a prosecutor came in a case that also resulted in a sentence of life in prison. There, the Supreme Court ruled that Fogleman had failed in his "duty" as an officer "of the State and the court to come forth with critical evidence." The court ruled that Fogleman's "error consisted of the withholding of significant evidence," thus denying the defendant a fair trial.[14]

To some, unfair trials that result in sentences of death or life in prison would seem more serious than a spate of vandalism—if that's what it was—by kids who were not yet teenagers. But, as law is a world unto itself, prosecutors can make life-threatening mistakes and not be held accountable.[15]

While Fogleman was forging his career on a path that seemed to be tracking his uncle's, Jason's path was laid by his mother. Because of her move back to Arkansas, Jason started sixth grade at Marion Elementary School, where word quickly got around that the new kid was on probation. Jason didn't know anyone, but he'd changed schools before. He'd found it easy to make friends. Even so, he wasn't prepared for the first day there. As soon as Jason's class went outside to recess, a short kid flew at him out of nowhere, fists flying. Startled, but quick, Jason avoided the blows. Then the short kid started chasing Jason, hollering like he meant to kill him. Jason kept well ahead but wondered: "What's up with this little guy? He must be nuts." Finally, a girl named Donna Spurlock yelled, "Hey, Jessie, leave him alone." The short kid stopped. Donna came to straighten things out. She told Jessie Misskelley, Jr., to promise not to mess with Jason anymore. Jessie promised. Jason shrugged. "Kids fight," he later said. "It's like that everywhere. It was just the playground hierarchy."

Jessie was a sixth-grader too, but in a different class. The two saw each other only at recess. Jason had no idea where Jessie—or, for that matter, where most of the kids at his school—lived. When Jason wasn't at school, the winding roads of Lakeshore Trailer Park constituted his world. The trailer park was home, but it was socially isolating. Most of his school friends lived in houses, either near the town's center or in subdivisions. They lived so far away he couldn't ride his bike there to play. Jason felt the physical separation as "sort of a cultural gap." But he also understood that the trailer park was only part of what separated him and Matt from their classmates. Poverty was the big divide. For the brothers, it was a good—and a not-so-good – thing when teachers brought them second-hand clothes.

Tastes in music also distinguished the brothers from most of their peers. Gail loved rock 'n' roll, and she'd passed that love on to her boys. But, although Elvis came to be revered in these parts after his death in 1977, four months after Jason was born, the region as a whole viewed rock with deep suspicion. Preachers warned that the devil was in it, ensnaring those who listened, using them for his purposes. Heavy metal was the worst. Gail didn't believe that and neither did Jason. "I was raised to listen to rock music," he later wrote. "My mom listened to it so I did too." By sixth grade, his fingers itched to play the guitar. Of course, for a family that couldn't buy eyeglasses, a guitar was out of the question.

Nevertheless, Jason did get a guitar when he was in sixth grade— if only for a night. 'A kid who lived around the corner from him had a guitar that sat, unused, in his closet. Jason asked if he could borrow it. The kid had a better idea. "I'll give it to you," he said. "But you have to give me all your rock t-shirts, all your cassettes, your Nintendo, your skateboard, your jacket—and your bicycle." Jason said they had a deal. Plans were made. At midnight, Jason loaded all the booty into a backpack, rode his bike to the boy's house and knocked on his window; the transaction was made. "I said, 'Okay, thanks,' and went home and jammed until like 7:30 or 8 in the morning," Jason recalled. "That's when I heard a knock on the door and there stood his mom holding all my stuff." Over time, Jason came to regard the episode as part of a pattern that ran through his life, one he described as "having and not having, experiencing and not experiencing, good stuff and bad."

Once Gail had divorced Jason and Matt's dad, Charles Baldwin, she never mentioned him to the boys again. There were no pictures of him in the house. It was as though he had never lived. But one day, after an absence of eight years, Charles Baldwin came back. Gail allowed him to see his sons only after he'd promised her that he would not reveal who he was. But the promise made no difference. Jason knew his father immediately. His memories—like those of the movies the two had seen together—were clear. However, as the adults seemed intent on believing the boys didn't know, Jason went along. The charade finally ended when the couple drove to a store where Gail got out of the car to buy cigarettes. The man turned around to Jason, who was sitting in the back seat, and asked, "You know who I am, Boy?" "Yeah," Jason answered. "You're my dad." When Gail returned, Jason's dad looked at her, jerked his head in Jason's direction and said, "He knows who I am." Furious, Gail ordered Charles to leave. Before he did, Jason recalled, his dad told him, "You should tell your mom to get you some glasses."

Even without glasses, Jason liked school and did well in it. He had the advantage of a last name that started with "B," which got him a front-row seat in Marion's alphabetically arranged classrooms. He could see the teacher and the blackboard. Though Jason had a couple of other strikes against him—poverty and probation— he had a gift for getting along. When Steve Jones, his probation officer, visited the school to check on him as the court required, the two would sit and talk. "I'd show him my report card," Jason said. "And sometimes when he came to the house to talk to my mom, he'd even buy us sodas. He was real nice and respectful. He never abused his authority. I always felt he thought it was a load of crap that we got arrested, but since we did, the visits were okay. They were just him doing his job."

By the time Jason got to seventh grade, his grandma's renters had moved out. She gave Gail and her three boys the doublewide by the lake. The boys loved having the dock and fished from it whenever they could, catching crappie, bass, catfish and brim, with their cat Charlie hanging around, doing some fishing himself. Gail would cook the catch with hushpuppies for dinner, and if the weather was good, she'd fry it—and they'd eat it—right there on the dock, tossing bread to the ducks as the sun set. Mrs. Littleton next door would be on her dock too, regaling the family with stories of catches from the past.

Life in the trailer beside the lake flowed between the ordinary tasks of home and school, the pleasures of music, art and goofing around, and visits with Jones, the probation officer. Eighth and ninth grades came and went. School was going well. But Gail had resumed seeing Terry. About a month after the family moved into the bigger trailer, Terry had moved in too. He'd quit his job in Memphis, saying that he would take care of the house and children while Gail supported the family of five, working nights at her job as a truck dispatcher in Memphis. "My mom and Terry loved each other, and there were promises to do better," Jason said. "But old habits die hard, I guess. They returned to the old patterns pretty quickly. I remember she'd be yelling at him, and he'd slap her, and I'd be, like, 'Stop!' and stuff, and Matt would be too, and he'd turn around and punch us."

Though Jason had no idea that Fogleman sat on the school board, he felt that he was getting a good education in Marion, and he appreciated it. However, he also realized by the ninth grade that not everyone valued school as he did. He knew, for instance, that Jessie Misskelley, whose family had recently moved to Lakeshore, was struggling, even in his special education classes. And he recognized that Damien Echols, one of the smart kids he knew, was just marking time in school. Damien was more than two years older than Jason, but the two were in the same grade, in part because Damien had had to repeat the fifth grade. In Jason's view, "Damien was just there because he had to be. He was pretty much a smart aleck. He didn't really have much respect for the teachers."[16]

For about a year and a half, while Jason was in the eighth and ninth grades, he and Jessie lived on the same street. "We got to know each other," Jason said. "We got to be pretty good friends." The two rode the same bus to school. "We'd play dodge ball or kick ball while we were waiting. We'd have a good time." Jason knew that Jessie had been charged once with theft of property, but having been judged by some people for being poor and by the court for the shed incident, he preferred not being judgmental.

As for the theft, Jessie told Jason that he thought he was doing a good deed. Walking home one day, he'd taken a shortcut through a field. There, he'd seen the strangest thing: a bunch of flags lying on the ground with no one in sight. He said he didn't even think about it; he just picked up the flags and took them home. He said he was going to ask his dad what he should do with them but until then he would protect them. However, before he saw his father to ask his advice, the flags were noticed missing, and someone had seen Jessie Jr. picking them up from the field. That's when Jessie Jr. was arrested and catapulted into the world of juvenile justice.

One day, while riding his bike in Lakeshore, Jason was surprised to see Damien riding his skateboard there. As it turned out, Damien and his family had moved to the trailer park too. Among the kids who lived there, Jason had far more in common with Damien than he did with Jessie, and before long, Jason and Damien were hanging out together. "Usually, that's how it goes," Jason said. "You spend time with friends who live close to you. It's hard for a kid to have long-distance friends. It's not like you had everybody in the world at your fingertips to choose from. He was there."

Connected by circumstance, the two became best friends. They'd go to each other's houses, play Nintendo, and listen to cassettes. Jason introduced Damien to Metallica, explaining how Metallica "can build all these different harmonies and melodies with their single instruments, and yet the music that they build independently becomes an instrument in itself, to make the overall song." In turn, Damien shared his appreciation of Pink Floyd, Guns n' Roses, and Nine Inch Nails.

Jason thought his mom was strict because she made him check in at home, in person, every hour. But Damien's mom was even more watchful. "A lot of times, I'd go over to his house, and his parents wouldn't let him have company or come out," Jason said. "I thought that was weird. But gradually, after his mom talked to my mom, she would let him come to my house. It was like going through an act of Congress just for us to play together." Often the friends only sat on the dock, chucking rocks into the lake. Sometimes Damien smoked cigarettes. Jason never did. "People thought we did drugs because we looked wild, but we didn't," Jason said. "We didn't need them."

Still, both boys were aware that their lives were not what they wanted. Jason understood by now that his mom suffered from depression, and he recognized the same illness in Damien. He believed that their friendship helped him. With few opportunities to do much else, the two did a lot of walking. "We used to walk to the local Walmart and bowling alley all the time," Jason said, "even when we didn't have any money. Neither one of us ever had any money. We definitely never had twenty bucks! We could maybe get five or ten to go to the bowling alley or the skating rink, where we would just enjoy being around people, especially the girls. That is basically why we went to these places: to meet new girls, shoot pool, and play video games."

Damien and Jason shared the clunk and splash of rocks in the lake, the fun of pool or video games, the prospect of meeting girls, and a sense of their lives' limitations. But they also respected their differences. Jason wore mostly blue jeans with t-shirts featuring the bands he liked. Damien dressed to distinguish himself. He preferred to wear all black—black pants and plain black t-shirts. Though Jason's family no longer went to church, Jason had read the Bible, felt a personal relationship with God, and "talked with Jesus like a brother." He could not remember a time when he did not pray. Damien, on the other hand, was more curious about religion, spirituality, and the possibilities of magic. The two didn't discuss that much. "I was a Christian, and I didn't care about the rest of that stuff," Jason said. "But I always supported his quest for knowledge."

The boys regarded their families differently too. In Jason's view, "Damien didn't have any respect for his mom or his dad, or even his sister, really." By contrast, Jason loved his mom. He respected and obeyed her. He accepted the responsibilities she gave him, like washing dishes, mowing the yard, taking out the trash, helping his brothers with their homework, and watching them when Terry, Sr., wasn't home. Jason also helped his grandmother and his neighbor Mrs. Littleton. Every now and then, he acknowledged, he got "resentful" because he didn't have "more nice things and more freedom." But his mom told him often how proud she was of him and how much she appreciated him, and to Jason, that love and approval mattered more than anything else.

In the spring of 1992, when Jason was nearing the end of ninth grade, Damien, seventeen, and his fifteen-year-old girlfriend, Deanna Holcomb, feeling thwarted by her family, decided to run away. As Jason recalled, it was an intense and complicated situation. Deanna's family had forbidden her to see Damien. In the void left by that edict, Damien had found Domini Teer. "Their love was passionate and wild," Jason said. "However, when Deanna started flirting again with Damien in the high school hallways, Damien responded. He would flirt with her during school hours, then after school, promise love to Domini. This worked until Deanna found out and gave Damien the ultimatum that if he truly loved her he would run away with her. In deciding to go with Deanna, he broke Domini's heart.

Damien and Deanna tried to talk Jason, who was thirteen at the time, into coming with them. "They said it would be a big adventure. We'd go to California and escape our miserable lives." But Jason declined, explaining that his mom and brothers needed him. "I tried to talk them out of it," he recalled, "but her parents forbade them to see each other, and they felt it was the only way they could be together."

The romantic escapade failed before it began, when Damien and Deanna, neither of whom could drive—let alone obtain a car—took refuge from a thunderstorm in an unoccupied house trailer. "That was a sad, dark day," Jason said. Damien and Deanna were caught and arrested. Damien was charged with burglary, breaking and entering, disorderly conduct, sexual misconduct, and terroristic threatening. At the time, Jason didn't know what had happened to his friend.

What he did know was that, right after Damien's arrest, Jason's mother grounded him for weeks because of the incident. Jason never understood why he was grounded because, after all, he'd chosen to stay home. While Jason was grounded despite his sound decision, Damien's family moved away to Portland, Oregon. The whole situation was hard. Because of the family's move and because Jason was grounded, he never got a chance to say goodbye to Damien's sister, Michelle. Only a few days earlier, he and Michelle had begun holding hands—and even kissed. Until Damien returned, Jason had no idea what had happened to him or his family. They were simply gone. For Jason, that summer passed strangely. He and Domini both missed Damien.

Gail was protective—but fragile. It wasn't unusual for her to freak out when an accident happened. Jason recalled one time in 1992, when his mom, his brothers, and some other kids were fishing from the dock, and Terry, who was seven or eight at the time, was rummaging through the tackle box. Inside the box was a knife that some cousins in Mississippi had given to Jason a few years before. Terry began whacking the dock with the knife and cut himself in the process. He wasn't seriously hurt, but when Gail saw the blood, Jason said, "She got real upset. She grabbed that knife and threw it into the lake."[17]

"Who knows what true loneliness is - not the conventional word but the naked terror? To the lonely themselves it wears a mask. The most miserable outcast hugs some memory or some illusion."

~ Joseph Conrad

Months passed before Jason saw Damien again. "He was gone that whole summer between ninth and tenth grades," Jason said.

"He was in jail, the training school, mental institutions—he went through all types of hell, all this crazy stuff. And then his family moved to Portland, Oregon." Damien went with them. But Oregon didn't work out.

Damien returned to Marion at the end of the summer of 1992, about when Jason started tenth grade. Jason learned that Damien had tried to enroll in school, that school officials had rejected him, and that he was on probation now too, though not assigned to Steve Jones. Instead, Damien was being supervised by Jones's boss, Jerry Driver.

Jason had experience with Driver. "He was a funny cat, very strange," he said. "He was large, with a full beard. Upon first glance, he reminded me of Santa Claus or Grizzly Adams, but upon talking to him, you knew that this man could not be either one of those noble men because he was too untrusting and very devious."

A couple of unsettling encounters had given Jason that impression. "I don't remember when I first met him," he said, "but I remember him coming to my house one time to ask me some questions about a BB gun and the railroad tracks. He pulled up in my drive and told me who he was and that he was investigating an incident that had occurred at the railroad tracks. Someone had shot something with a BB gun, and a person gave a description that supposedly matched me. He asked if I had a BB gun, and I said yes, but I had not shot anything up with it, besides the occasional water moccasin that crawled unwanted into our back yard from the lake. He still asked to see it, so I went inside and got it for him. He waited in his car. He looked at it and opened the place where the BBs go and dropped a few into his hand. He asked me if I ever used gold BBs. No, I always used the silver ones. 'Why is that,' he asked, and my answer was just because they came in a bigger pack than the gold ones and lasted longer. He then asked me about a laser that I knew nothing about. He said that was all and left."

Another time, when Jason was with Damien and Domini, the three ran into Driver at the local Walmart. "We were coming out of the store when we saw him," Jason said, "and he made some smart remark about us being a coven of witches or Damien being a vampire. I looked at him like he was crazy for saying such a thing, and Damien just laughed at his judgmental ignorance and stupidity, the way he laughs at everyone who picks on him for no true reason. Damien always laughed when people tried to hurt him." Jason admired his friend's ability "to shrug off things of that nature."

Besides placing Damien on probation, the court had ordered him to earn his GED, which he did. Damien had moved in with his adoptive stepfather, Jack Echols, in Lakeshore, intending to join his stepfather in the roofing trade. But the two did not get along, and when Damien started drawing Social Security Disability benefits—a result of having been diagnosed with bipolar disorder—he quit doing physical labor. A few months later, when Damien's mother and sister moved back from Oregon, Damien moved in with them.

Jason was glad to have him back. Damien said that the only reason he'd returned to Arkansas was that he'd had no friends in Oregon and that here, at least, he had Jason. "He didn't want to talk about all he'd been through," Jason said. "He just said it was BS and it sucked. I sensed it was a hard time for him. I didn't ask him a lot of questions. I definitely wasn't going to make him relive it."[18]

But Driver proved a constant reminder. "Driver just harassed him," Jason said. "Damien felt helpless and powerless, like they controlled his life. I was still on probation myself, but Steve Jones was okay. Damien had a totally different experience with Driver."

By now, Jason had known Jones for five years. He was used to having Jones "hound" him, as he put it, for wearing rock and roll t-shirts. Jason accepted this as Jones "messing around" with him and didn't care. But once Driver took charge of Damien, it was clear to Jason that both men "absolutely hated Damien." Jason wrote that Driver "told all the kids in the neighborhood that Damien was a Satan-worshipping faggot and that he hated blacks. This caused all types of trouble for Damien. Someone always wanted to kick him down, but he was smarter than that. He thought it was humorous, all the rumors about him. He didn't realize how seriously a lot of people took his name and what was said and how he looked. From then on, Steve Jones would lead the 'anti-Damien' campaign across Marion and West Memphis—he and Jerry Driver. They were not the only people in authority that hated Damien, either."

While Jason sympathized with the troubles clouding life for Damien, he was dealing with storms of his own. Life by the lake had its idyllic—and sometimes hysterical—moments, but mostly, inside the trailer, it had gotten rough again. And Jason, now fifteen, got into trouble again. In November 1992, he stole a six-ounce bag of potato chips and a thirty-two ounce bag of M&Ms from a Walgreen's store in West Memphis, and the manager called the cops. This was nothing like the shed incident. Jason knew when he lifted the candy and chips that what he was doing was wrong. As he was being arrested, the officer gave him a stern talking-to, "sort of man-to-man," Jason recalled, about how this wasn't the way to go. Officers took him to the jail and released him to his mother's custody.[19] Jason considers the shoplifting his first—and only—crime.

But it was more than that. By shoplifting, Jason had jeopardized the vision he'd embraced since childhood. He'd seen life as a kind of deal, believing that if he held up his end, the other side—whatever that was—would hold up its end as well. If he worked in school, he would graduate. If he helped his mom, she'd be able to take care of the family. If he kept his life on track, despite what he saw around him, it would lead him to something better beyond the trailer park. A shoplifting charge could have derailed that. Jason regarded the incident as serious—a warning he would heed. He remained on probation. He remained dedicated to his family. He remained serious about school. And he rededicated himself to his vision. He would not let down his end again.

But life was getting crazy. Shortly before Christmas, Charles Baldwin, Jason and Matt's biological father, reappeared again. This time, he took Jason and Matt away with him, to visit to his home in central Arkansas. There, Jason met his paternal grandparents for only the second time in his life—the first having been when he was four. The boys found themselves in a bigger house than they had ever known before, and they heard stories of a side of their family they'd barely known existed. Jason's dad told him he was going to buy him a truck and teach him to drive. The prospect tantalized, but the visit was short.

When Jason and Matt returned to Marion, they asked their mom if they could go back to live with their dad for a while—maybe spend the next school year with him. Gail went to pieces. "She had a nervous breakdown," Jason said. "She told us we didn't love her anymore. She tried to commit suicide. She slit her wrists and neck and stuff." (Jason paused a long time with that memory.) "Yeah, I found her," he said. "In the bathroom. Yeah, I called 911." After that, neither boy mentioned the idea of going to live with their father again.

Yet their resignation could not alleviate other tensions seething at home. Terry's abuse was becoming unbearable. About a month before the end of school, just after he'd turned sixteen, Jason threw Terry, Sr. out of the house. "It wasn't pretty," he recalled. In truth, it had been awful.

"Oh, man, it was bad. It was bad," Jason said. "He was beating my mom. I told him to stop. There was a big scene. I grabbed a baseball bat. I was telling him to stop and that this was unacceptable when he turned around and grabbed the bat and punched me with it. I went flying and landed in the hallway. Little Terry was in a bedroom right where I landed. He was about nine. He looked out and held out a little bat to help pull me up. I took that little bat, and this time I hit Terry with it. He hit the ground. I opened the door and said, 'Leave!'

"My mom freaked out on me for hitting him. Yeah, it was bad. I was like, 'Dang. How are you going to defend this guy?' He'd been beating on her for years and years, and beating on us, and now she's going to get mad at me for hitting him one time? After all this? I didn't want to hit him with the bat, but this had been going on ever since I was eight years old and had to go running down the street, getting neighbors to call the cops on him. It was crazy."

The present was grim, but Jason still nurtured hopes for his future. He had a girlfriend named Heather, whom he knew from school. Heather didn't live in the trailer park, but her folks liked Jason, and Gail liked Heather, so the parents helped the kids spend time together, skating at the rink or having dinners at each other's homes. "Between her mom and my mom," Jason said, "they always made sure they knew where we were at and what we were doing."

Mrs. Littleton next door liked him and wanted to repay him for his help over the years. When she'd return from shopping, he'd carry in her groceries and help put them away, and when she wanted to visit relatives in Tennessee, he would go with her so she wouldn't be on the road alone. When he told Mrs. Littleton that he'd landed a summer job at a grocery store, she promised she would match, "dollar-for-dollar," whatever money he earned.

Jason was to start the job on June 7, 1993, the Monday after school let out. With his pay and Mrs. Littleton's help, he planned to buy a car and some new clothes, and to put away some money. He felt he was on his way.

> "Everybody's got plans... until they get hit."
>
> ~ Mike Tyson

1993 was a big year in Arkansas. On January 20, Bill Clinton, the state's former governor, became President of the United States. Arkansans felt a sense of greatness at hand. But less than four months later, on May 6, 1993, fear gripped the eastern half of the state. It reached across the river, to Tennessee and Mississippi. It reached into Jason's school, where he heard the news in the halls: "They found some kids murdered in West Memphis!" Jason could only think of his brother Terry—just a year older than the victims. When he got home, his mom fretted about having to leave for work. She told Jason to stay inside and watch out for his brothers because a killer was on the loose. "The whole town went into an uproar of panic and hurt and frenzy," he said. "It was real serious and it hit close to home for everybody."

Even so, by the next day, he had other things on his mind. Just the week before, he had won an armload of prizes at the high school's art show, including a plaque for "Most Creative." The recognition felt good, and Jason thought he might find his way into a career in art. But those dreams still seemed far off. For now—killer or no killer—his thoughts were focused on his girlfriend, finishing the eleventh grade, starting his job, having some fun, and ultimately, buying a car.

But the vortex Jason didn't know existed—the unseen tornado—was drawing near. Within twenty-four hours of the murders, a West Memphis narcotics detective had already concluded that the killings bore "overtones of a cult sacrifice." The detective, Lt. James Sudbury, had already discussed his theory with Steve Jones, Jason's probation officer, and the two had agreed, as Sudbury later wrote, that of all the people they knew "to be involved in cult type activities," Damien "stood out" to them both as "capable of being involved in this type of crime." If Jason had known any of that, he might have been alarmed when Damien told him that Jones and Sudbury had come by his house on the day after the murders to talk to him. As it was, Jason wasn't even particularly concerned when two other West Memphis police officers came to his house on Sunday, May 9, three days after the murders, asking if Damien was there. "I put two and two together," he said. "By then, we'd seen the news and heard all the rumors about what had happened to the boys." He figured the police were talking to everyone, trying to solve the murders, and that struck him as reasonable.

In fact, Damien was at Jason's house. "They asked him if he'd heard anything," Jason recalled. "When he said, 'Yeah,' they asked, 'What have you heard?' Then: 'What do you think happened?' and 'Do you think it's possible that…?' Damien would say, 'Well, I guess…', and then they wrote it down as 'Damien said…' They asked, 'Do you think it's possible that Satanists would have done this?' I remember them asking that point-blank. And, of course, Damien, being open, and almost seeing himself as an expert, he wanted to offer what he knew to help."[20]

Damien was willing to imagine, to speculate. Not Jason. When the officers turned their attention to him, repeating similar questions, Jason told them, "I don't play no guessing games." Then Jason's mom showed up. "She came back home early that day," he said, "and she pretty much just ran them off."

That was the last Jason saw of the police. Even when Damien told him that the police had later taken him to the station to be questioned again, Jason still didn't think much of it. "I just knew something bad had happened to some kids, and that's all I wanted to know," he said. "I just didn't want to hear about it. I didn't want to think about it. I was just trying to live my life and get by with my family and stuff. I didn't give the cops much of a thought. I figured they'd sort it out in time."

All he knew on the last day of school, Thursday, June 3, 1993, was that on the following Monday he'd begin work at his new job and that, in the meantime, he planned to have some fun. That night he joined Damien at his house to watch some rented movies. Damien's mother and dad were going to the new casino across the river at Tunica, Mississippi. Jason said that, as they planned to stay there overnight, they'd rented a VCR and some movies "to keep us busy for the night."

Everyone was looking forward to a good time. But Damien's mother, Pam Echols, left with a word of caution because "apparently, all this time, Damien had been being harassed by the police," Jason said. "Pam told us, 'If cops come to the door, don't let them in. Act like there's nobody here.' She didn't want any drama. She said, 'Don't even let them in if they knock on the door.'"

When the adults were gone, the kids sat in the living room watching Leprechaun, a grade-B horror film. As usual, Jason sat on the floor, close to the television, to see. Behind him, Damien, his sister Michelle and Damien's girlfriend Domini sat on the couch. Suddenly, "Michelle jumped up," Jason said. "She thought somebody was in the front yard. She said, 'You know what Mom said. Act like nobody's here.' So we turned the lights and the TV off and went into the bedroom. But they were banging on the door. They said, 'We know you're in there. We saw the lights go out.' So then we came out and they arrested Damien. They told the rest of us to sit on the couch. Then they came back and arrested me. Michelle said, 'I want your names and badge numbers,' but they just told her to sit down and shut up.'"

Years later, Jason would compare the experience to a scene in the movie Saving Private Ryan, about the Allied troops' D-Day storming of the beaches in Normandy. At one point, the character played by Tom Hanks is overcome by the ordeal. His vision blurs. Time slows. The sounds of shelling grow muted. "That's exactly what I was going through right then, when they arrested me," he said. "Already I couldn't see, and I could hardly hear. I couldn't believe this stuff was happening. I was just in shock—a state of disbelief."[21]

CHAPTER TWO

JUVENILE DETENTION

June 4, 1993 - March 20, 1994

Jason sat in the back of a squad car, hands cuffed behind his back, struggling to understand. Damien was led off somewhere else. What was happening? He had no idea that Jessie Misskelley already sat bewildered in jail.

Indeed, Jessie sat in a cell at the West Memphis Police Department, battling his own shock and confusion. When he'd come to the station that morning, he'd thought he would help the police and then return home to his father. He'd cooperated with the detectives for hours, only to be told at the end, late that afternoon, that he would not be going home at all.

Jessie knew nothing of what Jason and Damien were experiencing at that moment, much less that he was the cause. Jessie's imagination would have had to reach even further to calculate the relief he'd brought to the police officers who'd arrested him. Before today, they'd had statements pointing to Damien, but nothing substantive enough to warrant his arrest, much less the arrests of Jason and Jessie.[22] But now, with all three teenagers in custody thanks to what Jessie had said, the department's month-long professional impotence was over. The pressure to find the killer or killers of three murdered children had lifted. Citizens could relax, as could the region's elected officials, who needed arrests to support their image of control. Until Jessie spoke into their tape recorder, the police had turned up nothing: no evidence and therefore, no case to present to the prosecutor. To Jessie's dismay—and to officials' relief—sometime on June 3, 1993, Fogleman and a judge decided that Jessie's recorded words alone provided probable cause to arrest him, Damien, and Jason.

As Jason was being driven to police headquarters, he did not know that what was unfolding around him was the result of events that finally had come together that morning, when detectives went to talk to Jessie. Jessie had no idea why the detectives wanted to talk to him, but he was not the kind of kid who would say 'no' to the police.

For hours, cramped in a small room at the station, Jessie told the detectives all kinds of things, most of which they themselves dismissed, knowing that they were inaccurate. With guided questioning, however, Jessie began giving answers in which the officers heard hints of plausibility—and possibility. Maybe the detectives believed the special-ed kid when he said that he had witnessed the murders and that he'd even participated in them. Maybe they excused everything he'd said that was mixed-up or contrary to their theory as the talk of someone too stupid—or too cunning—to tell a straight story. Or maybe they'd just heard what they wanted—and needed—to hear: a few disjointed fragments from an expendable kid who offered the police an escape from the onus of three unsolved murders. Detectives turned on their tape recorder twice while they had Jessie in the room. In total, they recorded forty-six minutes—about a tenth—of his interrogation. Even those forty-six minutes, however, made for a sloppy story. Jessie jumbled facts that were widely known, together with claims that the police themselves knew to be utter fiction. He contradicted himself so often police can be heard on the recordings attempting to straighten him out.

In contrast, parts of Jessie's disorganized utterances were treated with meticulous care. While junking much of what Jessie said, the officers accorded some of his statements the weight of solid evidence. Prompted by one of his questioners, Jessie had spoken the words, "when we had that cult," lending support to the theory that Sudbury and Jones had developed within twenty-four hours of finding the bodies. Jessie had witnessed Damien and Jason abusing and murdering the children. He had even said he'd assisted the killers, irrationally implicating himself.[23] Against a backdrop of nothing, the police saw these selected statements within selected recordings as more than sufficient. They presented them to the prosecutor as a legitimate confession to a heinous crime. In turn, Fogleman agreed that the police had built their case. And so did a judge, who immediately issued warrants for three arrests and for searches of the arrested boys' homes.

The police who grabbed Jason weren't rough. They simply read him his rights, put him into a police car, and drove him away from Damien's home. Dread—and night—enveloped him. At the police station, officers hustled him into a bright blue room. There, for what seemed like hours, they demanded: "Tell us what happened." When he'd start to respond that he didn't know, they'd interrupt him.

"I was trying to tell them I'm innocent. They said, 'Well, we've got your friend who says you aren't.' I thought, 'What friend? That can't be right.' I just thought they were lying to me. I had no idea they'd talked to Jessie or what he'd said. There I was, just put in this situation that was completely insane, untrue, and no one would listen to me. They just absolutely refused to listen to anything I had to say."[24] He did not ask for an attorney. Nobody called one for him.[25] Only later would it occur to him that something basic seemed to be missing. From movies and television he'd gotten the notion that, in America, people who were arrested were allowed to make a phone call. No one had offered him such an opportunity. He hadn't asked. How to demand your rights when you're arrested and in shock, he said later, "isn't something they teach you in civics."

Jason soon realized the strength of the police grip. "You can't say, 'You all got it wrong. I just want to go home,'" he recalled. "They're standing there. They've got guns. There's no way to escape it. It's not like being on the playground with a bully. You can't run from them." Utterly alone, he felt he knew nothing but the truth and that no one wanted to hear it.

When Jason would not confess, police officers took him to the county hospital, where technicians took samples of his blood, hair, and saliva, as well as prints of his hands and feet. He saw the activity as a good sign. If officials were taking samples from him, it must have meant that they had other evidence with which to compare it.

"Whoever did this crime must have left a handprint or a footprint or a hair," he thought. "They'll see that mine doesn't match, and that will prove my innocence, and I'll be able to go home."[26]

At one point, officers took away Jason's watch and clothes and put him in a concrete hallway with bars on two sides. He sat there "freaking naked" for two or three hours. Finally, officers returned with a blue policeman's uniform for Jason to put on. Before handing him the shirt, they ceremoniously removed the uniform's patches. The shirt hung off Jason's one hundred and twelve pound frame. When he had it buttoned, an officer took his mug shot.

The time in the hospital corridor seemed to stretch out all night, so Jason was surprised to see that it was still dark when officers hustled him into a squad car again, to return him to the West Memphis police station. Now he was getting hopeful. Maybe they'd already tested the samples and were about to send him home. But, no. After a huddled consultation, the officers moved Jason again—this time to the jail in Marion. "They weren't being very hospitable," Jason recalled. "They weren't explaining anything to me." He stayed in a cell in Marion's small jail, awake, for the rest of night.

With morning came another move. By now the sun was up. Still wearing the over-sized police uniform, he was driven back to the jail in West Memphis, where he was brought before a judge and charged with three counts of capital murder.[27] Had he been presumed innocent, someone might have considered the plight of a sixteen-year-old taken in the middle of the night and run through such an ordeal, without explanation or the benefit of a parent or advisor. But Jason was not presumed innocent. He was seen—and treated—as a kid who'd mutilated and murdered children. In fact, having been charged as an adult, he was not treated as a kid at all. He could do only what he was told: "Stand here." "Walk over there." And now, again, "Get in." Once again, without explanation, Jason was being moved. This time, he was in a van, being driven he knew not where. Looking out the window, he figured he was headed north when he saw that the van was passing by Lakeshore Trailer Park. Seeing that Jason had noticed, an officer remarked, "Take a good look. This is the last time you'll ever see it."

Jason knew his mom must be beside herself. Had anyone told her where he was? He knew she wouldn't be able to cope with hearing that he'd been arrested, much less charged with murder. But there was nothing he could do. He was shackled and cuffed inside an armed van. He was barely coping himself.

Though Jason had never traveled this far north, he noted that the fields he saw passing outside the van looked much like those around Marion. Yet everything about this ride felt threatening. After traveling in silence for an hour, Jason saw a compound surrounded by barbed wire. The van pulled to a stop outside a bland brick facility. Jostling him out of his seat, guards directed Jason into the building and then into a cell. Taking the blue shirt, they handed him an orange uniform and told him to put it on. Now he at least had a clue—but only that—about where he was being held. On the back of the shirt he was given were stamped the words, "Craighead County."

Saying little, a jailer removed Jason's shackles, then left him alone in the cell. It held nothing but a metal toilet, a concrete bunk, a mattress, and a small blanket. Jason sat on the bunk, trying to think. Eventually, silently, someone on the jail's staff brought him a tray of food and a plastic spoon with which to eat. That became the routine. No conversation. No access to TV, radio, or newspapers. No contact with other prisoners. No information. No one familiar. No one willing to tell him anything.

He understood that he was in shock. When days passed without word from his mom, he knew she didn't know where he was. He hurt at the thought of what she and his brothers must be enduring. He could only wait and hope for them to find him. Beyond that, he said, "I was waiting for somebody to tell me that things had been figured out and I could go home."

He did not cry. Rather, he said, "My primary emotion was one of disbelief and shock and expectancy—for this to be figured out and fixed. I kept thinking, 'They've got my blood and my hair and my footprint and fingerprints. They're going to figure this out any minute.'"

But no "any minute" came. For two weeks, Jason sat in his sterile cell—alone and without human contact, except for the guards who silently brought him meals. No one explained to him why he'd been charged with the murders or what might happen next. Gradually, he became unsure what day of the week it was. "Really, I was just put in a room and forgotten," he said. "All they did was feed me. Everyone was instructed not to speak to me, so I took on the practice of not speaking unless I was spoken to."

Then came a day when, without explanation, a guard opened the door to Jason's cell and told him he could make a phone call home. His mom frantically asked where he was. "I said all I knew was that the back of my shirt said 'Craighead County.' She said, 'I've been there twice and they told me you weren't there. They lied to me.' She had a million questions: How was I doing? How was I being treated? I said, 'I guess I'm being treated all right.'"

That wasn't true. Jason—sixteen and growing—was not getting enough to eat. "The food was all right," he said. "It tasted good. But there wasn't nothing to it. I think, at the time, I was going through my growth stage. It seemed like I was always hungry. Even right after eating, I'd still be hungry." But he didn't mention that to his mom.

As soon as she could, Gail made the one-hour drive to the juvenile detention center in Jonesboro, where she and Jason were allowed a fifteen-minute visit. They stood, separated by glass, in a special visitation cell. Jason could see that his mother was "disintegrating," but he could not reach out to touch her. "I couldn't cling onto anybody," he said, "and she couldn't either." Until officials allowed him that call, no one had told Gail where Jason was. She said she'd visited every jail in the area, including this one, but no one would tell her anything.[28]

Jason had suffered the past few weeks, but compared to his own experience, he felt his mother had endured "nine kinds of hell." She told Jason she'd fought with the police in West Memphis, explaining that Jason had been in school on the day of the murders, that he'd gone to school the day after, and that witnesses could vouch for his whereabouts every minute when he wasn't in school. But, she told Jason, nothing she said had mattered. A detective had even promised her that, if what she said checked out, Jason would be released. That promise had been a lie.

After Jason's first visit from his mom, he was allowed to see her weekly, but many times Gail could not afford the money for gas or the time off work. When she did come, she brought Matt and Terry. "It was great to see them," Jason said, "but it was sad too, knowing my mom was going through a breakdown." By the fall, Gail's boss had fired her. Neighbors and townspeople shunned her and her children. Everywhere Matt and Terry went, they were marked as a murderer's brothers. School quickly became unendurable, and even with nowhere else to go, they quit attending.

The winter of 1993 was one of the harshest ever for northeast Arkansas. Gail could barely afford to keep the trailer warm. Her visits to Jason grew fewer. When he did get to see his mom and brothers, the visits brought a grief of their own. He knew that he himself needed comforting, but the glass—and his mother's frailty—made that impossible. "I couldn't cling onto anybody," he said. "Mom was as helpless as I was. And fifteen minutes, there's not a lot you can really say, besides 'I love you,' and 'I'm doing well.' You can't even give each other a hug." Partings were the worst. "Matt and Terry would be saying, 'Okay, Mom, it's time to go,' and she'd be crying, saying, 'Why can't I take you home?'"[29]

After a few months of isolation, Jason was allowed a pencil and paper, so he could write letters home. "When they gave me the pencil, they told me, 'If you break the lead, find it, because if we have to come in and find that lead, it won't be pretty.'"

> **"One unerring mark of the love of truth is not entertaining any proposition with greater assurance than the proofs it is built upon will warrant."**
>
> ~ *John Locke*

Fogleman faced difficulties too, though of a very different kind. With the arrests and the pressure on the police department lifted, the burden of proving the teenagers' guilt now rested squarely on him. Some of Jessie's answers would help. Fogleman felt confident that any jury that heard the recorded parts of the boy's statements would find him guilty.

But the situation grew more difficult with regard to Jason and Damien. Although police had questioned both boys separately and intensely, neither was low-functioning, and neither had confessed. Fogleman had no evidence that positively connected them—or Jessie, either, for that matter—to any of the victims. Investigators had found a fiber at Jason's house that they said was "similar" to one found with the bodies, but that was pretty much of a stretch. Police had found no murder weapon. There was no indication that the alleged killers even knew the victims. And, despite all the talk of cults and ritual killings, police had found nothing at the scene— no altar, symbols, candle wax, nothing—that would support their unique theory of the crime.

Fogleman knew he had little of substance. So did his boss, Brent Davis, the district's chief prosecuting attorney.[30] But Davis worked out of an office in Jonesboro, an hour north of Marion. Locally, the job of prosecuting the teenagers would fall primarily to Fogleman. Facing the kind of case that could make or break a career, Fogleman launched an investigation of his own, using his subpoena power in hopes of finding evidence where the police had failed. Fogleman may have expected to have Jessie enter a plea bargain in exchange for a sentence of something less than death if he'd testify against Damien and Jason. Or, failing that, to have Jessie tried first, get him convicted, and then offer Jessie a reduced sentence if he would repeat his accusations against Damien and Jason at their trial. Either way, it would help if the public knew what Jessie had told the police.

Just how it happened remains unknown, but soon after the arrests, while a judge had ordered the arrest warrants sealed, a complete transcript of Jessie's recorded statements to the police was leaked to the region's biggest newspaper, *The Commercial Appeal* in Memphis. As a result, news media saturated the region with Jessie's clumsy account of stabbings, sexual predation, choking, and death, all intertwined with the names of Damien Echols and Jason Baldwin, and that mysterious, ungodly word — "cult."

During the seven months between the arrests and the start of Jessie's trial in January 1994, *The Commercial Appeal* ran more than seventy articles that included the words "cult," "devil," "Satanism," "evil," and "occult"—often in headlines. Television exploited the case's sensational aspects even more, with several media reporting claims that people had seen Damien dressed all in black even on hot summer days, killing dogs, carrying skulls, his fingernails filed to points, and carrying a staff as he walked. Reporters seemed to have no trouble finding people around Marion and West Memphis who were glad to describe Damien as "weird."

Jason presented a more singular challenge. As the summer of 1993 turned into fall and Jessie's January trial loomed nearer, the most damning information Fogleman had been able to develop against Jason—aside from what Jessie'd said—concerned the vandalism incident when he was eleven, the call about his shoplifting some chips and M&Ms, his preference for heavy metal music, and, of course, his friendship with Damien. Fogleman knew that none of that would support a request for the jury to sentence Jason to death—and death was Fogleman's goal.

By November, six months after the murders, the case against Jason still looked weak. But then, Fogleman got "a hunch." He said the idea struck him after a drive through the trailer park where Jason and Damien lived. Though the place was named "Lakeshore," Fogleman claimed that this was the first time he'd realized that it actually surrounded a lake. He said that's when it dawned on him: "If there had been a weapon, what better place to dispose of it than in that lake."

The prosecutor asked Arkansas State Police to search the lake, starting near Jason's house, and within minutes of entering the water, a diver arose with a knife. Years later, Fogleman said that the dive had been planned and conducted in strict secrecy. But, in fact, it was well publicized. The *West Memphis Evening Times* carried a front-page photo of the diver, still in the water, holding the knife in profile. An accompanying article explained that the knife was discovered within yards of Jason's house. A Memphis television station broadcast video of the recovery.[31]

> **"Insanity is relative. It depends on who has who locked in what cage."**
>
> ~ *Ray Bradbury*

Jason's only other visitors during his months in the regional jail were the attorneys assigned to represent him, Paul Ford and Robin Wadley. Jason was not much impressed with Wadley. He understood that Ford, the more amiable of the two, was his lead attorney, the one calling the shots. He also understood pretty quickly that Ford believed Damien was guilty. Jason never doubted that Ford believed in his innocence, but the split between Jason's view of the case and that of his attorney left Jason feeling unsure. It seemed to him that his attorneys and Damien's ought to be pulling together, but clearly, Ford thought differently.

Jason's only prior experience with an attorney had been that first summer in Marion, when he and the other kids were rounded up, taken to court, and threatened with reform school. He had no good memories of his court-appointed defender back then, but he told himself this time was different. He credited his lawyers with the sense of responsibility that he felt himself. He would not have let down the people who relied on him—in his case, his mother and brothers—so he placed his confidence in Ford and Wadley. He would treat them with respect because they were adults and that was how he'd been taught. And he would rely on them because they knew more about both the law and his situation than he did—and he had no other choice. Still, Ford's approach troubled Jason. "I felt, 'I've got to trust him to do his job,'" Jason said. "But he seemed like he couldn't get over Damien's weirdness and strangeness. After I told him I didn't do it, he said, 'Well, do you think Damien could have done it?' He'd always come back to that."

Ford's easy air of confidence was reflected, in part, by the way he wore his hair—tied in a ponytail at the nape of his neck. That was unusual for professional men in the area; it was exceptional for an attorney. Ford promised Baldwin he wouldn't cut his hair until Jason was home hugging his family. At least at first, Ford and Wadley brought Jason information he desperately needed. They were the ones who'd identified the "friend" who'd prompted his and Damien's arrests. Mostly, however, they wanted to hear everything Jason had tried to tell the police.

He told them: "I was cutting my uncle's yard. I was hanging out with my friend after cutting the yard, spending some of the money my uncle had paid me, playing video games at Walmart. There was a guy there watching me play video games. I didn't even know the guy, but he was just waiting his turn. Then, I went to a friend's house and bought a cassette. I talked to my girlfriend on the phone and ate dinner and saw my brothers and my mom's boyfriend. Just normal things that you do, those are the things I was doing that day. I wasn't out murdering anybody."

The attorneys asked a lot of questions, which Jason answered in detail. He told them he'd been with his mother and her current boyfriend, Dennis "Dink" Dent; with his brothers Matt and Terry; with his Uncle Hubert Bartoush; with Damien and Domini, Ken Watkins, and Adam Philips and his sister and her boyfriend. "I told them everybody I'd seen that day. I even told them about character witnesses like Mrs. Littleton and Mrs. [Sally] Ware," his high school art teacher. "I'd ask them, 'Have you talked to these people?' and they would say, 'Yeah.' But they wouldn't tell me anything more."[32]

Ford told Jason he'd fought to have Jason's trial severed from Damien's but that Judge Burnett would not allow it. Beyond that, the attorneys told Jason little about the development of his defense. He later recalled, "It seemed everyone had adopted this practice: don't tell Jason anything." In turn, Jason didn't ask questions. "I didn't know what to ask," he said. "I had no basis on which to ask. I just let them tell me whatever they had to tell me. The only question I ever had was, 'When do I go home?' Their answer was, 'At the end of the trial.' So that was the end of that."

The best part of the attorneys' visits was the food. Every time they came, Wadley would open his briefcase to reveal a pizza, two Mountain Dews, and a couple of Snickers bars for Jason to eat during their meetings. "I was starving to death in that place," Jason said. "I would drink the two Mountain Dews, and eat the two Snickers and the whole pizza whenever they would visit, crusts and all." Before coming to jail, he'd never eaten the crusts.

As bad as things were, he did not complain. He always slept well at night. "When I go to sleep it's over with," he said. Daytime was different.

He did push-ups for exercise, but otherwise, "You just sit there," he said. "You just think, hope and pray. It's not very romantic or dramatic. You're literally just sitting, waiting on breakfast, now waiting on lunch, then waiting on dinner. You're waiting on a visit, even though it's only going to be fifteen minutes and it's going to break your heart. You're waiting on a visit from your attorneys because they'll bring pizza and candy bars. And you're waiting on the unexpected."

Once, the unexpected was an order to go to the office of Joyce Cureton, the administrator of the juvenile detention center where he was held. Jason entered, ready for anything. Still, he was taken aback. A figurine of a wizard sat on the jailer's desk. "I was having this paranoid thought," he said. "'Is she really into this, or is this some kind of setup to draw me out?'" He learned later that Cureton was into collectables and that "her thing was wizards."

Jason said, "She asked me point-blank if I committed the crime. I told her I didn't. That's when she told me she'd had Damien as an inmate there the year before and that he'd gotten in some trouble there. All I'd known was that he was sent somewhere for running away, but I never knew where."

Jason understood it was hard for people, including Cureton, to accept that he was innocent. "They had this huge, insurmountable hurdle in their minds that had to be crossed, and it came from the fact that we were arrested. I was up against this thing, like, when people arrest you, you're automatically guilty," he recalled. "If you say you're innocent, they tell you, 'Yeah, that's what they all say.' Then, instead of people reacting the way you'd hope they'd react, they look at you like, 'On top of being a killer, you're a liar too.' It's tough. And if they don't react negatively, it's like, 'Okay, whatever. There's nothing I can do anyway. That's for somebody else to figure out. If you're innocent, they'll figure it out at the trial.'"

Cureton's reaction was the latter. "I could tell she was still holding onto what she'd been told," Jason said. "She didn't jump up and say, 'Well, I'm going to help you go home.' So the only people I came into contact with were powerless to help or refused to do anything. It was a weird, very helpless situation." He liked Cureton and the rest of the staff. But he also understood, "There was no way anybody could help. They were all wonderful and nice, respectful, and courteous. But, at the end of the day, they went home."[33]

After a few months, Cureton began allowing Jason outside his cell for about an hour a day or onto the outdoor basketball court for a half-hour once a week. The change gave Jason the chance to socialize with other inmates. As a result, he became a teacher. The jail offered inmates an opportunity to take the high-school equivalency test or GED. Jason didn't yet qualify to take the exam because it was limited to people seventeen and older. But that didn't mean that Jason couldn't tutor prisoners who did qualify. "I'd had a better education than a lot of those guys," he said. "Or maybe, my attitude towards education was just better." Jason was never assigned a cellmate, but he made some good friends at the jail; two decades later, he'd still remember their names.

The arrival of a camera crew at the jail came as another surprise. Jason had been denied any access to media. As a result, he still did not know that someone had leaked a transcript of Jessie's "confession" to a newspaper, where what he'd said had become front-page news. Jason didn't know that, for months, residents of the region, like Cureton, had been seeing and hearing reports that police viewed the murders of the West Memphis children as having been part of a Satanic sacrifice. So naturally, he had not known that the combination of the murders and the rumored, sensational motive had attracted the attention of a producer at a cable television network in New York. Within weeks of the arrests, Sheila Nevins at HBO had contracted with two documentary filmmakers to go to Arkansas to film the story, including the trials, if possible.

For the filmmakers, Joe Berlinger and Bruce Sinofsky, the assignment looked like a natural. "It seemed to be an open-and-shut case," Sinofksy said. "Three blood-drinking, Satan-worshiping teens had committed a horrifying act of violence. We saw that there were the seeds of a great drama."[34] It also looked like a long shot. No one could recall an Arkansas trial ever having been filmed before. But Arkansas law did provide for filming if—and it was a big 'if'—Berlinger and Sinofsky could get all the required permissions.[35] The filmmakers were friendly and dogged. They got to know all the key players in West Memphis, where the victims and Damien had lived; Marion, the county seat, where Fogleman, Jessie and Jason lived; Corning, where Jessie would be tried; and Jonesboro, where Davis and Burnett had their offices—and where Damien and Jason would be tried. Being able to extend some HBO money to the victims' families, as well as to the defendants' attorneys, helped with that task.[36]

Jason understood that the money the filmmakers paid his attorneys was to be passed on to his mother, though later he was informed that the funds had gone to his attorneys to pay for investigations that would help him in court. In any event, when Jason's attorneys told him it was okay for Berlinger and Sinofsky to record their conversations, Jason agreed. But the situation was a little confusing. "Most of the time, I was told not to say anything," he said, "whereas with these people, my attorneys gave me permission to talk, so it was kind of different." Gradually, the cameras became "just part of the experience."

And there was yet another surprise. "Steve Jones came to see me," Jason recalled. "It was me and Ms. Cureton in the room with him. We did not talk about the case. He seemed to me at the time very sad, like he had done something he did not want to do but had to or that he regretted it. I just remember the overall feeling of the visit. It felt like he was wanting to check up on me and express to me that he believed I didn't do it."[37]

Jason said that, by then, Cureton agreed. "But in the same breath," he added, "it was, like, 'But what about Damien?' It was a big hurdle. People just could not get over it: his history, his personality, his name—the whole Damien package."

The only other breaks in the routine of jail life came when Jason had to be shackled, taken from his cell, placed in a sheriff's van, and driven to a courthouse for one of the many pretrial hearings. The trips offered a release from seclusion, but it wasn't one he enjoyed. "There was one held in Corning, one in Marion, and maybe a couple in Jonesboro.[38] As usual, I couldn't see," he said. "And I didn't really understand anything that was going on. Nothing was being explained. The lawyers would tell me what the hearing was for and ask me if I understood, and I'd say, 'Yeah,' because I thought I should understand it."

But what happened inside the court wasn't the worst of it. "Getting in and going out of the courthouses was horrible. People can be so ugly and so nasty. There was so much hate coming off everybody out there. You know you've done nothing to deserve it, but people who know nothing about you think that they do. It was like a hate wall, just surrounding you, this insane, murderous rage."

His attorneys told him not to respond to the crowds at all. Jason could tell that the rage was intimidating, even to them. "The whole town wanted us dead," he said, "and they were the ones defending us. They were the ones walking into that. It had to have been tough." It was especially tough on Jason, the target of the rage, but he could not avoid the gauntlet. "You have no choice because you absolutely have no place you can go. You can't say, 'I think I'll just stay here in the jail today.' You're stuck in it until they get through with you."

Once Jason was returned to his cell and left alone, he'd try to frame the experience in some way that would not distort the person he wanted to be. Whatever the situation, he could find something from the Bible that applied to it. There at the jail, for instance, he'd met people accused of all kinds of crimes. He'd chosen not to judge them because, "Jesus didn't judge people. He pretty much forgave everybody, unless they were misusing religion or being hurtful. It was all about the love. That's what Jesus uses. You're supposed to love people, to uplift people, to make people better. That's what I learned from Jesus's teaching. That's why he's the guy. He's the big radical."

After enduring the judgment of crowds, Jason would resort to the words Jesus spoke from the cross: "Father, forgive them for they know not what they do." He reminded himself that Jesus had been falsely accused and jeered, and that he had responded with forgiveness. "So I tried to forgive them," Jason said of his accusers, "because I knew that if they knew I was innocent—if they knew the truth—they wouldn't be reacting to us that way. And I knew that that was the purpose of the trial: to get to the truth of it."[39]

A cold Christmas came and went. By early 1994, as Jessie's trial approached, many in the region were already satisfied that he,

Damien and Jason were, in fact, the killers. Among the few voices of caution raised was that of Bartholomew Sullivan, a reporter for *The Commercial Appeal*. He observed that Fogleman's case might not be so easy to prove. "Defense lawyers plan to tear apart an interrogation by two police detectives in which Misskelley asserted the nighttime murders took place at noon and that the bodies were tied up with rope, instead of shoestrings," Sullivan wrote. Noting that the knife found in the lake had not been discovered until six months after the arrests, he added that police would be "hard-pressed to explain why they waited until late November to search a lake behind Baldwin's house for what may be introduced as a murder weapon."[40]

Three days before Jessie's trial began, Sullivan wrote that Fogleman and Davis were "acting like this is just another murder case, despite its national attention, after revelations of sexual mutilation and police suggestions of a Satanic cult's role." He expected that, once the trial got underway, "The facts that have been slowly coming out . . . will be revealed in a coherent theory of the case." Since to this point, no "coherent theory" had been presented, Sullivan asked Fogleman what evidence he'd present to support Jessie's statements. "I can't comment on specifics," the prosecutor replied, "because I sincerely want these defendants to receive a fair trial."

As 1993 ended, Jason still had no idea where Damien and Jessie were. But when Jessie's trial began in Corning on January 19, 1994, with extensive TV coverage, news of each day's events spread through Jason's jail. Jason could not imagine that Jessie would be found guilty because what evidence supported his statements? Nevertheless, in the first week of February, Jason learned that the jury had not only found Jessie guilty but had sentenced him to life in prison—plus 40 years.[41]

For the prosecutors, Jessie's trial played out as simply as they'd hoped.[42] Hearing Jessie's own voice on the tape recording saying that he'd assisted Damien and Jason in one of the murders was all the evidence the jury needed. As the foreman later explained, "Just what Jessie said convinced me. You might brag about kissing a girl that you never did. But you don't brag about killing somebody. Why would you do that?"[43]

It was a win for Fogleman and Davis, even if the jury had not given Jessie the death sentence they'd requested. Now, the prosecutors hoped that the prospect of life in prison would nudge Jessie into turning against Damien and Jason, a change they badly needed. They hoped to use Jessie's conviction and his fear of what he faced in prison to leverage a deal. Through his attorney, they offered Jessie a chance at a term of years instead of life in prison—if he would testify against Damien and Jason in court, repeating what he'd told the police.[44]

But Jessie, who'd recanted the claims he'd made to police and pleaded not guilty at his trial, refused to cooperate. And because he refused to appear at Damien and Jason's trial and repeat those earlier claims, Davis and Fogleman were constitutionally barred from introducing even a word about what Jessie had said as they faced the trial ahead. That left them with serious concerns.

"We do not err because truth is difficult to see. It is visible at a glance. We err because this is more comfortable."

~ Alexander Solzhenitsyn

The prosecutors held a meeting with the victims' parents to explain the situation. Thanks to the HBO filmmakers who attended, a recording exists of that meeting. Fogleman framed the problem with losing Jessie this way: "All is not lost if he doesn't testify. But the odds are reduced significantly. I mean, we've still got some evidence."

Heading into Jason and Damien's trial, here's what Fogleman told the parents he had:

- Three fibers that even he admitted could not be linked to the accused "to the exclusion of all others."
- Witnesses' claim that, on the night of the murders, they'd seen Damien walking along a road near where the bodies were found; the problem was that these accounts placed Damien with a girl, not with Jason.
- Statements by two teen-age girls who said they'd overheard Damien at a softball field bragging that he'd committed the murders, and

- The statement of Michael Carson, a jailhouse snitch who claimed that Baldwin had privately confessed to him in lurid detail how he'd mutilated one of the victims; the problem here, Fogleman warned, was that the young man "might not be believed."[45]
- Then, as an afterthought, Fogleman added: "Oh, yes, and the knife in the lake."

In fact, there was one other element likely to help the prosecutors. Ever since the murders, now almost nine months past, publicity about the case had saturated this region along the Mississippi River. Though Jessie's recorded statements would be barred from Damien and Jason's trial, it would have been hard to find anyone in the region who had not heard something about the murders being linked to a cult, that a knife had been discovered in the lake by Jason's house, that Jessie had been convicted of the triple murder, and that a strange kid who'd dropped out of high school and called himself Damien was the leader of a cult.

On Ford and Wadley's next visit, they assured Jason that Jessie would appeal, and that his conviction could be reversed. Despite their attempt at comfort, Jason now understood that his own situation had suddenly become more threatening than he'd imagined. If a jury could sentence Jessie—Jessie!—to life in prison, what did that mean for him?

"I was already sitting in a jail cell for something I didn't do," he said, "so by this point, I was thinking that anything bad that can happen probably will. It was, like, 'Okay, what's next? Bring it on.' You get used to having bad stuff happen in your life. Anything that shows up, you're like, 'Of course, this would be the next horrible thing.' But in actuality, it went beyond that." The past months had been hard—hard and cold as the surfaces in his cell. Jason knew he'd survived this far, but he could not have foreseen how much further his courage would be tested or how spontaneously he'd respond.

The next time Ford and Wadley came, they brought Jason what they thought to be, not one, but two pieces of excellent news. The first was that Jessie had refused to testify against Jason and Damien. That was indeed a relief. But the lawyers' next bit of news hit Jason like a two-by-four. "I was sitting there eating pizza with Paul and Robin," he recalled. "And they said, 'The state wants to make a deal with you.'"

"What's the deal?" Jason asked. "They said it was, like, 'Fogleman will ask the jury to give you forty years if you'll testify against Damien.'" Jason looked at Ford and Wadley, the pizza forgotten in his mouth. "How can I do that?," he blurted. "All I can do is tell them where I was. They want me to lie?"

But Ford urged Jason to take the deal. "He said, 'Just say something. Save yourself.' But I was, like, 'Nah, this isn't right.'"

Ford looked amazed, frustrated, disappointed. The subject of Damien had always been a sore point between him and Jason. "I think Paul was doing his best," Jason said, "but when it came to Damien, I think he just saw all these alternative religions, his mental health record, his whole turmoil, and that affected his performance and his relationship with me." Though Jason was never allowed to read the transcript of Jessie's statements, Ford and Wadley told Jason that they contained graphic descriptions of him and Damien committing the murders. Sometimes Jason wondered if Ford even believed in his innocence. "Paul would ask me, 'Why would he lie? Why would he say all that stuff about you?' I'd say, 'I don't know why.' And they'd be off on a tangent about Damien being weird and his mental health record. And I'd be, like, 'I don't know why Damien is weird, but we didn't do this crime.' I figured, 'They're the ones with the law degrees. They're supposed to figure this out.'"

For Fogleman and Davis, the thrill of victory in Jessie's trial was dampened by the chance of defeat ahead. Although Fogleman had used his subpoena power to call in and question under oath dozens of Crittenden County residents, including several minors, about the murders, even that effort had not produced much. As he'd explained to the victims' parents, jurors might view the "some evidence" he had against Damien and Jason as thin, especially in a death penalty case. Jurors might question the belated discovery of the knife in the lake, they might suspect that the snitch in jail had gotten a deal for his testimony, and they might wonder if the girls at the softball field really had heard Damien from a distance of what they themselves estimated was between fifteen and twenty-five feet. The question of motive was an even greater concern. In Jessie's trial, jurors had gotten to hear Jessie talk about "that cult." Without Jessie there to repeat his statements at Damien and Jason's trial, the prosecutors worried that jurors might find it hard to believe that two teenagers had murdered three boys they didn't know for no discernible reason.

Any way the prosecutors looked at the trial ahead, they faced a predicament. They had no reliable physical evidence and no apparent motive. They needed an eyewitness. They needed Jason. Yes, they'd already passed word that, if he'd cooperate, they'd ask the jury to sentence him to time in prison rather than to death. And yes, he'd turned them down. But the prospect of a trial with no physical evidence beyond some "microscopically similar" fibers, no confessions, no apparent motive, and no one even to accuse Damien was enough for Fogleman and Davis to try to entice Jason with one more offer.

Jury selection had already begun for Damien and Jason's trial when Ford and Wadley returned to the jail to tell Jason that the prosecutors had sweetened their offer. This time, instead of death— instead of even a term of forty years—they would seek a sentence of only twenty years for Jason, if he would just testify against Damien. Jason told Ford "No!" He recalled: "I told them, 'Don't talk to me about it anymore.' I knew that if they kept talking, it was going to be a bunch of bullcrap about Damien."

Ford dropped the subject for the moment, but as opening statements for the trial drew nearer, Jason said, Ford urged him "a couple of other times" to reconsider and take the state's offer. "He said, 'Just testify against Damien. Say he done it. Get up there and lie.' I told him I couldn't help him with anything like that. 'I couldn't do it even if you said you'd let me go right now.'"

Jason had consulted no one and nothing but his conscience. He'd made the decision on his own to reject the advice of his attorneys. "I was not tempted," he said. "It was wrong. It was against everything I was brought up to believe in."

Jason was still sixteen. He'd already spent eight months in jail, much of that time in solitary confinement. And he was about to be put on trial for his life. Yet he was adamant. His attorneys were dumbfounded. "They couldn't believe it," Jason later said. "They urged me to take the offer. Paul used some horrible language. He was, like, 'What do you want me to do, tell Fogleman to take his deal and shove it up his ass?' The way he spoke was pretty vulgar—I think due to his frustration with it all. Paul was all about, 'They want Damien! Give them Damien!'"

It was Jason's style to be deferential to adults. But here he drew a line. Fogleman could ask that he be sentenced to death, if that's what he meant to do. Jason would not betray Damien to prevent that.

Back in his cell, he had time to reflect on the visit in detail. When he'd told Ford and Wadley that he would never testify that he knew anything about the crime because he didn't, Ford had said of Fogleman, "He either doesn't believe you or he doesn't care." Jason could not understand that. He considered the offers hideous. Diabolical.

If Jason lied, Fogleman would ask the jury to sentence him to a term of years in prison—a sentence that, if Jason behaved, would allow him to be freed in a few years. But if Jason persisted in telling the truth, Fogleman would seek his execution. Never in his short life had he encountered the type of mind, or the understanding of power, that could present someone in captivity with such a perverse choice. In the quiet of his cell, Jason pondered his own situation relative to Fogleman, wondering if it resembled what Jessie had faced with the police. Only one explanation seemed to make sense. As he put it later, "I guess some police and prosecutors get so used to putting pressure on people, and putting them in impossible situations, that they expect people to make stuff up."[46]

When Jason was a child, he'd believed that the world, essentially, would treat him as he treated it. If he were honest, life, in a sense, would treat him honestly in return. As he matured, he'd begun to realize that the bargain wasn't so simple. He'd come to understand that it wasn't an arrangement between himself and the world. The world would do what it would. Rather, Jason understood that the only pact possible—the deal that mattered—was the one he made with himself. Somewhere on the road to sixteen, he'd incorporated into his being a sense that integrity was sacred. That was his deal now, and he meant to uphold it entirely. Jason didn't know about other people, but he always slept peacefully at night.

"Show me a hero and I will write you a tragedy."
~ F. Scott Fitzgerald

As Jason's trial neared, Ford and Wadley revealed little about their preparation. Jason knew that Ford had fought hard, though unsuccessfully, to get his trial separated from Damien's, but couldn't see why that mattered. "I didn't understand it," Jason said. "I thought it was not a good thing for Paul to act like he thought Damien was guilty, just because he didn't like his attitude. To me, that was the point: he's innocent too."

What Jason did not understand was that he himself was but an asterisk, almost an inconvenient sidecar, to a proceeding that was lethally focused on Damien. Had Jason been tried by himself—before Jessie, after Jessie, or even after Damien—what would the case have been? That police had carted fifteen black t-shirts out of Jason's house (and only one white one!)? That he listened to Metallica? That a diver had pulled a serrated knife from the lake behind his trailer? No. Only the connection to Damien mattered—the connection that Jessie established in his rambling statements to police. Though media had scrutinized Damien's reputation for odd dress and behavior since the leak of Jessie's statements, there'd been little to report about Jason. He was too ordinary a kid. Linking his trial to Damien's gave Fogleman and Davis their only shot at convicting him—and at preserving their theory, as Jessie had described it, of three cult-involved teenagers savaging three eight-year-old children.

In the last week of February 1994, deputies drove Jason from the detention center on the outskirts of Jonesboro to the courthouse downtown for the start of his and Damien's trial. Jason knew the routine. "You get up and they take you out of the cell. They take you to a little bathroom where your court clothes are. The bailiff puts you in leg irons and waist chains. Then you get in the police car and drive to the courthouse. I always dreaded that. There'd be all these people full of hate, full of anger. It was not anything I would ever choose to go through, but you literally can't do anything but what they tell you to. It's like being a sheep led to slaughter. What's that sheep going to do?"

Still, Jason hung onto hope. He clung to his memory of lab technicians coming to his jail to take a second round of hair and saliva samples from him. That small episode had kept alive his belief that investigators had in fact found physical evidence against which they meant to compare the biological samples taken from him.[47] "I was still thinking, 'When the evidence comes back, it will back up what I've been saying.' I had it in my mind that eventually they were going to figure out that we didn't do this crime."

Jason also took comfort in his belief that Ford and Wadley had contacted all the alibi witnesses he had told them about, the people who would testify that they were with him while the victims were missing. "I figured that at the trial everyone would say, 'Well, Jason was doing this, Jason was doing that,' and everything would be all right." Jason believed that the lawyers had done everything he'd asked—and even more that they hadn't divulged to him. Ford and Wadley each assured Jason that everything was under control. "They just told me I was going to go home and not to worry."

When they arrived at the courthouse, Jason endured the jeering crowds, strengthened by his confidence that his attorneys had everything in hand. And, despite Jessie's conviction, he wanted to trust Judge Burnett. "You never want to think the worst of people," he said. "You always want to think there's some good there, that people are doing what they say they're doing. You want to give people the benefit of the doubt." He felt the same about the jury. But there was so much Jason didn't know. His faith in the entire proceeding might have been devastated on the spot had he known what tactics had been used—and allowed—to get Jessie to testify, even in the week before the start of his trial.[48]

Jason and Damien's trial began on February 22, 1994, George Washington's birthday. Joyce Cureton at the jail had given Jason some of her husband's shirts and socks to wear, clothes which she took home and washed and ironed each night because she "didn't want him going to court looking wrinkled."

Seeing in school had been a challenge, but the courtroom presented a bigger one. Jason recalled, "I couldn't see the jury. I could hear the judge, but I couldn't tell which way he was looking." He could see his own attorneys beside him, but little beyond them. He knew where Damien sat, and every now and then heard Damien's voice, but from where Jason usually sat, he could not make out Damien's face. Other characters in the courtroom were sketchy. "I began to know 'tall, thin,' that's Fogleman. The bigger man was Brent Davis." Witnesses came and went as vague, disembodied voices. Judge David Burnett, on his bench up front, loomed as an imposing but indistinct black shroud. The jurors, arrayed along one side of the room, amounted to a faceless block. At one point Ford asked Jason to assess the jurors and tell him what he thought of them. But the request was pointless. As Jason later explained, "I wish I'd had glasses at the time, but I couldn't see three feet in front of me." When he'd asked Ford if his mom and brothers were in the courtroom, the attorney said they were not, that they could not be present because, having been listed as possible witnesses, they were not allowed to hear other testimony. Visually limited and alone, Jason braced for what lay ahead. It passed in a blur. Ford promised Jason that, when the trial was over and he was allowed to go home, he would personally buy Jason a pair of glasses.

As Fogleman offered the state's opening statement, Jason heard for the first time almost more than he could bear about what was known of the crime: the brutalities inflicted on Michael Moore, Stevie Branch and Christopher Byers. Fogleman told the jurors that, as the trial proceeded, "the proof" would show "through scientific evidence, the statements of these defendants . . . and other evidence" that Damien and Jason caused the children's deaths.[49] However, even as the prosecutors called witness after witness to testify, it seemed to Jason that little they said had anything to do with him.

But then, on March 2, the third day of testimony, Davis called a kid named Michael Carson to the stand. As the kid walked into the courtroom, Ford leaned over and whispered to Jason, "This kid is about to testify that you told him you killed the boys. Remember the judge's orders: you cannot show any emotion." Jason had no idea who the kid was, and Ford's announcement was the first he knew of what

Carson intended to say. To Jason's amazement, he then heard Judge Burnett tell the jurors, "Ladies and gentlemen, you've already been told that . . . the evidence against both defendants should be taken by you and separated as it relates to each defendant. This witness's testimony will relate only to Mr. Baldwin, and you should give no consideration whatsoever of this testimony to Mr. Echols." Jason sat up, straining without success to see the witness. Jason was startled when Carson testified that he'd been in the juvenile detention center with Jason because he did not recognize his voice.

Carson said that once, after he'd played a game of spades with Jason, "We was scraping up the cards. I said, 'just between me and you, did you do it?' I won't say a word. He said yes and he went into detail about it."

Shocked, Jason whispered to Ford, "He's lying!" But Davis's questioning continued.

"You said he went into more detail," Davis said." What did he tell you?"

Carson replied, "He told me how he dismembered the kids, or I don't know exactly how many kids. He just said he dismembered them. He sucked the blood from the penis and scrotum and put the balls in his mouth."

Jason knew he had never been alone with the kid and that he had never said such a thing to anyone. He later recalled that, when he expressed his alarm to Ford, repeating that what Carson said was a lie, the attorney reassured him, "The jury can probably tell." But Ford never called Cureton or anyone who worked at the jail or who was incarcerated with Jason to challenge Carson's testimony.[50]

Later that same day, Fogleman called a member of the state police dive team, Corporal Joel Mullens, to testify about how, on Nov. 17, 1993, he'd searched the lake at Lakeshore Trailer Park "right behind the Baldwin trailer." When Fogleman held up a knife for Mullens to see, the officer identified it as the one he had found in the lake, "straight out from the pier where we were searching in front of."

Again, Jason was stung. "I told Paul, 'It's been in the lake all this time.' I talked to him until I was blue in the face. I was trying to think, 'What can we do to lend weight to our word? There's got to be some scientific way of showing that this has been in the lake all that time, like rust or snails' trails, something.' I tried to emphasize that to Paul, but they never did any tests like that, so we never had anything to show the court about that knife." Jason figured that, ultimately, the jurors were going to have to take the word of his mother and brothers about how, by whom, and—especially when—the knife had been thrown into the lake.

Several times, one set of lawyers or another would ask to approach the bench to speak with Judge Burnett in private. Jurors could not hear these conferences, nor could others in the courtroom, including the defendants. These were moments when Jason could relax a bit, but there was no way he could know what the attorneys and the judge were discussing, unless his attorneys returned and told him, which usually they did not.

In fact, many of those discussions focused on the trial's most sensitive—most critical—aspect: the idea that officers Sudbury and Jones had first suggested, that the police and prosecutors had finally embraced, and that had attracted HBO to Arkansas—that the killings were part of a Satanic ritual. Unbeknownst to Jason, Ford argued particularly hard during these bench conferences to bar the prosecutors from mentioning anything related to cults, the occult, or Satanism. Fogleman and Davis were working equally hard to find a way to introduce those topics as indications, they said, of motive. Burnett ruled that the prosecutors could not introduce "the issue of cult involvement" unless he became convinced, during an *in camera* hearing, that there was "competent evidence to establish that the defendant was involved in an occult or occultic type activities and/ or that this crime is indicative of a ritualistic occult killing."

However, a recording of one of those *in camera* sessions suggests that Burnett went further than waiting for the attorneys to present such "competent evidence." In a conference on March 3 that the jury could not hear, as Fogleman prepared to call Jerry Driver to the stand, the defense attorneys tried prevent Driver from testifying about his perception that Damien was involved in the occult. Though the official transcript of that discussion reflects only that Burnett said he would allow Fogleman to question Driver about having seen

"Damien, Jason and Jessie walking in Lakeshore wearing black coats and carrying staffs," the recording contains more of what was said. On it, Burnett can be heard inserting, apparently to the prosecutors, "If y'all want to spice it up a little bit and start talking about the devil, I'll listen."[51] He followed the comment with a chuckle. Ford did not report the exchange to Jason.

On March 7, five days after the testimony by Carson and the diver, Detective Bryn Ridge was called to the stand for his fourth appearance, and now, despite Ford's vigorous protests, Burnett allowed a line of questioning that opened the prosecutors' door. Fogleman asked Ridge if, during his interviews with Damien, he'd noted any tattoos. Ridge responded that Damien had his girlfriend's name tattooed on his right arm. He continued, "A cross between his thumb and first finger. An Egyptian ankh, he called it. And a pentagram on his chest."

All the defense attorneys objected. In a conference at the bench, they argued that the prosecutors' line of questioning violated Burnett's order bearing on the occult. But Burnett ruled that Fogleman and Davis were not out of line in "asking the witness to describe what physical features were on the defendant Echols's body." He added, "Nor have they violated the rule to ask the witness to describe what the defendant Echols said to them." Nevertheless, the judge asked Fogleman, "Do you anticipate any proof in the case to directly or indirectly link the defendant Jason Baldwin to occult activities?"

Fogleman waded full-in. "Your Honor," he responded, "that's something that will have to be talked about with the expert. It's my understanding that part of the involvement of somebody deal with obsession with heavy metal music, change in forms of dress, wearing all black and that kind of thing. And, your Honor, I believe the proof would show that he had, I wanna say, fifteen black t-shirts with the heavy metal thing . . . in his possession."[52]

Ultimately, Burnett ruled that he would instruct the jurors that they should consider "testimony relative to Wicca religion" only for Damien. Ford said, "That'll be fine, your Honor."

Ford was not sharing the content of these bench conferences with Jason. But when Fogleman's questioning of Ridge resumed, Jason could tell that the prosecutor was pursuing something new. Referring to Ridge's questioning of Damien, Fogleman asked the detective:

"What, if anything, did he tell you about the fact that water [was] present?"

"He said water was a demon type symbolism," Ridge answered.

"And, did he tell you anything about demonic forces?"

"Yes sir, he said that all people have a demonic force in them and that the person would have no control over that demonic force."

"All right. Did he say anything about the fact that the children were young?"

"Yes sir, he said that the younger the children, the more innocent they would be, and in turn the more innocent that person would be, the more power that would be derived by that killing."

Jason recognized the words as likely having come from Damien, but he felt he was hearing his friend's words perverted. Angrily, he thought, "They took what he said in innocence and twisted it on him, and they did it because he was Damien."

> **"Sometimes I wonder whether the world is being run by smart people who are putting us on or by imbeciles who really mean it."**
>
> *~ Mark Twain*

The following day, Fogleman called Dale Griffis to the stand. Griffis described himself as a captain from a small Ohio police department, now retired, who had developed an expertise "in the area of cults and nontraditional groups, occult groups." He also claimed to have earned a doctorate degree in the subject. However, under questioning by Ford, Griffis was forced to admit that his Ph.D. had been granted by a now defunct diploma mill.[53] The defense teams objected to allowing Griffis to testify as an expert witness, but Burnett ruled that Griffis was qualified—helping to buttress the prosecutors' claim that Satanism was behind the murders.

Jason could only listen helplessly as Fogleman struggled to formulate his question for Griffis. In essence, Fogleman asked: "If you assume that the testimony showed that the defendant, Jason

Baldwin, sucked the blood from the penis of one of the victims, that... this crime occurred on May 5th or 6th of 1993, that there was a full moon and that there was the absence of evidence of blood at... the scene : based on those factors and the information that you reviewed, do you have an opinion as to whether or not the murder of Michael Moore, Stevie Branch and Chris Byers is occult inspired or the occult is involved?... What is your opinion?"

Griffis responded that, "they were using the trappings of occultism during this event."

Later, Fogleman asked, "Now, while we're talking about it, can you define what we mean when we say 'the occult'?"

"Sure," Griffis responded. "'Occult' is like an esoteric secret science religion. And there are different types to it. There's paganism, which is white witchcraft, and there's Satanism, which is black witchcraft. Some shamanism has been put in there which is Indian folklore occultism. They go back in the area of paganism prior to Christianity."

Jason had lived in the area around Memphis, West Memphis, and Marion long enough to understand how such talk would sound to a jury. His trial had turned into the opposite of what he had hoped. Instead of a focus on science, "secret science religion"—whatever that meant—had become the centerpiece.

Now Griffis was explaining that there was a difference between "traditional occult groups" and what he called "occult cult groups." With Fogleman's encouragement, he told the court that "traditional occultists follow rules set out by various prescribed manuals for services and so forth," whereas "an occult cult group usually follows that of the leader, and—it could be anything." Questioned further, he explained that "an occult cult would start out with an experimenter, usually one who practices alone in an unorganized manner, a self-styled occultist—and we are talking here only in the field of Satanism. And this person has some kind of problems in life, and they use the trappings of occultism to get along. Then we have an occult cult group, and this has a little charismatic leader and some followers."

Jason could have been blind and still seen where this trial was headed. "I was listening to their reasoning," he said, "but that didn't make it true." So he was barely surprised the next day, after the state rested its case, that Damien's lawyer's called Damien to the stand. At first, Jason simply listened, as Damien answered questions put to him by his own attorney. What Jason heard his friend saying sounded true and reasonable.

But then it was Brent Davis's turn, and Jason heard the prosecutor hammering Damien about "a fellow named Aleister Crowley." It wasn't a name Jason knew. On the other hand, Jason wasn't surprised to hear Damien tell Davis that he knew who Crowley was, though he added that he hadn't read any of Crowley's books. When Davis observed that Crowley believed in human sacrifice and that "children were the best type of human sacrifice," Jason heard Damien agree. With a sense of nausea, he felt hope slip away for those scientific samples he'd counted on for so long. Whatever approach the defense might try, it was clear that the prosecutors' plan was to link Damien—and himself by association—to the murders via the obscure but scary-sounding words 'cult,' 'occult' and, worst of all, 'Satanism'.

Davis handed Damien what he called "a copy of some documents," asking Damien if he recognized the three pages.[54] Damien said they appeared to be pages on which he'd written "different alphabets or, like, translations where you could write things that nobody could read." When did Damien write those? Davis wanted to know. "Are you sure you have not done those since you were arrested, while you've been staying in the jail?" Damien was not sure. "Whose names are written on that document," Davis asked. Damien answered: "Mine, Jason's, my son's, one that says Aleister Crowley—"

"Who?" Davis interrupted.

"Aleister Crowley," Damien repeated.

Davis seemed intent on establishing that Damien had written the pages since his arrest, while he was held in jail. Damien acknowledged that he had. But the episode evolved into one of the most disturbing of a trial that was troubling overall. It developed that Damien's attorneys had never been shown the papers Damien was handed, as is required in criminal cases. Damien's lawyers objected and, in a conference at the bench, demanded to know how and when the prosecutors had obtained the documents. Fogleman replied: "It was after the trial started."

Jason could not hear what was transpiring. Nor could the HBO film crew. But the prosecutors' audacity was stunning. Challenged by Damien's defense attorneys, they admitted they'd acquired "a copy" of the papers from the jail where Damien was being held. Turning to Burnett, Damien's lead attorney, Val Price, told the judge, "We'd like to know who in the jail has been going through my client's personal items." His indignation rising, Price added, "There's gotta be a chain of evidence." Turning to the prosecutors, Price demanded, "Does the state have the original?" Davis answered, "No."

"Whoa—" Price said, astonished. Finally, Davis acknowledged, "I think we got it from some jail personnel."

By now Burnett had decided that the documents lacked the necessary legal basis to be admitted into evidence. But Damien's lawyer pushed further: "We ask for a mistrial, too." Burnett said simply, "Denied." Price moved to strike Damien's testimony about the papers. Again Burnett said, "Denied." The judge rationalized, "The witness identified it as being his. He identified the time and place of the authorship and that testimony is before the jury, and it was basically without objection. The only objection that's been made was to the tender of the documents themselves, which I'm sustaining."

Price wanted Burnett to hold a hearing on how the prosecutors had obtained Damien's papers, but the judge refused that too. In fact, he told the defense attorneys that, if they wanted to know how the state had obtained Damien's possessions from the jail without a search warrant and had delivered copies of them to the prosecutors, they would have to investigate it themselves. Exasperated, Ford said, "Your Honor, it goes to the area of prosecutorial—"

"Misconduct," Price said, finishing the other man's sentence. Burnett, however, said that he believed jailers had a right "to go through the belongings of a person in a penitentiary or a jail."

Nevertheless, in their zeal to associate Damien with the writings of Aleister Crowley, the prosecutors had been caught in a serious violation. And when court reconvened the next day, they were ready to admit that they'd been guilty of an "inadvertent oversight"—one that Davis admitted violated the state's Rules of Criminal Procedure. However, Burnett, an expert in the Rules of Criminal Procedure, did not deem the "oversight" serious. He decided that, though the prosecutors had "technically violated" the rules, the matter did not constitute prosecutorial misconduct, and that it had not prejudiced Damien's and Jason's cases. He ordered that the pages not be shown to the jury. But he also ruled that what Damien had said about them would stay on the record, thus allowing the prosecutors to continue to refer to them. It was a huge win for the prosecutors. Despite their admitted violation of the state's trial rules, the damning link between Damien Echols, Jason Baldwin and Aleister Crowley had been established.

So much of this happened in bench conferences, between the attorneys and Judge Burnett, that Jason barely knew about it. He was focused on his own defense. He was anxious for Ford to begin calling his list of alibi witnesses. And he was anxious to testify himself. Though Ford did call a fiber expert to dispute testimony by a state crime lab technician about fibers that prosecutors claimed could have come from Jason's house, Jason was mystified that he wasn't calling anyone else. Every day Jason entered the courtroom expecting that this would be the day that Ford and Wadley would come roaring in with his defense. And every day he left with those expectations unfulfilled. Why was Ford not calling his mom and his brothers? Why wasn't he calling Ken Watkins, Uncle Hubert, and Adam Philips? How were the jurors going to know that he couldn't have murdered those children because he'd been in school the day of the murders, and after school, he'd met with Ken, cut his uncle's grass, gotten paid by his uncle, and then bought a cassette tape from Philips with the money? Who was going to tell them that he'd shown up at school, as usual, the day after the murders? Jason sat in his chair, gripped by a growing bewilderment. "It seemed like the only thing that mattered was that Damien was weird and I had black t-shirts," he later said. "That was all they talked about through the whole trial."

Then suddenly—Fogleman was approaching the jury to deliver his closing argument! It took a few moments for Jason to realize what had happened. The trial was drawing to a close, and Ford had not called a single witness to provide his alibi. Nobody—not his mother, his uncle, his mom's boyfriend, his friends, the Asian guy at the Walmart, his teachers, or Ms. Cureton from the jail—no one had spoken up for him. Ford hadn't even let him speak up for himself. "Every time I asked them about testifying, they just put me off," he said. "They kept giving me the runaround, saying, 'You don't need to testify.' Ford said it wouldn't matter what I said up there. Whatever I said, the prosecutor was going to twist it and use it against me to the jury. I couldn't make them let me testify. I trusted that they were doing what they were supposed to be doing—and I had no idea what that was."[55]

On the other hand, he'd understood Ford's argument that Jason wasn't required to prove his innocence; that it was the state's burden to prove his guilt, which the prosecutors had failed to do. Ford pointed out that Fogleman and Davis had produced the lake knife, a jailhouse snitch and testimony about t-shirts—evidence, he assured Jason, the jurors would see as flimsy. Jason figured the argument made sense, but he found no comfort in it. He remembered once believing that "sense" would have gotten him out of jail, when the physical samples from him didn't match the killer's. That had not happened; his confidence in logic was waning.

"Think back," Fogleman was telling the jurors. "Remember when Mr. Davis was cross-examining Damien Echols? And he said, 'On the sheet of paper that you wrote in jail, whose names are on there?'" Fogleman reminded them: the names included those of Jason and Aleister Crowley, "the proponent of human sacrifice who says that the younger the victim, the better."[56]

Jason's stomach turned. Instead of introducing physical evidence at the trial, the opposite had happened! Here was Fogleman telling the jury how strange it was that so little evidence had been recovered. Now he was telling the jurors: "We've got a crime scene that's clean. The killers were very meticulous about removing any evidence, hiding the bicycles, hiding the clothes, hiding the bodies." Nevertheless, he concluded, when everything known was taken together, "the evidence was that this murder had the trappings of an occult murder. A satanic murder."

On March 17, the trial was over. The prosecutors and the defense teams rested. The judge gave the jurors their instructions and sent them off to deliberate. Jason sat still, in disbelief. "I was putting it together—that it was over," he said. "All I could think was, 'I didn't get to testify.'" For weeks, his mom had waited outside the courtroom, barred from entering because she was listed as a witness. But she'd never been called to testify.[57] Even as Jason was led back to the jail for the night, knowing that the jurors would return the next morning to decide his fate, the weight of what happened had not sunk in. The full shock of it would not even begin to hit until the afternoon of the following day, Friday, March 18, when the jury returned from its deliberations to pronounce Damien and Jason guilty.

Ford seemed to have feared it, ever since Burnett had not allowed Jason's trial to be severed from Damien's. Now, he explained to Jason that Arkansas trials consist of two phases: guilt and penalty. With the guilt phase over, the jurors would have to decide Damien's and Jason's sentences.[58] But back in the jail that night, awaiting that decision, Jason didn't care. He had already spent two hundred eighty-seven nights in the detention center. At this point it made no difference to him whether the jury sentenced him to death or life in prison. Death. Life. Or a single day in prison. All were the same. The only word that mattered now was "guilty." The judge had repeated it three times to him—once for each of the children: Guilty. Guilty. Guilty. Each time, the word exploded part of his world. How could he have been found guilty?

For nine months in jail, he'd held himself together with faith. He'd hung on to an inner certainty that here—at trial—the mistakes that had sent him to jail would be exposed. His alibi would be established. Everyone would understand that he would not, could not—had not—hurt a soul. God would make things right. The truth would set him free. He would go home with his mother and brothers. "I didn't think there was any possible way they could find us guilty when we didn't do it," he said. "Not in America."

"It does not require many words to speak the truth."
~ Chief Joseph

The next day, Saturday, Judge Burnett read the jury's sentences. Death for Damien. And for Jason, three sentences of life in prison with no chance of parole. The teenagers were called to stand before Judge Burnett. Jason could not detect the robed man's expression as he told Damien precisely when and how he was to be executed. When Burnett asked Damien if he could offer any legal reason why his death sentence should not be carried out, Jason heard his friend, standing beside him, respond, "No, Sir."

Then Burnett turned to Jason. Now it was Jason's turn to offer a legal reason why his sentence of life in prison should not be imposed. "Mr. Baldwin?" the judge inquired. *Sotto voce*, Jason answered, "Because I'm innocent."

No one who knew Jason Baldwin would have described him as confrontational. His demeanor, especially around adults, and particularly those in authority, tended towards polite compliance. Throughout his trial, he'd not spoken on his own behalf. He'd even struggled to control his facial expressions because Burnett had warned at the start of the trial that anyone making emotional outbursts would be removed from court. Yet here he now stood, challenging the entirety of the legal proceeding against him. He had not rehearsed his words. He'd not known the question would be asked, much less how he would respond. He kept his voice emotionless. In the courtroom, his voice sounded remarkably steady. But to himself, it sounded small and pathetic, like the squeak of a trapped animal.

"Pardon?" the judge asked, leaning forward. Jason repeated what he thought was obvious. "Because I'm innocent," he said.

Burnett banged his gavel. The jury had concluded otherwise, he said. And that was that—which it was, because Burnett knew what Jason did not: that legally, once the jury reached its decision, any talk of innocence had become pointless. With the guilty verdict, "innocent" had died as "a legal reason."

With numbing abruptness, the trial was over. Jason left the courtroom quietly. No one heard the scream that was arising inside him: "Can no one see the truth?"[59]

Jason never confronted Ford about why he had not called any alibi witnesses. He'd never thought to question whether Ford had been banking on those "deals" Fogleman had offered. He never asked why his mother and brothers were kept out of the courtroom—and thus away from him—if they were not going to be called to testify. What he understood was this: that "why?" was a futile question and that no answers mattered. "I never confronted anybody about anything," he said. "All I knew was I was completely beat down."

Jason's attorneys patted him on the back, offering a mixture of hope and half-hearted comfort. "Ford was like, 'Well, I'll have you out in a year on appeal,'" Jason recalled. "And Wadley was like, 'You get in there and get in with some church-going guys and you'll be all right.' I could tell that they probably didn't think I was going to survive. They were definitely concerned, but they were, like, there wasn't anything they could do about it."

What Jason's attorneys failed to realize, there in the post-trial chill, was that something far scarier than prison loomed in their young client's mind. He was alive, yes; but, as deputies strapped him into a bulletproof vest, he felt something vital inside himself dying. If truth didn't matter—and farce could so easily prevail—what was the meaning of justice? Hobbling from the courthouse in shackles, it wasn't the loud, cursing crowd that tormented him. Now, the agony that bound him was this: in a world where a trial such as this was called just, what—Law? Country? God?—what was left to believe in?

CHAPTER THREE

DIAGNOSTIC

March 21, 1994 - May 20, 1994

On that Saturday, March 19, 1994, when Judge Burnett sentenced Jason to life in prison, the teenager's seventeenth birthday was still more than three weeks away. The winter sun had set when deputies drove him from the courthouse back to the county jail. There, he was not returned to his former cell but led to a new one in the part of the juvenile section reserved for females, which was no longer occupied. He learned it was the cell in which Damien had been held throughout the trial. As soon as Damien was sentenced to death, deputies drove him straight to the unit of the Arkansas Department of Correction that housed the state's death row. Jason was told he'd be taken to a different prison on Monday.

Years later Jason recalled: "I was holding up okay when I came in, until Ms. Sue, Ms. Pat and Ms. Joyce all gave me hugs and told me how sorry they were and cried. And then, I cried too. I cried it all out, and I made up my mind then to never cry again. We all prayed for things to come out good, that my family would hold up, and that, no matter what, for God to bring the truth to light that I am innocent and that the real killer(s) should be brought to justice, and that Damien, Jessie, and myself be set free. They also prayed that God would protect me while I had to stay in prison."[60] The reality of Jason's new life was beginning to dawn on him. He realized, "The people who wanted to change the verdict had no power to do so, and the people who had that power refused."

Prison trustees who worked at the jail were assigned to watch Jason in his cell around the clock. Officials feared he might try to kill himself. This was more than grim isolation. It was grim isolation under constant observation. On Sunday, Cureton asked one of the prison trustees to speak to Jason about the life he faced in prison.

"He told me what to expect and how I should not trust anyone there, no matter how friendly they acted towards me," Jason said. "He informed me that prison is a violent place, full of hateful people, and that I, especially being as young and small as I was, would always have to be on guard. 'Great,' I thought. He then told me that I would be okay, and he gave me ten dollars out of his own pocket to carry with me."

Next, guards took Jason to the jail library, where his mother and brothers were waiting. They would be allowed thirty minutes for what jailers call a "contact visit." For the first time in more than nine months, he was not separated from his family by glass. "My mom gave me a big hug. I had wanted to hug her for so long, and now that I could it was bittersweet because it wasn't the hug that we had been planning for all year. I was supposed to be hugging her after they found me not guilty and we were heading back home. Now, instead of this being a hug of victory and happiness, it was one of sadness. We did not want to let one another go. I knew it was tearing her up inside to have to let me go on to prison, where we both knew that I did not belong."

Jason had endured two hundred eighty-nine days in jail, a bewildering trial, and the shock of being found guilty. He had just been warned of what lay in store for him in prison. And now he saw his little family being crushed from all sides by trauma. Jason knew his mom was close to breaking. "I told her I'd be all right," he said. "I told her what Paul had said—that they were going to appeal it and I'd be home soon—and that I still had good confidence in Paul. My brothers were trying to be strong, but my mom . . . it was like part of her was gone, like she wasn't even there. There's no way to explain it. She was saying things that didn't make sense." Here—with his mom, Matt, now fourteen, and Terry, nine—he was the man of the family, and he was headed to life in prison. Engulfed by pain, he tried humor. Before his arrest, he'd stood almost eye-level with his mom, but now he realized he'd grown about ten inches taller. "Whoa," he laughed.

"You got short!" He play-punched each of his brothers and told them to be strong. "No tears," he said, "and that goes for you too, Mom."

Seeing them with so little support, Jason felt he could not let his mother and brothers know how badly his own faith had been shaken. "So I smiled and told them that I would be okay and not to worry about me. I did my best to show them that I wasn't afraid, that no matter what, we must stick together as a family, to not lose hope and to have faith in God and what is right. That we must never lose sight of these things, no matter how hard it got and no matter what people might say, because they do not know what they are talking about anyway. Our love would get us through this, and God would work out a miracle for us."

The half-hour expired and Jason was torn from his family again. He had no idea when he would see them next. As guards led Jason away, he realized that, while he'd been in jail, his family had endured something worse. At school, Matt and Terry were called Satanists. The family's yard was set on fire. Bricks were thrown through the trailer's windows. His mom lost her job. "In a sense," Jason said, "I had been protected from the horror of it all, being locked away in a cell with no one telling me really what was going on and being said. It was the toughest on my mom and brothers, who had to live out there where all the lies and rumors were being told and spread, lies and rumors they knew were untrue." He understood that, whatever fate awaited him in prison, his family faced grim prospects as well.

On Monday morning, guards cuffed and shackled Jason for the three-hour ride from the jail in Jonesboro, in Arkansas's northeast corner, to the Arkansas Department of Correction's Diagnostic Unit in Pine Bluff, about one hundred and fifty miles south. He carried with him his Bible and thirty-five dollars: the ten dollars from the trustee, twenty dollars that Cureton had given him, and five that his mother slipped into his hand as their visit ended. He climbed into a van with six other prisoners.

"I got a seat next to the window, and I watched as the country went by. I looked at cars and their occupants, remembering when we used to go on trips, my mom, brothers and I, and how we would drive way out into the country, in Mississippi, to my Aunt

Janette's house, and how it would be a long trip, and I would watch the country pass by through the window just the same, except during those trips I was eager for the arrival. This one I wasn't. I was thinking that it would be okay if the destination never arrived, that we could just keep on driving forever and ever, or maybe the officer driving would take me home and say, 'Sorry, Mr. Baldwin. We found out it was a mistake for you to be with us all along. Here, go on home.' And I would get out, the cuffs and shackles would be taken off of me, and I would praise God and run into the house and give my mom and brothers that big hug that we had planned and everything would be okay again."

Instead, Jason brought his mind back to the fact that he was really being driven to prison—a truth that was confirmed when the van approached a big brick building surrounded by barbed wire: the prison system's Diagnostic Unit. "My heart starts beating really hard now," Jason said, "and my breathing speeds up. I see the guard towers. We pull up to one and the officer driving speaks to another officer up on the balcony, and he says he's got seven from Craighead County, and yes, Jason Baldwin is one of them. At the sound of my name, my heart just stops. This is really happening. I am going to prison for murder. Everything seems to be happening in slow motion. The officer in the tower lowers a milk crate on a rope, and the officers up front drop their guns in the basket and it is hoisted away. Then the little bar in front of the van is raised up, and we enter the grounds of the prison."[61]

> **"Things are going to get a lot worse before they get worse."**
> ~ *Lily Tomlin*

Jason felt the free world slipping away as he moved toward the building. "I am led out, the shackles biting into my ankles," he said, "the chains dangling from my waist to my handcuffs. I hold onto my paper sack that contains a few letters from my mom and brothers, my Bible and the little bit of money that was given to me, and I walk through a gate. Into the building I go. I set foot into prison. It is dark, but my eyes get used to it."

Adaptation, while essential to prison survival, does not assure it. Jason's eyes adjusted quickly. Intuitively, he knew that the challenge ahead would be to discern where he could adapt—and to decide where he would not. "An officer comes and takes the cuffs and shackles and chains off. I am told to wait in line with the other guys to be processed. I wait, and eventually I reach an old man who takes inventory of all that I have. He takes my money and tells me it will be put onto my account. 'My very first account,' I think to myself— so different from what I had planned."

"Then I am in a room standing in front of three people sitting in front of a table with a bunch of papers in front of them. It's some type of hearing board. They are all sharply and nicely dressed. I am conscious of my orange jail jumpsuit. They tell me to get naked. I must not have heard them right. This time it is an order: 'Get naked,' they say. So I take off my clothes until I am in my underwear. 'All of it,' they say, so I take them off too and stand there in front of them and their hateful stares. One of them says, 'You think you're tough, don't ya?' I think to myself, 'Yeah, I've got to be tough to survive all of this.' I've got to be and my mantra is born: 'I am tough.' I say that out loud. And then one of them says to the others, "He won't be tough for long," and they all laugh. It is humiliating.

"Someone told me to hold out my arms. I couldn't even see who was talking. I know there was one rude voice. He sounded like he probably hates everybody who comes through there. He told me my number—103335—and told me not to forget it. Then somebody came over and pretty much looked at everything, looking for tattoos, birthmarks, scars—that kind of thing.

"They asked me my name and my charge and how much time I'd been given. They asked me, 'Did you do it?' I had no way of knowing if this was part of their job or if they were just curious or what, but it was the same at the jail. Everybody always asked that—the inmates, the guards, everybody.

"Then, an old white man, an inmate, comes to me and tells me to hold out my hands, and he pours a foul-smelling liquid into them and tells me to put it everywhere I have hair. It is delousing shampoo, he says. Then he points me to a shower spigot in the corner and I am to shower there in front of all of them—the board's hateful stares and now this old man's hungry-looking one. I tell him not to look at me—and I stare directly into his eyes. He bows his head and turns around, and I learn then that I will survive.

"After I have showered, the old man gives me a clean towel and points to a bench where some clothes are neatly folded: a white prison jumpsuit, some boxers, and socks. I dry off and try to put the boxers on, and I can't even get them over my hips they are so tight. The old man is looking at me again and smiling that dirty smile. I tell him he better get me some boxers that fit and do not play any games with me because I do not play. I was warned of people like him from the guy at the county jail—sexual predators. I tell him I am in here for murder. He asks did I really kill someone. He says that I do not look like a killer to him. I tell him that is what I am in here for so he better not mess with me. I wasn't lying. It does not matter that I am innocent; I begin to see that now. It works, and he gets me some boxers that fit.[62] I soon learn that I should stop being shy about getting naked in front of people because it is nothing for an officer to tell you to take off all of your clothes for a strip search."

Entering prison is a form of death—removal from civil society—so it's fitting that a prisoner's initiation includes being stripped naked, cleaned, inspected, and finally clothed in white. Prisons themselves have much in common with cemeteries. With walls and gates and rows of cells like graves, they are places set apart from normal life. There, prisoners are supposed to shed their corrupted pasts, as in death. When they leave—if they do—they must be legally resurrected, to begin life anew. Such, anyway, is the theory.[63]

New inmates go to the Diagnostic Unit first so that prison officials can assess them physically, mentally and emotionally. The assessment is supposed to help officials determine how much of a problem a new inmate might be, what skills or handicaps he might have, and where he should be permanently housed. Jason remembered that his physical exam was minimal. A nurse told him to strip to his boxers, instructed him to touch his toes, and asked if he had any allergies. He was quickly classified as M-1, which meant he was in perfect health. No one asked about his vision. No one checked his eyes.

Guards escorted Jason to Five Barracks, where he was put into Cell 5. He would stay there, alone, for a month. On Tuesday, his first full day in the cell, Jason realized that he was not being treated like the inmates around him. Other men in the barracks shared cells and were allowed out for their meals, but food was brought to Jason, and he ate it alone in his cell. Other inmates got to go outside together for daily yard call, but, again, officials kept Jason separate. Once a day, a Catholic chaplain accompanied Jason to the prison's basketball court for a solitary hour of recreation.

Jason understood that he was being protected. The staff and inmates at the Diagnostic Unit all knew about his case. They'd heard about the three Satan-worshipping teenagers who'd killed the three little boys. They knew of Michael Carson's testimony that one of them—Jason Baldwin—had bragged about putting one of the boys' testicles in his mouth. Jason knew he was seen as a monster. He knew there were dangerous people around him. And he knew that many of them would consider it a good deed to kill him.

On Wednesday, police escorted him to his first meeting with prison officials. This was where the warden and some of his staff gave new inmates their standard introduction. "It was like, 'We're not the ones that put you here. It's our duty to keep you safe. We're not going to have any problems out of you, are we?' They told me what I should expect from them and what they expected of me. They let me know it didn't matter to them whether I was guilty or not. I was in their care, and they weren't going to treat me differently from anybody else. But that wasn't true. They were already treating me differently."

Twenty days after entering the Diagnostic Unit, Jason welcomed his seventeenth birthday on April 11, 1994. That was the day he learned that, six days earlier, Kurt Cobain had killed himself. It was also the day he received his first letter from the outside world. The letter came addressed simply: "To Jason Baldwin, somewhere in prison." The writer was a teenage girl, younger even than Jason, who lived in Millington, Tennessee, near Memphis. Included with the girl's letter was a separate one from her mother. The girl's mother explained that she was allowing her daughter to write to Jason because they had both seen a news clip of him protesting his innocence—and they had believed him. The girl wrote that she believed Jason was "not in a position to be turning down a friend."[64]

"I got a laugh out of that," he said. "It was probably one of my first laughs in a long time."

Plus, it was good to have a friend. It would have been better to have a girlfriend. But teenage prospects of love, hugs, kisses, sex and dreams—none of that had any place in the life Jason saw ahead. He recalled that once, as a kindness, one of the guards had brought him a romance novel to read. (Perhaps surprisingly, romances are a popular genre in prisons.) Jason's vision problem was myopia; he was nearsighted, which is why he'd always been able to read his books for school. But these books were a different matter. He told the guard, "I can't read this stuff." Later, he explained: "A kid going through puberty? No. I didn't need to be reading that."

After three weeks at the Diagnostic Unit, Jason got his first prison visit with his mom and brothers. "My mom wanted to know how the prison was and if everyone was treating me okay. I told her that I was doing well and that it was just like a country club. I told her the unit chaplain, Chaplain McKraken, a real neat old white guy, likes to come and talk to me about God and we play basketball together. I tell her, 'He may be old, but he can play! He beats me every time! Plus, there is another old white guy who likes to come to see me too. He brings Bible study booklets, and I have been reading those while I am locked up in my cell."

The main question his mother and brothers had for Jason concerned the prison food. "I told them it was absolutely terrible! I said it is unfit for even a dog and that, if we were to put a plate of the stuff in front of Bear or Charlie (our pet dog and cat), they would just turn their noses up at it! At that, my mom took out some change and asked one of the officers who was supervising our visit if she could buy me a soda, a candy bar, and some chips out of one of the snack machines out there, and thankfully he let her. Of course, she couldn't buy me something without buying my brothers something too, so we all snacked and sipped sodas while we talked. It was so good to see them again." Unlike the visits in the county detention center, Jason got to have physical contact with his family here. The visits were also longer than what he'd been allowed at the county jail. Still, he said, "They always ended way too fast, and it was always hard to let go. The guards told us 'one hug and one kiss for the beginning and ending of the visit,' but this rule was impossible to keep because my mom and brothers couldn't leave me there with just one hug to part with."

"Not being able to govern events, I govern myself."
                                                                ~ Michel de Montaigne

Part of Jason's medical classification hearing had included a meeting with a department psychologist. "She tried to put me on some medication which I refused," he recalled. "My reasoning was that there wasn't anything wrong with me. The only thing I was experiencing emotionally was because of what I'd been through. There was nothing to be medicated. She wanted to put me on Zoloft, which was experimental at the time. She said, 'I want you to take it and tell me how you feel.' She said, 'Your family has a history of mental illness and suicide.' But I'm like, 'No. I'm not suicidal in any way, shape, or form.'"

Jason reasoned that, if he complied with the order to take antidepressants, administrators could claim he was being treated for depression and place him in the Suicide Prevention Unit, or SPU, where he would be under closer supervision. He decided that was not going to happen. Before his arrest, Jason had seen the film *One Flew over the Cuckoo's Nest* with Jack Nicholson. And already, in his short time at the Diagnostic Unit, he'd observed "the guys from the SPU walking down the halls, doing the Thorazine shuffle." He didn't want to take Zoloft because, as he put it, "If they put me in SPU, I had no idea what could have come next."

Sure enough, members of the classification board asked Jason if he would like to stay long-term at the Diagnostic Unit, on the SPU ward. "They told me that Jessie was already there and that I would have my own cell and everything. They tried to make it sound really nice. I didn't trust them. They told me that if I didn't go to the SPU, their only alternative would be to send me to the Varner Unit. Then, they proceeded to tell me how horrible that unit was and that, if

Checkout Receipt

Tommy Douglas
Mar 08 2018 10:57AM
****

Dark spell : surviving the sentence /
BOOK
4235298
Due Date: Apr 05 2018

Practice to deceive /
BOOK
2975911
Due Date: Apr 05 2018

Pretty little killers : the truth behind
BOOK
3727741
Due Date: Apr 05 2018

He killed them all : Robert Durst and my
BOOK
4879103
Due Date: Apr 05 2018

TOTAL: 4

* *
Items due by closing on date shown.
To renew your material go to our website
www.bpl.bc.ca
Or call our telephone renewal line
604-293-0034
* * * * * * * * * * * * * * * * * *

The library will be closed on Good Friday
Mar 30,
Sunday Apr 1 and Monday Apr 2 for Easter.
* * * * * * * * * * * * * * * * * * * *

I were to go there, I would not survive. They told me Varner was Gladiator School. It did not sound like a happy place, but I would go if I had to. I'd already heard enough about SPU to know that I did not want to go there. They were already trying to dope me up so I wouldn't be able to think clearly. I could only imagine what they would do if I were in a psyche ward. 'No,' I said, 'you can send me to Varner if that is what it has come to. I refuse to be so doped up that I cannot even think about fighting for my freedom.'"

Whatever might happen or be done to him, Jason at least wanted to be in control of himself. He refused the medication. "I might have been a little paranoid," he admitted later. "I was just glad they didn't jump on me and hold me down and shoot me with a needle."

The officials' next proposal was to place Jason in protective custody, or PC, at the Cummins Unit. There, as in an SPU, he would have been closely watched. But again, he refused. "PC is where they put inmates who are too feeble to defend themselves, or who might be targeted by other inmates for injury or even murder," he said. "They might call it 'protective custody,' but usually it turns out not to be protective. I knew that just from seeing the behavior of people. Being in PC means you can't stand up on your own two feet. It means you're singling yourself out for even more abuse." Coincidentally, a film had factored into this decision too. By sixteen Jason had seen Brubaker, the 1980 film starring Robert Redford that was based on true events from a few decades earlier at Arkansas's Cummins Unit.[65] He'd heard that going into PC at Cummins was "the worst thing you can do because that's where the worst predators are." No. Jason would not agree to PC.

A new side of Jason was showing itself. He'd always been compliant—at home, in school, in jail, with his attorneys, and, until now, here at prison. Never before had he refused an adult's order. But here, all bets were off. This was his life. He had little control over anything in it. Where he could control it, he would.

Of course, some decisions carried consequences. That's especially true in prison, where no refusal of an order—however insensible— is tolerated. What administrators saw was a super-high-risk kid who was refusing to take medication, accept protective custody or go into an SPU. Exasperated, the warden ordered Jason sent to punitive isolation, or what was called "the hole." For the staff, it meant that he could be protected there. For Jason, all it meant was more isolation.

Even by now, Jason was an old hand at the deprivation called isolation. He'd endured months of it before his trial. He knew that, in prison, conditions in the hole were worse than those on death row, where televisions, radios and books were allowed—except that prisoners in the hole weren't put there to await execution. Stays there were limited to thirty days unless a hearing were held where an inmate's time was extended.

Yet he understood. "They didn't have too many choices about where to put me. I didn't sense any ill will in it. It was just like they were seeing me being put into a messed-up situation and they were trying to do the best they could within the parameters they were allowed. And they weren't allowed to do much. I felt they always wished they could do a lot more." Nevertheless, "I was alone, just like I'd been at the jail. You work out, but mostly you're just sitting in there. It sucks. The only advantage is that nobody's trying to kill you."

There was, in fact, one other advantage. While Jason was in the barracks, in a single-man cell, he'd have to wait while guards marched the other men past his cell, naked, to the showers. Then, after everyone else was finished, he'd be taken out and marched, naked and alone, past all of them for his shower. "I had to walk past all them in their cells and listen to all their negative mutterings," he said, "and I couldn't even see them. It was like being surrounded by monsters all the time." But at least, in the hole, when he got to shower, no other inmates were watching.

Still, everyone—including Jason—knew that he could not remain there indefinitely. Unless an inmate faces new charges, he can only be kept in "punitive" for thirty days. A place had to be found for him somewhere in Arkansas's vast penitentiary system—a system filled with adults. Jason, skinny and seventeen, stood convicted of killing three children—about the worst crime there is. On top of that, his case was charged with rumors of Satanism and sexual mutilation. Everyone in charge had reason to worry about him. "They really feared somebody was going to try to do something to me," he recalled, "and then, on the other hand, the mental health lady was afraid I'd do something to myself."

The warden assigned a sergeant to keep an eye on Jason and to do things for him that other inmates were allowed to do for themselves, like go to the prison's library or commissary. The sergeant would also take Jason—alone—to the basketball court. "He was always professional," Jason said. "He'd say, 'Hey, I'm going to treat you with respect, you treat me with respect, we'll get along just fine.' He'd tell me, 'If somebody comes running at you, tries to do something to you, get behind me.'"

For all their concern, however, no one on the prison staff realized yet that Jason could barely see. Nor did he tell them. Since his arrest he'd adopted a policy of not speaking unless spoken to. He kept to himself. He didn't mention it to anyone when he learned, at the end of a month at the Diagnostic Unit, that Burnett had just dismissed a motion that Ford had filed seeking a new trial. He did not let himself feel fear. "I'd already experienced so much in my short little life—so much bad—that I'd ceased to be afraid," he said. "And I'd ceased to be shocked. King Kong could have come knocking the walls out and stuff, and I'd be like, 'Well, I didn't see it coming, but now that it has, well, okay.'"

That proved to be a reasonable outlook. After Jason had spent a month in the hole, administrators decided where to place him. Near the end of May, almost two months exactly after his arrival at the Diagnostic Unit, the sergeant showed up at his cell door. He held out a two-piece uniform for Jason: white pants and a white shirt that had his name and a laundry number on it. The unstated message seemed to be, "If you're not going to cooperate, we're going to treat you like everyone else." The sergeant said, "You're going to Varner."

CHAPTER FOUR

VARNER

May 20, 1994 - January 31, 1998

In 1994, Varner was the toughest unit in Arkansas. Just seven years old, it was built for high security, to house thousands of the state's young male offenders—a combustible population. Inmates and staff alike knew that there were times when the place verged on boiling out of control. The word reaching Jason was that it was run by gangs of African-Americans who were "tearing the place apart," and that they were especially hard on white guys. "I knew it was going to be rough at first," Jason said, "just like being the new kid at a new school on the playground. I remembered being in the county jail with guys who were in there for robbing, breaking into houses, and so on. But, like anybody, once you got to know them, they were cool. My overwhelming feeling was only that I was resolved to get through it."

Jason enjoyed the thirty-five mile ride from Diagnostic to Varner, deep in east Arkansas's farm lands. He would end up staying there for four years, from May 1994 to February 1998, years that saw O.J. Simpson's arrest, the slaughter of half a million Rwandans, a jetliner crash near Long Island, release of the movie Titanic, and reports of a woman named Monica Lewinsky having some kind of an affair with the president. Of course, Jason's survival at Varner did not make news, but as improbable stories go, perhaps it should have.

"I went with several other guys," he said. "They all wanted to know about me; they had seen me on the news. It seems like everyone knows my name but I don't know theirs. They all ask the same thing, why did you kill those boys? I tell them that I am innocent and that just shocks them. Rarely does anyone ever believe me. It hurts because people find it so much easier to believe that I am a crazed killer rather than a normal teenager."

The van drove around the barbed wire fence of the institution, to the "sally port" or prison gate at the back.[66] There, guards took the handcuffs and shackles off Jason. They pointed to a concrete sidewalk about two hundred fifty yards long and ordered, "You just follow that walkway to those doors." Jason stood amazed. For more than a year, he had been used to going where he was told—but always accompanied by guards. "You mean, I should walk all that way alone?" he wondered. Walking unescorted, as he'd been instructed, Jason felt strangely elated. "It was just a small taste of liberty."

The first person Jason met at Varner after arriving at the sally port was a stern, older man whom Jason knew only as Mr. Patton. As the prison's classification officer, he determined where inmates lived and worked, and what privileges they were entitled to, based on their classification or "class." In prison, class is rigid and determined by several factors, including the inmate's crime, length of his sentence, and disciplinary record. Class, which determines everything in a prisoner's life, is designated by a numeral and a letter. An inmate's letter class can rise and fall between a low of C or a high of A. But, while Jason could aspire to a numerical classification of one, he understood that his letter classification could never rise above C because he was to suffer a life without the possibility of parole. He saw the C for what it was: C stood for Condemned.

The classification officer told Jason he would start out, like most new inmates, as a Class 2-C. He gave Jason roughly the same welcoming speech Jason heard at Diagnostic, except that Mr. Patton added this: "Stand up for yourself." The officer then turned to his inmate clerk, George Rhoades, who was also serving life without parole. Mr. Patton said, "Mojo, show him your scars." When Mojo lifted his shirt, Jason drew back. He later recalled, "He had a scar that ran from his naval to his rib cage. A guy had stabbed him for no reason and practically gutted him. And it had happened just a short time before. He'd healed and was on his feet again. I was, like, 'Oh, this is going to be fun.'" Jason and Mojo would become—and remain—close friends.

New inmates were called "short hairs" by the prison system's veterans, inmates and staff.

The classification officer assigned Jason to work on the prison's hoe squad, where almost all new inmates start out. But before work would begin that Monday, Jason had to be assigned to a barracks. Up to this point, he had been confined to single-man cells located in larger cell blocks. Varner was different. It was built with what are called open barracks. At the time, the only single-man cells at Varner consisted of several old railroad box cars that had been converted into cells for punitive isolation, the hole. Jason was assigned to Seven Barracks, the first barracks assignment for everyone who entered Varner's doors. Barracks One through Fourteen held inmates who were assigned to hoe squad detail, a surviving remnant of the South's slave trade.

When Jason left Patton's office, he was told to head left. His new home, Seven Barracks, would be just past the control center. Jason walked out the door, but as he passed the control center, he heard a crazy riot of banging and gonging, as if thousands of drums were being beaten at once. Looking up, he saw a three-story wall of bulletproof glass crisscrossed with chicken wire. Behind that were metal bars, and hanging onto those bars were people. Men of all description were literally climbing the walls. The awful drumming came from them, beating on the bulletproof glass. Their faces were contorted with rage, hate, and glee. All their mouths formed vulgarities. Spittle flew over the windows. Jason walked slowly to the center of the hallway, trying to stay as far away from the spectacle as possible, his jaw dropped. It was the hate wall from the courthouse again. It had found him here. The men were pointing at him. He was the object of all that hate and rage.

"Of all the wonders that I yet have heard, it seems to me most strange that men should fear; seeing that death, a necessary end, will come when it will come."
~ William Shakespeare

A voice barked above it all from his side of the glass, "Get behind the yellow line, Inmate!" The speaker was a large guard in a blue

Arkansas Department of Correction uniform bearing the insignia of a sergeant. Jason quickly moved out of the center of the hallway, towards the thundering wall of hate. Careful now not to stray beyond the yellow line drawn just three feet from the wall, he walked slowly down the length of the barracks, just a foot away from the glass, making his way the hundred feet or so to the Seven Barracks door.

The men behind the wall of glass sustained their violent frenzy. They had been watching Jason on the news for a year, talking about the murders and how sick and horrible he was. They'd been expecting Jason. And now he'd been delivered. Their excitement to get a piece of him was madness. He thought to himself—not for the first time—that surely, here, was what the Bible spoke of when it told the tale of Legion. The men on the wall looked possessed.

When Jason finally made it to the metal door that marked the entry to Seven Barracks, the large guard who had yelled at him looked down and asked, "Are you ready?" Jason gulped, looked up and nodded. The guard looked down and asked Jason again, "No, I asked, 'Are you ready?'" He put a lot of meaning into the question this time. Jason felt it. He raised his head and straightened his shoulders a bit, summoning his courage and standing taller. Readjusting his grip on the paper sack containing his worldly possessions, he managed to say, "I'm ready."

Before the sergeant opened the door, he said something else to Jason. "Stand up for yourself in there. If you do, I've got you. If not, they do." Jason looked up into his eyes and nodded once.

Then the sergeant opened the door and Jason stepped into hell. He fought as hard as he could and likes to think that he gave as good as he got, but he knows that just isn't true. Jason had just entered a fifty-man barracks, and every man in it wanted a piece of him. There was nothing fair or pretty about it. All the rage and anger that had been building up for over a year over the senseless murders of three children finally had an outlet.

The sergeant was true to his word. Every now and then, when Jason was overwhelmed, he would come in with his pepper spray and let his own fists fly, pulling men off the boy. In those days, it was rare for anyone to be locked in the hole for fighting, as that space was reserved for stabbings, which, at this time in the unit's history, were an almost daily occurrence. After breaking up the fights, the sergeant would ask Jason how he was holding up. Jason would respond that he was okay, even as the men around him screamed, "Catch out, bitch!" It did not take long for Jason to learn the words' meaning.

This was a time when Varner held mostly African-Americans— young men who, for a variety of reasons, simmered in deep-seated anger. Within the prison, these inmates had developed their own culture—one they held tightly in common, regardless of what different gangs they may have belonged to back on the streets. Here, on this old plantation, where everyone was treated as a slave, these young men shared a double bond: they knew that they belonged to a race that had been enslaved by white Americans, and they knew that their race was now disproportionately being assigned to the latter-day slavery of imprisonment. They directed their fury at any white inmate unfortunate enough to enter Varner. In short, they were accustomed to beating the white guys out of "their" barracks.

To "catch out" meant to give up. For a white inmate, it meant conceding that he couldn't take the beatings anymore and asking to be transferred for his own safety—usually to protective custody. Any inmate who didn't catch out but who quit resisting was expected to become a sex slave, to be passed around, used and abused, in order to win "protection" and make the beatings stop.

Jason refused to catch out. And he never quit resisting. When the sergeant came in and broke things up and asked Jason if he was "all right," he was really asking if Jason was ready to sign up for protective custody. When Jason said "I'm good," he heard some men around him shout things like, "We've got a tough one, boss!" and, "He ain't no punk bitch but we gonna fuck'm up for killin' those kids!" Jason would grin through bloodied lips, taking what little victories he could wherever he could because, muddled as he was, it seemed he'd heard a compliment in there.

After fighting in Seven Barracks for several hours that first Friday night, Jason won a moment's respite as things began to slow down.

By then, he'd felt blows from everyone in the barracks. As he sat in the dayroom, holding his head in his hands, and watching the blood from his face pool between his feet, he thought about his trial and the testimony about the boys' wounds and how much they must have bled. He felt an infinite sadness at how much violence seeks to destroy the innocent.

That's when officers announced shower call. The shower at Varner was built to accommodate one hundred men at once, so men from two barracks were called at a time. Seven Barracks and Eight Barracks showered together. The men in Eight Barracks hadn't been let loose on Jason yet and were beside themselves with anticipation. So Jason's battles began anew in that shower. It was a long, brutal and ugly ordeal, but Jason was not raped. The fighting went on and on, but the culture dictated that you would not be raped if you fought. "When guys stopped standing up and fighting," Jason said, "when they said they were tired of fighting, that's when they ended up becoming sex slaves." Jason never stopped fighting. The universe beat and pummeled its rage onto his body all weekend.

At 5:30 Monday morning, Jason was led out for his first prison job, laboring on a hoe squad under Arkansas's delta sun. Slaves and prisoners before him had bled and died at this place. He had no idea how many. All he knew was that he was a different person from the kid who had once looked forward to this day: a different Monday in a different summer working a different job for different reasons.

"I remember when I first went out there into those prison fields under the hot blistering May sun," he said. "My skin had turned white from being locked in a cell for nearly a year at the county jail during the trial and for the two months at the Diagnostic Unit. I welcomed the sun and it blistered me. It burned my nose, ears and neck, but it felt so good to be outside again. The hoe squad major at the time used to take me up alongside of his truck and make me march while he held his gun on me, telling me not to fall behind or he would kill me for escape. He was mean and cruel but he was not a liar. I knew he wanted to kill me—every day of hoe squad he wanted to—but God stayed his hand."

Jason understood that the major was not the only person who would relish the opportunity to kill him. In the hierarchy of prison, his crime made him lower than scum. Yes, he was convicted of murder, but Varner held many who'd killed. Killing a child, though—that was worse. And killing a child as part of a Satanic ritual that included sexual mutilation? Even in the harshness of Varner, that was beyond depraved. Jason was marked, and he knew it. "The way Fogleman spun the story," he said, "touched every single group's hate buttons."[67]

Jason worked on the hoe squad for sixty days under supervision of horse-mounted guards called riders. There was a school at the prison, and Jason wanted to get his GED, or General Education Development certificate, which is the equivalent of a high school diploma. But he'd heard the riders "talk bad about people who signed up to go to school to get out of work." He decided that, before signing up for school, he would try to earn the guards' respect. "As limited as my choices were," he said, "I wasn't going to make one that would reduce my chances around there."

Summer—and the intensity of work in the fields—drew to an end. Jason had survived his first two months at Varner. Having completed his mandatory stint on the hoe squad, he was eligible to appear before another classification board. This one consisted of the warden, the assistant warden, the field major, the building major, and most other department heads at the prison, and it presented him with the opportunity to have his class raised a notch, to 1-C status. Any member of the board could prevent that, but no one objected. Next, Jason was asked if he had any work experience. He told them, "I was about to get my first job when this junk happened." Concluding that Jason had no skills, the administrators assigned him to work in the kitchen.

While working in the kitchen, Jason applied to attend school and earn his GED. But he was told the program was not available to him because he had "too much time." In other words, inmates sentenced to life in prison did not need education and therefore should not take up space in the prison's educational programs. In response, Jason filed a grievance against the administration. It was the only grievance—or official complaint—he would ever file. He was just seventeen and had been in prison for less than a year. "I choose my battles," he explained. "Having a crappy mattress? I'm not going to win that battle, and it's just going to label me a trouble maker. But my education was something worth fighting for."

The prison relented.[68] Jason worked the morning shift in the kitchen, from 3:30 to 11:30 a.m., and then went to school from noon to 3:30. Free-world teachers taught the classes, and when an inmate passed a preliminary test, he could take the GED exam. "It was all very simple, very rudimentary," Jason recalled. "All I had was a tenth-grade education, and I never had taken any higher levels of math." Still, within thirty days of starting school, he'd earned his GED.[69]

From his start as a dishwasher, Jason worked his way into the bakery that served twenty five hundred men daily. "The kitchen was freaking hot, and the oven was huge," he said. "You could drive a car into it." But this was heat with benefits. While bread baked, Jason could take a breather in the kitchen's air-conditioned office and listen to the radio. The job seemed so relatively normal that Jason forgot the constant presence of watchful guards. Jason's first experience with getting nabbed by "the police" came while he was a baker. He had found a quarter in a hallway and pocketed it, even though he knew that, in prison, free-world money is contraband. Nor was that the worst of it. A bit earlier, another inmate had helped Jason out when he had a headache by giving him two Motrin capsules that the other inmate had received from the infirmary. Jason had swallowed one and kept the other. It too was contraband.

"There was this officer who saw me as someone who just got to prison and didn't know prison ways," Jason said. "He had the philosophy that every inmate has something they're not supposed to have." The officer shook Jason down, found the quarter and the Motrin, and hauled him to the warden's office.[70] Jason said the meeting went something like this: "They said, 'We don't want to bust you on this,' and I was thinking, 'I agree it's petty.' They said you can get out of this if you tell us what this certain clerk was doing. Write a statement. I was, like, 'I don't even know this guy.' They thought I was lying, so they wrote me a disciplinary for it."[71]

Years later, Jason wrote a poem about that shake-down:

The List Nefarious: Contraband.

Holy Bible
Yellow legal pad full of notes
Polaroid of family
a Motrin
a quarter
one Speedstick deodorant—dry
a bar of state soap
a white three-inch toothbrush with flayed bristles
a clear tube of Maximum Security Toothpaste—made in China
two Top Ramen—chicken flavor
one coffee cup, coffee-stained and plastic

Opening my locker box
he is determined to find
contraband

Looking inside
you may decide the box
is empty

but it is not.

Picking up The Holy Bible
he flips the pages
they go f-l-l-l-l-l-l-i-i-i-p-p-p-p
as he thumbs The Book
upside down

a single photo floats
to the ground

a young woman with blonde hair
and three equally blonde boys
in tow
the one laughing is me

my arms strain against the chains
as his boot covers the photo
dismissively

the deodorant and toothbrush
scrape along the bottom metal
of the box as he shoves them
aside

his boots are black
polished to perfection
I can see my brother's spiky hair
and crooked smile
peeking past the cleats
as if willing me to remember
the days we played
hide and seek
amidst rows and rows
of soybeans and cotton
"Ollyollyoxenfreeeeeeeeee..."

he doesn't touch
the state soap
leaving it to congeal in the box's corner

instead he reaches for
the brown stained plastic
coffee cup
further in the box
he leans in deep
for his prize
his boots grind away
at my mother's face
something brown and muddy
where her eyes once shined
gone is her smiling mouth
that kissed us good night
"Sweet dreams, sweet dreams,
sweet dreams..."

"Aha! What's this?"
He asks, twinkling in his eyes
rattling and rolling its contents inside

He empties the cup into his palm
His eyebrow shoots up
"Ooooooooh" he sings in triumph
as a quarter and Motrin
tumble into his hand
"That's contraband."

Inside prisons, as outside, information can be power, a unit of exchange, something to be bartered. Likewise, not having information—or having it but being unwilling to turn it over—can get a person hurt. Jason wasn't a snitch, and in the case of the errant clerk, he didn't even have the information the police wanted. For his silence, Jason got busted from 1-C to 4-C status and ordered back to the hoe squad. Jason returned to the fields clueless as to what awaited him.

"Emptiness is filling me to the point of agony."

~ Metallica

"It was summertime," he recalled, "and we were coming in from hoe squad. It was very bright and hot. When you would come in from outside, it would take a minute for your eyes to adjust. I had just stepped inside the door when somebody just threw me in a choke hold. I saw stars. I had tunnel vision. I knew it was over with. So I started fighting as hard as I could. Somehow I got loose. But then, somebody hit me. I spun around and I saw three guys. I was trying to run away, but I ran straight into this big dude. I mean, he was big. He held me up over his head. I was upside down, perpendicular to the floor, and I could see that I was at eye-level to the exit sign over the door. Then he just brought me down as hard as he could onto the concrete floor. And I was out."

The next thing Jason remembered was the sensation of having a long, lighted wooden match stuck up his nostril. Someone was kneeling over him with smelling salts. "It felt like fire inside my head, and my head felt like broken pottery. I tried to raise my hand up, and it was like the gears in my shoulder and arm didn't work. Then I passed out again."

When he woke up in the infirmary, he had no idea how long he'd been out. He saw Mojo and heard him say, "JB, man, you all right?" Then he passed out again. Over the next several hours, Jason would come to and pass out several more times. Once he heard a sergeant ask, "Is this one of the guys who jumped on you?" Jason tried to focus his eyes, "I can't see," he said. "Bring him closer." The inmate's face was shoved close to Jason's. Jason said, "Yeah, that's one of them." Then he passed out again. He remembered the warden coming— and passing out again. He couldn't stay conscious for more than a second or two.

At some point he realized that a night had passed and he needed to use the restroom. He tried to shift out of the bed but collapsed as soon as his feet hit the floor. He passed out again, and this time when he woke it was night, and he was still on the infirmary floor. He managed to stand up, and realizing that he could, he walked out of the infirmary. "A nurse asked me, 'Where are you going?' I said, 'To the barracks,' and I walked to the barracks. I had a real headache. The guys in the barracks gave me some contraband Motrin, and I went to the bathroom."

Having left the infirmary, Jason was still assigned to the hoe squad, so guards demanded that he go out to the fields. "They didn't give me a sling, or anything for the pain, and ordered me to hoe squad. I didn't go. So they wrote me a disciplinary." That meant he had to go before a prison judge. When Jason made his appearance, he recalled, "The judge said, 'You're the guy with the broken bones?' Then he said, 'Okay," and let me off the squad for a couple of weeks."

Even when Jason had to return to work, he could barely climb up onto the tractor, and once in the fields, he couldn't keep up with the work. That angered another inmate, who was about to attack him for that. But Jason had some defenders. As he recalled, "Another guy knocked that guy flat out." It was Montavious Gordon, a kid who'd spent time in the Craighead County Detention Center with Jason and who believed in his innocence. Eventually, a doctor called Jason to the infirmary again, where he was given some x-rays. The images showed a fractured skull and a broken collarbone. The doctor gave Jason some exercises to do to rehabilitate his shoulder.

There were two TVs in Jason's barracks. One Saturday, about a week after Jason's short stint in the infirmary, one of the sets was tuned to Soul Train, and the other to a movie. Jason was sitting in front of the one showing the film, when another inmate came over and flipped the dial to Soul Train. "I'm looking pretty rough," Jason recalled, "but I said, 'Hey, I'm watching that movie.' We exchanged a few choice words, and I ended up watching the show. Well, later that night, when I was on the toilet, a few guys come into the bathroom. One of them jumped me. He kicked me in the face and chest. I ducked my head and he punched my forehead. I heard his hand break or pop. I jumped up and hit him in the jaw. Just then a sergeant came in and took him off. The back of my head was broken from the earlier incident, but the front of my skull was thicker. Everyone's is. My head was not further injured, but it hadn't stopped hurting from the original injury. I had blood draining from my nose forever, big thick clots for a month, like it was coming from my brain."

That was Varner. "People were trying to kill each other in there every day, every hour," Jason said. "There was so much hate." Besides "Gladiator School," Varner Unit was also nicknamed "Little Saigon." Prisoners who'd been to other units knew it as the ADC's toughest. Guards knew they had their hands full and often felt at risk. Jason said, "It was nothing to see a building major walking around with a black eye. It was pretty rough. I got into lots of fights. I got the crap beat out of me for years. But I'd go straight back into the same barracks. I didn't run from them. You earn respect by going back in. For me, that meant just being myself. By just talking to people. Or by standing up for myself in fights. But it doesn't happen overnight."

Violence was not limited to the Varner Unit where Jason was. In 1995, an inmate at another unit got out of his cell and stabbed a guard to death. News like that made it out of the prison, but most other news did not. While some prisoners were isolated within cells in each prison, the prisons themselves were isolated, located in rural parts of the state, unconnected to public transportation, distanced from most of the cities where relatives lived. When Jason arrived at Varner, even telephone calls to families were prohibited.

But in 1995, Arkansas caught up with most other states and began allowing prisoners controlled access to telephones. People from the free world could still not call in, but prisoners could make calls to a limited number of people who were pre-approved by the corrections department—and who were willing to pay steep charges to accept the collect calls. Jason's mother could not accept many collect calls, so he mostly wrote to her. But news was withheld on both ends.

When his stepfather Terry died, nobody told Jason. He, in turn, never told his mom about the broken collarbone and fractured skull.

Jason hoped not to die in prison, young or old, but he could see no way out other than death. His trial attorneys, Ford and Wadley, came to visit him once to show him the direct appeal they would be filing on his behalf with the Arkansas Supreme Court. The legal system had already brutally failed him. Yet Jason signed his appeal. "The only hope I had to hang onto," he said, "was the system itself."

Most people think, as Jason did, that the appellate system of their state and nation is dedicated to righting wrongs that occur in trials. That is only narrowly correct. Courts of appeal review trials to satisfy themselves that procedures were duly followed—in other words, that the trials were technically correct. These courts don't want to second-guess juries. They rarely second-guess judges. Many have long-established practices of viewing disagreements "in the light most favorable to the state." People filing appeals often lack the funds to hire attorneys, much less private investigators. And the points they can raise on appeal are limited. If the criminal system were a pyramid, the trial would be its broad base, where the opportunity to present evidence and arguments and to challenge proceedings is greatest. The direct appeal, such as Ford and Wadley had prepared for Jason, forms the next layer of the pyramid. But now, the pyramid is narrower, as are the arguments that can be presented.

The lawyers discussed the document with Jason and had him sign it. "I thought it should work," he said. "I'm not an attorney, but it sounded good to me. I was always hopeful and never wanted to think that what's going on is going to be hopeless. You always want to think it will open their eyes."

Again, he hoped that the truth would matter to someone. But Jason felt that his conviction had placed him, not just out of sight, but out of mind as well. Much like his trial, his first year in prison passed in a literal blur. After he'd been there long enough to understand how prison operated, he requested an eye exam. As a result, the state of Arkansas issued him a pair of eyeglasses—the first he'd worn in his life. "Until then," he said, "I really wasn't aware of how blind I was." But the cheap, state-issued glasses scratched and broke easily.

Jason said, "Guys would be walking around with tape all over them, holding them together." Eventually a friend on the outside smuggled in a better pair of contraband, free world glasses. Normally, guards overlooked the obvious violation, but they—and the inmates— knew that a crackdown (and confiscation) could come at any time. [72]

In January 1995, Danny Williams, a drug counselor from Jonesboro, wrote an anguished letter to Jason about Michael Carson, the teenager who testified that Jason had confessed to him his participation in the killings. Williams explained that he had been Michael Carson's drug counselor in the months before Jason and Damien's trial and that he had told Carson what was publicly known about the murders. The letter gave Jason a new, clearer vision–something like getting glasses—that Jason could now apply, in retrospect, to his trial.

"Every word that he said in court was told to him by me," Williams wrote. "This young man then went to the police and stated that you had confessed these details to him while in detention together." Williams said he contacted Ford and expected to be called to testify as a witness for Jason's defense, but that he later learned that he "would not be allowed" to tell the court what had happened. "I cannot tell you why because I do not know," Williams said. "They said it had something to do with the fact that the information was privileged." Williams continued, "Jason, I cannot begin to tell you how sorry I am. I have never done anything that I regret more than this incident . . . I would give anything in the world if I could take back the comments that I made or change what happened, but again, you know that is impossible." Williams understood that his letter had no legal value.

As if to underscore that point, in February 1996, the Arkansas Supreme Court unanimously affirmed Jessie's conviction, despite admitting qualms about his age and mental abilities. Ten months later, in a ruling handed down two days before Christmas, the court also unanimously affirmed Jason's and Damien's convictions.[73] In the longest opinion the state's high court had ever issued, it dismissed every one of the forty-four points that lawyers for Damien and Jason had argued on appeal. The court found, for example,

- that Damien's and Jason's trials could be properly joined because "the crimes were part of a joint scheme or plan";
- that the verdicts in their cases were supported by "substantial evidence";
- that Griffis was an acceptable expert witness because he "had much more than ordinary knowledge of nontraditional groups";
- that introducing evidence of Damien's beliefs did not violate the First Amendment because those beliefs were "relevant to a crime";
- that a book on the history of witches was relevant because it showed Damien's "interest in the occult"; and
- that because "one witness testified that appellant Baldwin had told him that he had dismembered one of the boys, sucked the blood from his penis and scrotum, and put the testicles in his mouth, and [because] an expert on ritual killings stated that one of the facts that led him to believe that the killings were cult-related was that one of the victims had been castrated and had the blood sucked from his penis, there was sufficient evidence of appellant Baldwin's participation in occult activities, and the trial court correctly allowed the evidence."[74]

That opinion, written by Associate Justice Robert H. Dudley, came as a blow, but by now, Jason was getting used to blows. "You always want to hope," he said. "But when the news comes back negative, you're not even shocked. Then something else would get filed and you'd get hopeful again."

After that, Jason saw no more of Ford and Wadley.[75] He was without a lawyer, and though he did not know it, he was in urgent need of one. When the Supreme Court affirmed his conviction on direct appeal, that ruling started a crucial clock ticking. Jason did not understand that the clock resembled one on a bomb, or how, once it detonated, hopes he might have had would be lost. That was something else that kids aren't usually taught in civics. In the world of law and prisons, however, the countdown now underway mattered enormously—whether he knew it or not.

The legal reality was, now that the state Supreme Court had affirmed Jason's conviction, his options were rapidly narrowing. He had few opportunities to appeal left, and his time to file the next one was running out. He needed to file a petition claiming that his attorneys had not adequately represented him. In Arkansas, that appeal based on "ineffective assistance of counsel" is called a Rule 37 petition.[76] Many inmates never file Rule 37 petitions because they lack an attorney, they don't understand the requirement, and the time allowed for them to file runs out. If that happens, the failure at this stage of the process can block all future attempts at redress. If Jason did not file his Rule 37 petition in time, he would be "procedurally barred" from ever presenting that claim. Yet Jason, at nineteen, did not know this. His trial over, he no longer had a state-appointed attorney, and his mother certainly could not afford to hire a private lawyer. He was quite alone.

But then, unexpectedly, a lawyer who had no obligation to Jason stepped in to help. Jessie's attorney, Dan Stidham, paid Jason a visit. Stidham knew that, because Damien was sentenced to death, he would be appointed a federal public defender. Stidham knew that he was going to stick with Jessie, to see that his Rule 37 petition got filed. However, he also recognized that no one was looking out for Jason. After the state Supreme Court's ruling in December 1996, the youngest of the three West Memphis defendants had no one.

Of the six attorneys who had been appointed to represent the accused teenagers, only Stidham was—and remained—outspoken about his client's innocence. Now, having filed what amounted to an ineffective-assistance-of-counsel petition against himself on behalf of Jessie, Stidham went out of his way to help Jason file the same petition for himself. Stidham made the long trip to the prison at Varner to help Jason compose a Rule 37 petition that he could file pro se, or "for himself." Because of that kindness, Jason was able to file the crucial petition in March 1997, before the court's deadline passed.[77]

From the vantage of prison, courts appear indifferent to time. While the legal process ground on, Jason's life at Varner did too. Day followed day amid the yells and smells, sights and fights, chaos and general perversity of mass incarceration. A raw brutality charged the place, making life hard for everyone there. For Jason, the experience was harsher still because of the general assumption that he had sadistically murdered children. "When I was working and around people daily, I'd tell them I didn't do it," he said. "But they didn't care. Most of them said, 'Well, that's what they all say.' Others said, 'So you're a murderer and a liar too.' It was like I was on trial every day with every person I met."

Except for a few people like Mojo—and Clayton "Smitty" Smith. Smitty was serving fifteen years for the armed robbery of a gas station. He and Jason were close to the same age and had entered Varner at close to the same time, but Smitty's background was different. He'd graduated from high school and become a Marine. "But when he got out," Jason said, "he got in with the party crowd. He tried something that no one should ever try because once you try it, it's got you. He got into drugs."

In prison, Jason said, "Smitty grew up a lot. He changed and got off those drugs. He was driven to achieve and excel. He didn't whine and cry a lot about what he was going through. And he had good taste in music. He liked the same things I did." The two became good friends.

Smitty's rack, or bunk, was next to Jason's. "One day his laundry didn't come back," Jason recalled. "He was a field clerk and he had to go to work. Well, I had a clean shirt, so I said, 'Take it. Go to work, and when you're done, stop by the laundry and pick up yours.' Of course, my shirt had my name—'Baldwin'—on it.

"At end of the day, he gave me back my shirt and he said, 'I'm sorry, man. I will never ask to wear one of your shirts again.' When he came out wearing that shirt that said 'Baldwin,' the field boss saw him sitting in the field security area and thought he was me and he flipped out. Smitty was like, 'Just one minute in your shoes, and I'm ready to get out of it. All that hate. I've never experienced it.' I was like, 'Yeah, you get used to it.'"

"There is a crack in everything. That's how the light gets in."
~ *Leonard Cohen*

Outside the prison, however, the hate that had surrounded the trials where the trials were held and that now followed Jason in prison was meeting a challenge. Call it amazement. Or curiosity. Or both. In June 1996, HBO released *Paradise Lost: The Child Murders at Robin Hood Hills*, the documentary film that Berlinger and Sinofsky made from footage they'd recorded before and during the trials. While Jason endured the danger and humdrum of prison, the film that became known simply as PL1 was introducing him, along with Damien, Jessie, the families of the West Memphis victims, Fogleman, Davis, and Burnett—all the players in the West Memphis saga—to the world. The documentary would win two Emmy awards and raise viewer interest in the trials.

"The film is really about the justice system, about poor man's justice," Sinofsky later said. "It's about the sadness and the desperate nature of trailer parks in poor America. But in many ways, it's also a life-affirming film. It makes you look at your own children and the people you love a little more intently. You can see how fleeting life is."

At first, neither Jason nor anyone he knew had seen *Paradise Lost*, but as years trickled by, new people entering prison would come to him and say, "Hey, I watched the video." Officers let him know that they were pulling for him. "That helped me a lot," he said, "all through the years."

Jason began to get excited letters from people who'd seen the film. "They were amazing," he said. "In them, there were so many nuggets of hope: people saying, 'We're not going to give up,' and 'We'll do whatever we can to make sure this case isn't forgotten.' One of the letter-writers, a teenage girl in Arkansas, became a regular correspondent and remained a bright spot in Jason's life for years. Three others, Kathy Bakken, Grove Pashley, and Burk Sauls, friends in Los Angeles, were moved enough by the film to call Arkansas officials to inquire what had become of Jason, Jessie and Damien since their convictions. When the Californians learned that the appeals had been denied and that they were all still in prison, Kathy, Grove and Burk—or "KGB" as they became known—wrote to the men and followed their letters with a visit to Arkansas, where they met with each of the men in prison.

Bakken was surprised by her meeting with Jason. Of the three, she found him to be most different from the kid she'd seen in the film—"a deer in the headlights," as she recalled. "Nowhere do you get a sense of how sharp and quick and optimistic he is," she later reported. For all his youth and naivety, she saw him as "the brain."

While in Arkansas, the Californians also contacted Stidham. Pashley remembered sitting in the attorney's office on Nov. 1, 1996, and viewing the crime scene and autopsy images of Stevie, Michael and Christopher for the first time. "Once I saw these images firsthand," he said, "I knew that there was really no turning back from this thing." Out of that experience grew the website WM3. org and the call to "Free the West Memphis Three." Soon, a fourth California supporter, Lisa Fancher, would join the fledgling effort.[78] In a stroke, the three Arkansas trailer-park kids had a unifying name. They were the West Memphis Three, or the WM3 for short. And they had a slogan demanding their freedom.

A documentary film, serious viewers and compelling questions combined with the fast-forming Internet to forge a movement unprecedented in U.S. legal history. As it began to grow, "Lots of people wrote letters to me," Jason said. "The most common denominator of what they wrote was, 'We believe in you,' 'Hang in there,' 'We're praying for you,' 'We've got your back.' It's an amazing thing when you get letters every day from people you don't know. You've got the very real possibility that your best friend will be murdered by the state, and at the same time, you get letters like these." Many correspondents said they were writing to Damien too.

People sent books through Amazon.com, so Jason always had something good to read, and many also sent money, which went into his commissary account, from which he could buy items not issued by the prison. The amount there ebbed and flowed. Any time his account topped $500, Jason sent the money to his mom. "The amount of support was just extraordinary," he said. "If it weren't for all those people, life in there would have been horrible—a lot worse than it was."

Though hundreds of letters made their way to Jason, Damien, and Jessie as a result of *Paradise Lost*, most viewers who were moved by the film never contacted the men. A dentist in Tennessee said his initial reaction to *Paradise Lost* was that "the West Memphis Three were probably guilty and the state's case wasn't portrayed accurately by the filmmakers." He added that, "Like most people, I trusted the authorities more than Hollywood." A woman in Oklahoma recalled that after watching the film when it premiered on HBO, she and her husband "just looked at each other and said, 'What the fuck just happened there?'" When *Paradise Lost* made it to European TV, it gripped a twenty-one year-old man in Denmark who had never before heard of the faraway case. After seeing the film, he said, however, "I couldn't stop thinking about it."[79]

Some viewers with similar reactions began Internet chat rooms, where strong feelings flew back and forth about the brutality of the murders, the quality of the investigation, the conduct of the trials, and the defendants' guilt or innocence. For a long time, the documentary, the book *Blood of Innocents* (which was published in March 2000) and viewers' reactions to what the film and book chronicled were about all the public discussed. But gradually, in addition to the Californians, a few people from Arkansas, Tennessee, and elsewhere began going to the West Memphis Police Department, the Arkansas Supreme Court, and other public sources to search for case-related documents. As these primary sources were located, they were copied and put online.

The Tennessee dentist said that's when he got "emotionally hooked" on the case. "Reading actual case documents and the strong opinions from both sides drove me to try to find out what really happened," he said. The woman in Oklahoma found the WM3.org website, "and immediately, that day, put a check in the mail" to get a "Free the West Memphis Three" t-shirt. Christian, the man in Denmark, said, "For the first six months or so, I was going back and forth in my mind as to the WM3's guilt or innocence on a daily basis. There wasn't a lot of information available on the Internet back then, but after reading it all, and particularly after learning that Jessie Misskelley had made a post-trial confession, I came to believe they were guilty."[80]

Though unnoticed by most of the world—and certainly by officials in Arkansas—a storm was beginning to form. Media in the Memphis/West Memphis area reported on the release of *Paradise Lost*. A

Memphis paper quoted Sheila Nevins, the HBO senior vice president behind the documentary, voicing doubt about the verdicts. "I think that if reasonable doubt is the issue in this country, not so much guilt or innocence, then there sure is reasonable doubt there," she said. "These kids were guilty until proven innocent. But they weren't sophisticated enough to prove it."[81]

Some news, like reports on the HBO film, filtered into prison TVs. Guards and newly sentenced inmates brought in other news. Letters and visitors carried still more. One way or another, Jason heard a fair amount about some of the people he'd known back in Crittenden County. He heard, for example, that shortly after his and Damien's trial, Chief Inspector Gary Gitchell, who'd led the investigation into the murders, had resigned from the department and moved across the river to Memphis. He knew that, soon after the trial, Fogleman had run for judge and been elected. He heard that Jerry Driver, the juvenile officer who'd given Damien so much trouble, had resigned from his job after an audit of his department revealed missing funds, and that Steve Jones, Jason's own probation officer, had also soon resigned and left Arkansas.[82]

What little news Jason heard about the victims' families was tragic. On November 6, 1994, about six months after Jason entered Varner, Terry Hobbs, the stepfather of victim Stevie Branch, assaulted his wife, Pam. When Pam's brother, Jackie Hicks, intervened, Terry Hobbs shot Hicks in the abdomen. In June 1995, Dana Moore, the mother of victim Michael Moore, struck and killed a pedestrian on a rural road in Crittenden County. The victim happened to be a relative of Jason's from his mother's side of the family. Dana Moore pleaded guilty to driving while intoxicated. And on March 29, 1996, Melissa Byers, the mother of victim Christopher Byers, died under mysterious circumstances, after she was found unconscious at the new home in north-central Arkansas she shared with her husband, John Mark Byers.[83]

Yet that news, sad and interesting as it was, had no impact on Jason's life. He was nineteen years old, in prison for life, aware that many now believed him to be innocent, but locked into the unrelenting reality of life in a dangerous prison. Day after day, he survived by standing up for himself, working hard, and treating everyone—staff and inmates alike—with respect. By the time he was taken off the hoe squad and reassigned to the kitchen, he'd learned the basics of life behind bars. "You get to prison, you're a slave," he said. "If you work in the kitchen, you work twelve-hour days, seven days a week. Then, when you get in and you're waiting on shower call, you might wait an hour. You can't lie down on your rack because you're nasty. The whole time is working and waiting and crashing from being tired. Or it's fighting— trying to figure out who stole your stuff while you were gone and things like that."

Everyone assigned to the kitchen starts out in the dish room. Many quit and go back to hoe squad because, while the outdoor work is hard, men who work on the hoe squad get rainy days, weekends and holidays off. They also get a lunch break. By contrast, kitchen duty is longer and there are no days off. On top of that, a kitchen worker is constantly around food but not allowed to eat except at chow time, like everybody else. There was "a lot more food" at Varner than he'd had in the juvenile jail, Jason said, "but it was not as good."

On Jason's second kitchen assignment, he again started in the dish room, then moved to the serving line. "But that didn't last long," he said. "I got into a bunch of fights. When I got there, before I got glasses, I couldn't see people. I think people coming through the line took advantage of that." From the serving line, he went to sweeping, then, once again, back to the bakery. "I baked bread and dessert," he said. "Ten runs of bread of fifty loaves each, and cakes, cobblers, and crisps. We had giant mixing pots, bigger than I am, and a certain recipe you had to follow. It was scorching hot. Our one oven was probably bigger than a Hummer." He stayed in the kitchen and worked hard, he said, because, "I never wanted to incur any disrespect or loss of respect."

He brought the same philosophy to fights, which came his way often due to the nature of his conviction. "For example, they called me 'Baby Raper,'" he explained. "I'd say, 'That's a lie.' Then they'd say, 'You calling me a liar?' and the next thing you know, they're swinging at me, and I'm swinging back. I've never swung at anybody first. Never have in my life. I've never spoken disrespectful to anybody in my life. But I always stood up. I might not win—that one on the toilet was the only one I ever really won—but eventually that's how people started respecting me. It was just for my attitude. Even in the middle of fights, I wouldn't call people names. I couldn't take it personally, even though it was personal to me."

Jason's steadiness began to pay off. He was moved up to Class 1-C status, the highest classification possible for him. Two and a half years after his arrival at Varner, around Christmas 1996, the warden gave Jason his first job as a clerk, the equivalent of a white-collar job in prison. Jason got the job because of his class and because he knew how to type. Thanks to a typing class he'd taken back at Marion High School, Jason became the nighttime count-room clerk. Each night he would call the guards and ask, 'How many guys you got in the barracks?' If the number didn't match the number the roster said were supposed to be there, Jason would ask, 'Who's out?' If the guard couldn't say, he'd tell the guard, 'You'd better go count your barracks again.'"

The job offered Jason his first opportunity to work on computers. The count-room where he was assigned used only typewriters, but other clerks worked for officials, such as the building major, the field major, and the classification officer, whose offices used computers. And some of those clerks gave Jason their passwords. When work was slow, as it often was at night, Jason could get on their computers. Thus, at night, alone and unmolested, he learned Windows 95, Microsoft Office, Access, and other valuable programs.

For a nearly blind kid living in a place where few had expected him to survive, getting to work on computers was a big step up. It would have been great if the computers had also been linked to the Internet, but in prison, such an incredible link to the outside world was beyond imagining.

"What is art but a way of seeing?"

~ Saul Bellow

It may have been late 1997 or early '98, close to five years after the murders. One morning at about 2:20 a.m., Jason found himself being shaken awake by Mojo. It was confusing. Mojo didn't even live in Jason's barracks. "Get up and get dressed," Mojo whispered. "What's going on?" Jason asked. Mojo responded, "You trust me, don't ya?"

Possibilities flooded Jason's mind. "This dude has some kind of escape plan or something," he thought. "I'm not sure I want to." But it was Mojo, so he got dressed. The two left the barracks and went down the quiet hall to the unit's visitation area. Mojo was a clerk too, with access to the prison's visitation area, and his shift covered this time of night. He was relaxed and acting like a host at a grand event. "He's like, 'You drink Mountain Dew, don't you? You want a burrito? Grab a couple of chairs.'"

Mojo worked for a field major, but sometimes he also did paperwork for other officers, in exchange for small privileges. He'd called in some of those favors to arrange this particular night. "So he gets me out and we set down," Jason said. "He had this TV on a rolling cart. There's a tape in the VCR. He pushed 'play.' And it was *Paradise Lost*. Jason had met the film's makers. He'd received letters from people who'd been shocked and moved by the film. But he had never seen it himself. He didn't know how he'd feel as he sat down to watch a documentary about how his life had been derailed.

Crime scene footage of children's pale, bent bodies on the muddy bank of a ditch hurled him back to the most horrifying part of his trial. The difference was that he could see the images now, not just hear them described. There was aerial footage of Lakeshore Trailer Park. And there was his mother, insisting, "I know where he was, and I know he's innocent!" She looked so much younger then.

Jason saw himself too. At sixteen, he had curly hair and a few pimples, his smile showed a crooked front tooth. He wore the orange jump suit from the jail and talked about his pet iguana and his cat. How young he'd been too when he'd told the filmmakers, "I can see where they might think I'm in a cult because I wear Metallica t-shirts and stuff like that, but I'm not into nothing like that. I couldn't kill an animal or a person."

And there was Damien, the friend he had not seen in more than three years, just as Jason remembered him. For the first time, Jason could see the half-wink and confident nod that Gitchell gave at the press conference the morning after Jason's arrest, when he assured the region that, on a scale of one-to-ten, his case against the teenagers rated an "eleven." Jason had never before seen the rants of John Mark Byers, the father of Christopher Byers, promising to see the three accused in hell; the venom of Christopher's mother Melissa Byers as she spat, "I hate these three—and the mothers that bore them"; the anguish evident as the parents of Michael Moore wondered about their son's last moments; or the angry, whacky way Pam Hobbs, the mother of Stevie Branch, told a television reporter she believed the accused were Satanists because "They look like punks."

With the start of Jessie's trial, Jason pulled his chair close to the prison TV. He wanted to get a good look at Burnett. And at Fogleman, finally, too. Even though Jason was well aware by now that he'd been arrested primarily because of what Jessie had said to police, it was eerie to see the point at Jessie's trial where Gitchell pushed a button on a tape recorder and then to hear the damning words in Jessie's own voice: "I saw Damien hit this one boy real bad, and then he started screwing him and stuff… and then Jason turned around and hit Stevie Branch and started doing the same thing."

Those were the words, Jason thought—the words that had changed his life. It was shocking to hear them from someone he'd considered a friend. Yet Jason could not feel so much as a thimbleful of anger towards Jessie. By now, Jason knew that Jessie kept his head down during the trial because that's what his attorney had told him to do. Jason understood that Jessie was trying to comply with what someone in charge—in this case, Stidham—wanted, and Jason figured that is what Jessie had done during his police interview. "In his mind," Jason said, "he was saying what they wanted him to say. He was put into an impossible situation." Jason reserved his anger for the police. "There was no call for what was done to him."

Watching Jessie slouched in his chair, his forehead braced against the defense table, Jason thought that any juror would have at least harbored doubts about Jessie's so-called confession, especially after Stidham pointed out key details—like when the murders occurred and what the boys were bound with—that Jessie had gotten wrong.

Yet Jason could also see the easy assurance with which Gitchell had brushed those errors aside, saying, "Jessie simply got confused." Jason reacted, "Of course, he got confused! You'd been messing with him for hours!" But what futility! One of the other things Jason knew was that he almost certainly would not be sitting here, watching this film in prison, if the jury had chosen to believe the confused kid over the confident cop.

In the film, it looked like the whole trial had played out that simply. Jason knew that the reality had been much the same. The jurors heard Jessie implicate himself, as well as Damien and Jason, in the murders, and that had been enough for them to find Jessie guilty and sentence him to life plus forty years in prison. Jason had never seen the courthouse where Jessie was tried. He watched the sad scene of Jessie being led out of the building, much as he had been, wearing handcuffs and a bulletproof vest. Jessie was strong for such a little guy, Jason thought. The top of Jessie's head barely reached the shoulders of the deputies escorting him.

It was hard in a different way for Jason to watch footage of the victims' parents. "You understand how much pain they're suffering," he said. "I can understand them wanting to blame who the police told them to blame." Yet, watching, he knew that even now, "I couldn't say anything that would console them at all."

Everything about the film was hard. As Jason watched the meeting between the prosecutors and the victims' parents, where Davis and Fogleman tried to explain to the parents why, right after getting Jessie convicted, they were offering him a reduced sentence, Jason realized that this meeting had occurred at the same time that Ford and Wadley were conveying the prosecutors' offers of a reduced sentence to him—if he would just testify against Damien. It was sickening to realize how hard those men grasped for his and Jessie's testimony, even as they held out their list of weak evidence to the parents. Sickening and pathetic. He wondered, had the prosecutors been counting all along on their ability to get Jessie and him to buckle, to be so scared of a possible death sentence that they would lie about Damien? With so little else to go on, had that always been their plan?

Jason could hardly believe it when he heard Fogleman telling the parents after Jessie's trial and before his and Damien's that all would not be lost if Jessie refused to testify, then adding, 'But the odds are reduced significantly.' It was grimly fascinating to see Fogleman outline for the parents the evidence he and Davis felt they had for the trial ahead: "a couple of fibers," statements of people he called "the Hollingsworth clan," remarks made by "some kids" who said they'd overheard Damien admit to the killings at a girls' softball game, "a guy that was in jail with Jason who says that Jason made some incriminating statements to him," and "the knife that was found in the lake behind Jason's house." Fogleman concluded, "So that's what we've got, but that's all that we've got." Davis told the parents that the odds of convicting Damien and Jason without Jessie's testimony were about "fifty-fifty."

It was incredible for Jason to hear the prosecutors acknowledge that they were willing to seek the death penalty for him and Damien with evidence that, by their own calculation, was no stronger than random luck, unless they could wrangle accusatory testimony from a kid who was known to be mentally challenged. It was beyond him to think that they—that anyone—would seek execution for defendants whose guilt they didn't feel dead-certain they could prove.

The scene struck Jason especially hard for what it did not contain: any mention of the occult, the strange and disturbing motive that, just two weeks later, assumed such prominence at his and Damien's trial. Here, in *Paradise Lost*, was Fogleman saying that the list of evidence he'd recited was "all" he and Davis had. Jason knew that, by the time this was filmed, Fogleman had been working on the case for almost nine months. Until now, seeing the film, Jason would have thought that Fogleman's speech to the parents would have included the pitch he'd used so effectively at trial; that he might have said, "And, of course, we have the most important evidence of all, which is evidence of the killers' motive, and that is that they were involved in a Satanic cult." After being bludgeoned with the occult at trial, Jason was perhaps most upset at hearing no mention of the word in this part of the film.

Then, of course, there was the real evidence that had been collected but that the West Memphis police claimed to have "lost" the samples of blood and mud left by a "disoriented" man in a Bojangles' restaurant near the crime scene on the night of the murders. Long before seeing the film, Jason had concluded the department's bungling of the Bojangles' evidence marked the turning point in the case. He believed that two tragedies occurred as a result: the first was that, in losing that evidence, investigators lost their most critical lead in discovering the killer or killers; the second was that they consequently shifted their attention to Damien and his associates, as Driver had been urging them to do. "After they lost the Bojangles' evidence, all the rest was intentional," Jason said. "Damage control."

But all that was hindsight. He could think whatever he wanted, but the reality was that he and Mojo were watching inside a dark prison. He noted with irony that it would be here, watching his younger self on trial—that he would see the courthouse and the characters who had surrounded him then clearly for the first time. Enduring the actual trial had been difficult enough. But this time was actually harder. Then, he'd had hope. Then, he'd felt sure that the jury would see how contrived the state's evidence against him was. Now, however, he knew how this movie ended. The evidence against him and Damien was nothing but cobwebs. Nevertheless, here he sat, locked between walls of iron. The contrast between the spectral evidence spun in the film and the grim physicality of prison hit him hard. And the film kept hitting:

- There was the lake knife that Fogleman made out to be so important, and yet, there came the state's own witness, Detective Mike Allen, responding when asked if he was saying that the knife was the murder weapon: "No, sir. I'm not telling the jury that."
- There was another state's witness, Dr. Frank Peretti, of the Arkansas Crime Lab, saying that, though the mutilation of Christopher Byers was supposed to be part of the "occult ritual," he could not explain how a killer could have so skillfully removed the skin from the boy's penis in the ditch, where blood would have been washed away—or alternatively, why, if the mutilation was performed on the banks of the ditch, virtually no trace of blood had been found there.

- There was Michael Carson, from the juvenile detention center, acknowledging that, yes, he had kept quiet for more than six months after hearing Jason confess to killing the boys, but explaining that he'd finally come forward just before the start of Damien and Jason's trial because he'd seen the victims' parents on TV and realized "how brokenhearted they were."

- There was the 12-year-old whose face wasn't filmed, describing how she'd heard Damien confess to the murders at a softball field, but also admitting that she had not been "close" enough to Damien to have heard anything he'd said before or after that confession.

- There was West Memphis police Officer Bryn Ridge, admitting that he'd "lost" blood scrapings taken from the Bojangles' restaurant, near where the bodies were found, yet feeling confident enough to testify that Damien had read "horror books" by the likes of Stephen King and, when asked if he found that strange, responding firmly, "Yes, I did."

- Most disturbing of all, of course, there was "Dr." Dale Griffis, the state's "expert" in the occult, talking about the full moon that had risen on the night of the murders, the "symbolic importance" of water, blood and the number three. One word hovered in Jason's mind as he watched the state's parade of witnesses: "Crazy."

The spectacle was familiar—yet not. What he was now seeing Jason had experienced first-hand, but at the age of sixteen, and with his life hanging in the balance. He'd learned a lot since then, and by now he'd read all the state Supreme Court's reasons why the trial had been, procedurally, just about perfect. But he'd never read a transcript of it. Watching *Paradise Lost*, Jason remembered the sense he'd had at his trial that Burnett was "calling the shots." He had the same sense seeing the film.

To Jason, the whole show seemed to be summed up at the end, when Fogleman, having reminded the jurors about all "this Satanic stuff," pointed at Damien and pronounced, "There's not a soul in there."[84] Just as Jason remembered, when all was said and done, that's what the state's case had rested on: a lacework of unsupported claims, the testimony of a charlatan, and language from the Inquisition.

For Jason, *Paradise Lost* was both awful and fascinating to watch, like seeing a film of a car crash in which you were almost killed or of a disaster that ruined your home and swept away your family. Yet such comparisons weren't quite apt, either. There was something off-kilter about this tragedy. It wasn't as straightforward as a car crash or as indifferent as a natural disaster. Jason saw more clearly now the veil of officiousness that clothed the case. The trial looked dignified and formal, but it rested on clever absurdity.

For all in the film that rattled Jason, it held one shining moment when someone spoke a plain and beautiful truth. That someone was his mother. Overcoming all her frailties, Jason saw his mother in a scene he'd never known had taken place. There she stood outside the courtroom, confronting all the forces arrayed against her son—and making more sense, it seemed to Jason, than anyone else in the film. "It's kind of like the Nazis, you know," she was telling the filmmakers. "They can just take somebody's word and come in your house and take you away. And, basically, that's what they did, because of what Jessie told them, even though it had all those inconsistencies in it."

Afterward, just as after the trial, Jason felt indignant. "What I found insulting was how, if Damien said anything, Brent Davis and John Fogleman would twist it around," he said. "I found all that stuff repulsive. And it really got everything and everyone away from the real issue of who committed the crime." Still, Jason thought—then and now—that Damien had conducted himself well. "He was honest. He wasn't hiding anything. He was totally operating under the security of what you're taught about being an American: that trials are fair, that you have the freedom to educate yourself, and that you have the freedom to worship whatever religion you want. He was being totally honest and saying all that under the premise that, 'I might not live the way you do, but in America, that's okay.'"

As soon as the credits began to roll, Mojo jumped up and said, "JB, you're going home, man!" But Jason was not elated. The film had taken a toll. "It's hard to see yourself going through all that stuff again," he later explained. "And I could see the people I wasn't able to see while it was going on—my mom and Little Terry—there in the courtroom at my sentencing. After it was all over, I could see in the video that my mom was trying to get my attention. It was painful for me. So while Mojo was jumping up, I was just kind of sitting there in a daze and reliving it all. Seeing my mom and Little Terry that close to me and not even knowing they were that close to me at the time, and seeing how much pain was in her face, I was like, man, I wish I could have just said, 'Hey, Mom, I love you and everything will be all right.'"

Back in his rack, with time to think, Jason experienced a rush of conflicting reactions. He realized how much better able he was now to "absorb" the experience of his trial than he'd been at sixteen. Back then, he'd literally taken to heart the notion that the jury would consider Damien, Jessie, and him innocent until the state proved they were guilty. Tonight, though, he'd seen his trial more clearly. Going into it, he said, "Everyone knew we were guilty, so everyone made sure there was something to support that." At his trial, Jason expected the jurors to want to be shown evidence. Tonight he realized that the jury had simply "let Fogleman dramatize and ostracize us."

In fairness, he also acknowledged to himself how lame his defense team had been. "The jurors heard Michael Carson, but they didn't hear my alibi witnesses. They weren't allowed to hear stuff that was available even then. So they were only getting one side of the picture." Reflecting from yet another angle, he thought, "It's supposed to be a jury of your peers, but people on the jury were so far removed from a character like Damien, they could hardly relate to him. And even if they'd been able to, the picture they got of him from the prosecutors was so vilified, it probably wouldn't have made any difference."

Scenes of Jessie, Damien, and himself being led in handcuffs into and out of courtrooms—alone and so estranged, from each other and from the mobs around them—had been especially hard to watch, despite Metallica's familiar music in the background. As hard as prison had been for him, he'd felt anew "how much pain Damien's family and Jessie's family and my family were put through during all that." Seeing *Paradise Lost* had reminded him "how the whole community turned against us."

As for seeing himself back then: "Oh, man. That was the worst. Everything about it was bad. Just seeing myself going through that, all the time thinking, 'Justice will prevail.'" Watching his world collapse, he'd heard himself warn his younger self on the screen: "Dude, you had no idea!"

Chris Byers   **Michael Moore**   **Steve Branch**

The murders of the three eight-year-old boys on May 5, 1993 still haunt West Memphis, Arkansas and many who've followed the case. The mother of Stevie Branch and the stepfather of Christopher Byers no longer believe that the West Memphis Three committed the crime.

Photo courtesy West Memphis Police Department.

From a young age, Jason admired the way the members of the band Metallica could "build all these different harmonies and melodies with their single instruments," yet combine their individuality to make "the overall song."

Photo courtesy West Memphis Police Department.

Ron Lax, a prominent Memphis private investigator, volunteered to help the attorneys assigned to represent Damien, Jason and Jessie soon after he learned of the teenagers' arrests. Attorneys for Damien and Jessie accepted the offer. Jason's attorney declined.

Photo courtesy Vita Zelikov.

Bruce Sinofsky (left) and Joe Berlinger went to Arkansas soon after the teenagers' arrests to record the film that would become *Paradise Lost: The Child Murders at Robin Hood Hills*. This photo, from 1993, shows Jason as he awaited trial in the juvenile detention center in Jonesboro.

Photo courtesy of Joe Berlinger, all rights reserved.

On November 17, 1993, more than five months after Jason's arrest, a diver for the Arkansas State Police retrieved a serrated knife from the lake behind his house. Years later, prosecutor John Fogleman said he had requested the search on a "hunch," yet media were informed of the dive in advance.

Photo courtesy Kathleen Burt/West Memphis Evening Times.

In one of the most remarkable scenes from *Paradise Lost: The Child Murders at Robin Hood Hills*, prosecutors Brent Davis and John Fogleman tell the victims' parents that, "All is not lost," without Jessie's testimony at Damien and Jason's pending trial. However, they estimated their odds of convicting the two would be about "fifty-fifty."

Photo courtesy of Joe Berlinger, all rights reserved.

Jason could not understand why his lead attorney, Paul Ford, did not call any of his alibi witnesses to testify or allow him to take the stand in his own defense. Jason said that every time he asked his lawyers about letting him testify, "They just put me off, they kept giving me the runaround."

The only evidence linking Jason to the murders, aside from the knife recovered from the lake by his house, was the testimony of Michael Carson, a young offender facing multiple charges. Carson testified that while he and Jason were jailed together, Jason told him he'd "sucked the blood from the penis and scrotum" of a victim, "and put the balls in his mouth."

Jason said he did not know who Carson was when the teenager took the stand. He said that, as Carson was being sworn in, Ford leaned over and whispered to him: "This kid is about to testify that you told him you killed the boys. Remember the judge's orders. You cannot show any emotion."

The gate at the Arkansas prison system's Diagnostic Unit remains much as Jason described it: "The officer in the tower lowers a milk crate on a rope and the officers up front drop their guns in the basket and it is hoisted away. Then the little bar in front of the van is raised up and we enter the grounds of the prison."

In 1994, when Jason entered prison, all of Arkansas's young male offenders were housed in the state's sprawling Varner Unit. By the time Jason arrived, the seven-year-old prison had developed such a reputation for violence that guards and prisoners alike called it "Gladiator School."

Photo courtesy Arkansas Department of Correction.

For a time, prisoners' families were allowed to purchase Polaroid photos shot by other inmates with a department-owned camera. This was taken during Jason's first stint at Varner, after he'd gotten his first pair of contraband glasses—and before the department limited how long inmates could grow their hair.

Photo courtesy Antonio Williams.

In 1996, while Jason was at Varner, Associate Justice Robert H. Dudley, a former prosecutor and judge from Jonesboro, wrote the Arkansas Supreme Court's unanimous opinion affirming his and Damien's convictions. At about thirty thousand words—a third the length of this book—it found "no reversible errors" in their trial.

Photo Credit: Portrait by Larry Bishop photographed by Meghan Sever.

The influence of the first documentary Berlinger and Sinofsky produced on the West Memphis case cannot be overstated. The film's release in 1996 led to broad discussion on the Internet, websites devoted to case records, fundraising on behalf of the men in prison, new attorneys and new investigations.

Photo courtesy of Joe Berlinger, all rights reserved.

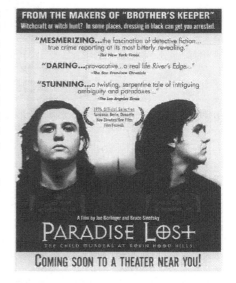

The Californians who began and maintained the influential website, WM3. org—Lisa Fancher, Kathy Bakken, Burk Sauls, and Grove Pashley—made several trips to Arkansas to attend court hearings and visit the prisoners they named the West Memphis Three. Here the four are shown with Damien, who was housed on death row at Arkansas's Supermax Unit.

Photo courtesy Burk Sauls.

Grove Pashley, a professional photographer and one of the founders of WM3.org, shot many of the iconic images that were used to publicize the prisoners' plight. No words need accompany this one he took of Jason at Varner.

Jason occasionally saw Jessie, when they happened to be assigned to the same unit. Reflecting on Jessie's confession, Jason said: "I guess some police and prosecutors get so used to putting pressure on people, and putting them in impossible situations, that they expect people to make stuff up."

Photo courtesy Grove Pashley.

This author visited all of the men in prison, starting soon after their convictions. Here she is shown with Jason at the Grimes Unit, where he clerked at the prison's school. When Jason first entered the new unit, guards dropped tear gas into the entire barracks in what was called "a demonstration of power."

Photo courtesy Grove Pashley.

In the late 1990s, musician Eddie Vedder of Pearl Jam asked John Philipsborn (shown,), a San Francisco attorney experienced in trial and appellate work, to take a look at the status of all three cases and propose a starting point because, as Philipsborn put it, "there was a lot of material that hadn't been looked at very well."

By the time Jason was put in solitary confinement at the state's Supermax Unit, DNA findings had raised suspicions about Terry Hobbs, the stepfather of Stevie Branch, whom police had never questioned. A hair found inside a knot binding Michael Moore showed a high probability of having come from Hobbs.

By eight years after the murders, interest in the West Memphis case had spread worldwide. For a 2001 hearing at the Arkansas Supreme Court, organizers of the WM3.org website asked supporters who could not attend in person to send postcards representing their countries and states. Thousands did, creating a banner hundreds of feet long.

While this book ends in 2007, with Jason still in prison, he was able to tell his story because he, Jessie and Damien were freed in 2011. Events leading to that remarkable piece of legal history will comprise the final book of this trilogy. Here, Jason is shown with Holly Ballard, one of the supporters who attended the event at the Crittenden County Courthouse in 2007. They married in 2013.

Photo courtesy Sarah Woodrow Collier.

CHAPTER FIVE

GRIMES

February 1, 1998 - July 31, 2001

Memories from *Paradise Lost* pummeled Jason well beyond that night. For the first time, he had seen—seen!—events that surrounded his arrest, plans which were laid while he waited in jail, and the officials who conducted his trial. The images took their time working their way through his brain, knocking over this misconception, bulldozing that belief, returning him to an all new square one, raising a riot of new questions. Jason was no longer a shackled sixteen year-old kid being run through the machinery of law. He was now nearly twenty-one—a man, whose maturity had been bought at the price of his youth. He'd spent the last five years enduring some of the harshest brutality his country could legally offer, from the threat of death at his trial to the day-to-day threats at Varner. He'd entered the system young, trusting and visually impaired. He was none of those things now.

He'd survived, at least so far, both physically and spiritually. He had not succumbed to meanness, though meanness surrounded him. He'd become a man with hope but without delusions. He hadn't graduated from high school, but he'd earned his GED. Instead of studying art in college, he'd come through "gladiator school." Varner had turned out to be everything they'd warned him about at Diagnostic. "Windows were knocked out. Fights were constant things," he recalled. Yet, in that environment, he'd managed to find a measure of peace and respectability as a count-room clerk. One morning, as Jason was coming off the graveyard shift, a supervisor stopped Jason in the hall. "Are you going to

Grimes when it's open?" the supervisor asked. "I'm looking for somebody to go over there and run our school."

Rumors had circulated for months about the two new prisons being built in northeast Arkansas. One would be for men, the other for women, and they were going to be run by a private company, the Wackenhut Corporation.[85] The men's unit would be named after Sgt. Scott A. Grimes, a prison guard who was stabbed to death the year after Jason entered prison.

Jason had heard that the Grimes Unit would be for young offenders, twenty-one and under, who were entering with nonviolent charges. He waited to hear more. "Do you work on computers yet?" the supervisor asked. "Not officially," Jason answered. The supervisor said, "Well, I've talked to people about you, and they say you could go over and run the unit's school."

Jason understood the prison's staffing dilemma. With prison populations burgeoning, the state could not afford to hire enough employees, and among those who were hired, turnover was high. As a result, reliable inmate clerks were needed throughout the system. Without them, no unit could function. A good clerk serving a life sentence was especially valuable.

Administrators recognized the clerks' importance, and so did the clerks themselves. In every unit they formed tight-knit groups, stayed in the same barracks, and tended to hold onto their positions, especially if they liked their supervisors. Jason enjoyed being a count-room clerk, and he liked his supervisor a lot. He realized that the new prison was probably finding it hard to recruit qualified clerks who were willing to leave their current posts to work at the new unit's school. On the other hand, given a choice between the job he was doing and clerking in a school, Jason would choose the school. The decision was made easier when his friend Smitty agreed to go and clerk in the school, too.

"So after that," Jason said, "instead of going back to the barracks, I'd go sit in the school and watch the clerks. I learned all three of their jobs; school management, running the office, and running the computer lab." In February 1998, two months shy of his twenty-first birthday, Jason and Smitty boarded the prison bus for the three-hour drive north to the just-opened Scott Grimes Unit.

It wasn't what he'd expected. "When I got over there, they put me into 1-Delta, a barracks with two-man cells. I get in there and I notice that everybody in this barracks has a murder charge. Why is that?" The answer wasn't long in coming. "Once they got the place built, Varner just got rid of everybody who'd been giving them trouble. They dumped all their knuckleheads into Grimes. It was the same thing that happened just before I got to Varner. So all these guards at Varner were telling the Wackenhut guys, 'You won't be able to handle these guys.' So the guys running Grimes were really aggressive starting out. Their entire message was: 'You're not going to do here what you did at Varner.'"

Inmates at Grimes were separated by charge, so Jason, despite his Class 1-C status, was in with the murderers. Within each group, the men were separated alphabetically. His roommate was André Blair. "The first thing I noticed was that the TVs in the barracks were twice as big as at Varner, and the barracks had microwaves. And the food wasn't farm food. It was like school cafeteria food, prepared at the women's unit. The women fixed food for both units, and the men at Grimes did the laundry for both. The food was awesome."

The staff was on heightened security alert. "All they kept saying was, 'This ain't Varner,' Jason recalled. "The school was not up and running yet, so when I first got there, they pretty much just kept us in lockdown in our cells." Gradually, the staff began to let the men into the commons area, and not long after that, violence erupted. Jason was using the telephone when he saw, all of a sudden, an inmate walk over and swing a chair at the back of a captain's head. Jason hung up and walked to his cell. Within seconds, a voice came over the intercom instructing everyone to go immediately to their cells, that the doors were about to be locked and that they had better be inside.

"Of course, there were guys that did not go in their cells," Jason said. "And, sure enough, they brought in the goon squad. It was a search team. They were dressed all in black. They had shields, batons, and gas masks. The barracks was built with three tiers, and there were pipes coming down from the ceiling. All of a sudden, these canisters of tear gas start dropping down from the pipes. The doors to our cells are solid steel, so I get my towel and put it in my sink and get it wet. I put it on the floor in front of the door. They were using some kind of pepper-based gas that attacks the mucus membranes. They never had done anything like that at Varner. Varner wasn't designed in cell blocks. It was open barracks. So they'd spray a person with mace but not attack the whole barracks."

The steel door on Jason's cell had a small, shatter-resistant plastic window strengthened with something like chicken wire. Guards could see in and inmates could see out. The doors electronically locked. Jason stood at the window and watched. "After they threw the gas in," he said, "they came in and they beat them dudes. There were five, six or seven guys outside, and they came out there and just beat them down. There was a stairwell right by my cell. I saw them dragging a guy by his feet. His hands and feet were tied with zip ties. They were dragging him down the stairs on his belly, and his chin would bounce on every step."

Time passed. Jason hoped the incident was over. But no. "After a good while, they come around and opened everybody's bean flap"—the slot in the door that opens from the outside through which food trays can pass. "They told everybody to strip down to our boxers. They said, 'You will strip down. This is not Varner.' So I look at André. He looks at me. I've already seen what's going to happen when you exhibit disobedience. So André and I strip down to our boxers."

Guards told the men to stick their hands out the bean hole. "They take a plastic zip tie and wrap it around my wrists, and they make it tight," Jason said. "I mean, it's biting to the bone. Of course, me, I understand that these people are like in a hornets' nest that's been kicked. There's no reasoning with them. They do Blair the same way and tell us to go sit down on our bunks. Then, they open the door and order us out. 'Over by the wall! Bend over and kiss your ass! On your knees! Heads against the wall!' Pretty soon, everybody that didn't stay out and fight is out there. But there's still some gas, and now my nose is running because I'm out in it. It's just a gross, messed-up, compromised situation—and painful. It's a concrete floor, and I've got bony knees. My hands are aching. It's really bugging me. But I'm not going to say anything. I'm not going be the one they get. My runny nose—it was what it was."

As Jason recalls, guards had at least a hundred men against the wall. The warden, a man who'd worked for Wackenhut prisons all over the world, strode along the line like a general. "'This isn't Varner,' he says, "and he's got in his left hand, while he's talking, he's got a whole box of freaking toothpicks. He puts one in the right side of mouth. He chews on it. He moves it to the left side. Then he spits it out and gets another one. I've never seen anything like it. He was ripping through them things. He's telling us how we're going to be good or we're going to be punished. Then, he has us stand up and march outside into the hallway. We're marching down the hallway, and we get all the way to the last window, and they tell us to get up along the wall again, only now they tell us to lie down on our bellies. They've got all the guys with the big time, and that includes me, of course. So they're putting down what's called a demonstration of their power. And after we sit out there for a while, with the warden giving us his speech with the toothpicks where other guys in their cells could hear, there was one guy who said something about his hands, and he got summarily dealt with."

That was Jason's welcome to Grimes. Eventually, the men were marched to the prison gymnasium, where a nurse looked them over. She went to Jason first and asked if he could wiggle his fingers. An officer beside her cut the zip tie. The nurse asked, "Are you okay?" Without waiting for an answer, she said, "I'm going to take this one with me down to the infirmary." When circulation returned to his hands, Jason was put back in his cell, where he and his roommate stayed on lockdown for several, chaotic days. Important parts of the prison, such as the commissary, that were manned by inmates weren't running yet. "Guys were complaining," Jason said. "Tensions were high." As with Varner, no word about the troubles at Grimes made it into the Arkansas news. That would have been unlikely at any time, but the gassing occurred in 1998, when the impeachment of President Bill Clinton dominated the nation's—and Arkansas's—news.

Within a few months of Jason's arrival at Grimes, the staff got the new prison structured, inmates' got their original classifications back, and talk turned to starting the school. Jason was more than ready to be let out of his cell and get back to doing a job. The day finally came when Mac Kennedy, the civilian teacher hired to run the school, showed up at Jason's door. Kennedy said, "Baldwin, I need to get this school up and running." Jason replied that he was ready but demanded, "Get me out of here." Kennedy made the move happen, and Jason was returned to his trustee status in a twenty-five man open barracks. Smitty went to work in the school with Jason in the computer lab. "But then Smitty got out," Jason said, "and after he got released, I ended up running all of it." By 1999, conditions were quieter at Grimes.[86]

Jason heard that Damien's lawyers had filed his Rule 37 petition and that Judge Burnett had held eight days of hearings on it, staggered between May 1998 and March 1999. Jason knew that, after that, Edward Mallett, a lawyer representing Damien on his appeal, had argued that Damien's trial lawyers had compromised themselves by accepting five thousand dollars from the HBO filmmakers to offset legal expenses.[87] He also knew that Mallett had called in an expert who said that a wound on the face of victim Stevie Branch could have been a bite mark made by a human. The question was, if the wound was a bite mark, who—or what—had made it? Jason, Damien and Jessie all agreed to have impressions taken of their teeth to establish that, if the human bite theory turned out to be correct, they could be excluded as the source. Once again, Jason allowed himself to hope that science would come to his rescue. "I was excited about everything that came out," Jason said. "Things like a bite mark on Stevie Branch—I'd say, 'Okay, this is going to be it.' If an expert says, 'Whoever killed them bit them,' I say, 'Yeah, get my impression made.'"

Otherwise, for Jason, the arguments were interesting but abstract; at this point, he had neither an attorney nor any idea how results favoring Damien might also favor him.[88] All Jason could do was live his life, which, at that time, revolved mostly around his work. He loved his job at the school.

"The staff, the people who I work with—they make me feel like just another guy on the job, not an inmate in a white suit," he said at the time. "They care about me. Every day, we talk and debate over what's going on with my case, and they know—they know—I don't belong here. It's weird, to be so liked in the place where I work, doing something I enjoy, and yet to have to walk out of here every day, back into the population, where the security runs the show and how different that is. In here I'm treated nicely, fairly, and respectfully. But when I step out of where I work, I am ridiculed, picked on, and treated with the utmost prejudice. If I could I'd just bring my bed and things down here to the school and stay!"

Other inmates can make life in prison miserable, but their power can't compare to the power officials wield. A corrupt or malicious officer can make an inmate's life hell, and there was such a man at Grimes. While it seemed that half the men at Varner had wanted to kill Jason, at Grimes, it was a particular captain who first made his hostility known. When Jason arrived at the new prison, the captain informed Jason that he did not just dislike him; he hated him. The captain never explained why. Jason assumed that, like most others, the man saw him as a Satanic child-killer. Whatever the captain's reasons, Jason distinctly remembered the captain telling him that he and his officers intended to treat Jason "with utmost prejudice."

The captain proved true to his word. He looked for opportunities to give Jason grief, especially in the one part of Jason's life that actually brought him joy. She was a slip of a girl from Little Rock, the same age as Jason, who had been writing to him since shortly after his conviction. She wrote regularly, as did he, and she visited him often, starting at Varner. But, bad as Varner was, Grimes—and that captain, in particular—was another matter. Here, when she visited Jason and he held her hand, the captain came out and told her to leave. Holding hands was allowed, and other couples were doing much more, but as the captain had promised, Jason was being treated with prejudice. After having been a Class-1 inmate for five years, he was busted to Class-2 for holding his girlfriend's hand. He was denied mail and phone calls for thirty days and visitors for sixty days.[89]

"Other guys were out there kissing their girlfriends, but they were overlooked," Jason said at the time. "I have been blessed with a lot of friends and support, and I know that I will be free someday. That makes me happy and gives me hope. I can even smile and work at getting an education and all kinds of stuff while I am in here. But no matter how good things may be going, there is always a deep sense of sorrow inside of me." He said he felt that sorrow "always"—except when he was with his girlfriend. When the captain ordered her to leave, "We were singled out and punished."

The school became Jason's sanctuary, encompassing him in something as close as he could get to the life he wanted, work he valued, and people who cared about learning. The free-world teachers shared a lounge that had chairs, a table, and a refrigerator. They couldn't bring inmates food; that would breach regulations. But nothing said they couldn't bring extra for their lunches and leave it in the refrigerator. "Every one of them was like my grandma," he said. "Every one of them was trying to fatten me up. They were like, 'We left a bunch of food in the fridge that needs to be disposed of.'"

Jason did mainly administrative work, tracking attendance and grades. As most students were working for their GEDs, the school sorted them into levels. The ones at Level Five were almost ready to take the exam. Those at Level One had trouble adding, spelling and sometimes even writing their names. Of the five hundred men at Grimes, Jason estimated that at any time, about four hundred, on average, had dropped out of high school and lacked their GEDs. He saw many reasons for that grim statistic, all of them interconnected. "Every little thing contributed," he said. "You can't pull any of it out. Poverty. Poor neighborhoods. Drugs. Taking up crime at young ages. A lack of positive role models."[90] He recognized that culture too played a role. Though a regional prejudice against heavy metal music may have helped convict him, Jason, for his part, found nothing to like in rap. To him, it represented the sound of "glorified violence and drug culture," and he'd seen "a lot of guys in prison as a result of it."

"Some people walk in the rain, others just get wet."
~ Roger Miller

Jason worked at the school from 7 a.m. to 4:30 p.m. When a few college courses were offered, he signed up for any classes he could fit into his work schedule.[91] In addition, he became a peer counselor. Administrators at Grimes chose Jason to be one of fifteen inmates who would live with prisoners who, "had been addicted to either alcohol or drugs and who were ready to leave that part of their lives behind." The idea was that Jason, having endured some tough experiences himself, would be able to serve as a role model. The counselor's job was to show the men in the program that, as Jason put it, "As difficult as things may be, you still have a choice. Even though the choices might suck, some suck less than others." Though he was younger than most of the men he counseled, Jason understood that it would not be easy for them to change practices that had brought them to prison. "They don't usually know what to do besides what they have always done," he said, "which is to be a 'fuck up.'"

Inmates flowed constantly into and out of the program. One evening, while Jason was fixing a meal he'd bought for himself and some friends at the commissary, a new inmate walked in. Seeing Jason, the new man approached. "I don't know if you remember me," he said. Jason did, instantly. Standing before him was one of the men who had cracked his skull and broken his collarbone at Varner. The man apologized and asked Jason not to hold the incident against him. Jason knew that this was more than a simple apology. The inmate needed to complete the prison's substance treatment program to apply for an early release, and he needed Jason's approval to complete the program. "'I accept your apology," Jason said. "I forgave you long ago." Then he invited the new man to join in the dinner.

Life got better still when a friend smuggled a tape deck into the prison for Jason. He listened to Metallica, Nine Inch Nails, and the Deftones. Guards retired or resigned and were replaced by new guards who had not heard all the horror stories about the men being transferred from Varner, so they tended to be not so rough. Through letters and phone calls, Jason kept in touch with the four Californians who'd founded the website with the bold intent to "Free the West Memphis Three." He heard news from them, from the local TV, and from newcomers to the prison. He learned, for instance, that Judge Burnett had rejected all of Damien's legal arguments and denied his Rule 37 petition.[92] He also learned that Damien had married a woman from New York named Lorri Davis, with whom he'd been corresponding for years. But one of the best surprises for Jason in 1999 came by mail directly to him: a warm letter from his high school art teacher, Ms. Sally Ware.

She wrote: "I didn't hear anything around town when Damien was here for his hearing. Seems like things are kept kind of hush-hush around here." Noting that Jason had been in her class for two years, which she calculated to have been "three hundred and forty classes," Ware assured Jason, "I knew you couldn't have been involved in the West Memphis murders. For you to be capable of doing that, it would make Dr. Jekyll turning into Mr. Hyde look like Minnie Mouse." Besides, she added, more soberly, "There was no evidence against you."[93]

Grimes offered one thing that most prisons did not: space. The barracks at this unit were bigger than he'd ever been in and the day room felt "humongous." In the beginning, inmates had access to recreational items in the day room, including Hacky Sacks. Jason had been introduced to the foot bag at Varner by none other than a relative of Damien's stepfather, who happened to serve a short time there. "We kicked a little bit," he recalled. But a novice needs room to practice keeping a stuffed sack in motion without using hands, and Varner had no such space.

At Grimes, Jason picked up a Hacky Sack and found that, "right there where you lived, you had all the room you needed." Gradually, kicking the Hacky Sack became a central, grounding, and comforting part of his life. "I don't meditate," he explained. "Not that I have anything against it. I just have no experience with that. So I'd just put my headphones on and kick the Hacky Sack for physical exercise, to—not tune out but—tune in. It's like the same feeling you get when you go walking or jogging or biking. You get this oneness feeling, especially when you get caught up in it, and you're not losing control of it, and an hour has gone by and you're drenched in sweat, and you got to take a shower, and you feel good."

As equipment broke down or disappeared from the day room, most was not replaced. That forced Jason and other prisoners to make their own faux Hacky Sacks, using cloth from old uniforms, popcorn kernels for fill, and a pattern for sewing a baseball. They had needles and thread because this was a time, now gone, when prison uniforms still had buttons and commissaries still sold sewing kits.

Sometimes, when Jason was kicking, other people would jump in, kick a bit, and jump out, but mostly he kicked alone. Eventually, he got good enough that he could kick in a very small space. A fellow inmate, Dung Thai Tran, enjoyed watching Jason kick. "That your discipline," he'd say.

As a counselor, Jason got to know hundreds of inmates in a more than casual way. Part of his job was to assess them, for purposes of their early release. But he didn't judge. Most of the inmates assigned to him were African-Americans—men who'd grown up in street gangs that had supplanted their families. "Their father might not have been there. Their big brothers were in gangs. They grew up in gangs, and there they went—selling drugs to make money to help mom out—or whatever. And then the next thing you know, they're in prison. I guess they could have refused to deal, but who knows what the scenario was? To go against all that takes tremendous will power. And people who decide to go against it might not even survive the decision."

He offered counseling and learned in return. He met many men who were shaped by experiences that made his own look rich by comparison. After all, he had a caring mom who, he knew, loved him. And, while a couple of prosecutors had attempted to have him killed, at least he'd never felt the fire of a bullet through his flesh. "In prison I met so many people that had been shot multiple times," he said. "It was unreal, I couldn't imagine being shot or making the decision to shoot someone else. But these guys just acted like it was nothing, just a normal thing. Lots left with the same state of mind they had when they came in. Some would come back. Some, you would hear they got shot and killed after they were released." He learned: "You can tell a person what to do or not to do until you're blue in the face, but it's always their decision. And, again, what opportunities do they have?"

Besides restraining inmates physically, prisons affect the inner workings of every person inside them, including staff, and the effect on each person is different. Some prisoners, especially those in solitary confinement for long periods, go mad. Others, whose mental health was marginal when they committed their crimes, deteriorate further.

By contrast, some inmates adapt well to prison, finding in them the structure they couldn't create for themselves outside. Some inmates get mean or meaner, some find strength and purpose in faith, some succumb to lifelong dependency on a government institution, and some leave, only to return again and again, like yo-yo dieters. A very few find in prison a sense of freedom such as is rarely encountered even in the "free world." For these, mastery of self can transcend their physical confinement—at least at times. This was the case for Jason.

Whatever an inmate's personality, it's never easy living surrounded by chain link, coiled razor wire, iron bars, concrete walls, yelling, disrespect and despair. Men who considered their punishments fair fared better. But for men who were wrongfully convicted, hurt or outrage over the injustice torqueing their lives could push the bounds of sanity. The odd thing about Jason's early twenties in prison was that, even as he faced life in prison, he thrived in studying and handling responsible jobs. Meanwhile, Jason witnessed the lives of his younger brothers crash and burn.

Neither Matt nor Terry had returned to school after Jason got locked up. Gail lacked both the emotional and the financial resources to pack and leave Marion, and, living there, her boys could not endure the stigma of being a convicted child-killer's kin. As years passed after the murders, the families of the victims, the families of the convicted, and everyone associated with the murders continued to suffer from the crimes, in countless different ways. In 2000, Jason said, "I just wish there were some way that I could motivate my brothers to finish school and learn a trade or go to college. I see so many kids here in prison that do not have either hope or guidance to keep them out of this place." Yet he understood why Matt and Terry had dropped out. "They could not stand the talk, the gossip, or the jeers of everyone there about me."[94]

"The highest and best form of efficiency is the spontaneous cooperation of a free people."
~ Woodrow Wilson

Attitudes in the Arkansas-Tennessee section of the Mississippi River delta were hard-set against the three men in prison. Jason knew that. Gary Gitchell, the former chief of detectives for the West Memphis Police Department, summed up the easy acceptance of the verdicts that characterized much of the region when he told a reporter: "You've got a lot of circumstantial evidence is what you've got. There's no smoking gun. This is not a smoking-gun type case."[95]

What he did not know—and what no one could have foreseen at the end of the twentieth century—was how forces of new media would impact the West Memphis convictions. Jason understood that many people outside Arkansas found the case outrageous. But he also understood that no one quite knew how to fight what was wrong with the case—especially since the state Supreme Court had found nothing wrong.

Nevertheless, new media was driving the case into uncharted territory, a fresh American landscape. Significantly, the murders of the three boys in West Memphis occurred at a turning point in the public's ability to see into trials. Because the Sixth Amendment to the U.S. Constitution establishes the right of an accused person to a "public trial," citizens can physically enter a courthouse, as in *To Kill a Mockingbird*, and watch almost any trial, providing there's enough room. But between the country's founding and the end of the twentieth century, it became less and less practical for most people to keep track of—much less attend—the growing number of trials conducted in local courts. In most places, especially as the War on Drugs began to ramp up, even members of the media could not report on all the trials being held. In addition, prosecutors were winning more and more convictions through the use of plea deals, avoiding trials entirely.[96] Public awareness of judicial activities plummeted. A troubling disconnect between the courts and the citizenry took hold.

But public interest in certain cases remained high, as Court TV (now trutv) demonstrated in 1993—the year of the West Memphis murders—when it broadcast the trial of the Menendez brothers in California and HBO dispatched Berlinger and Sinofsky to document the case in Arkansas. In 1994, Court TV proved the strength of viewer interest in high-profile cases with its live coverage of the O.J. Simpson trial.

While the role of cameras and television was being debated in the mid-90s, the public gained access to new technologies that would impact courts. The West Memphis murders and trials roughly coincided with the public debut of the World Wide Web and the introduction of email. Ownership of personal computers and smart phones soared during the 1990s. By 2000, WM3.org had already been online for four years, and emails about the case were flying. Ironically, the West Memphis trials, with all their talk of the occult and Satan, occurred at the dawn of a media revolution. Perhaps there is some significance in the fact that this was not the first time that "witch" trials coincided with a technological revolution involving media.

During the sixteenth and seventeenth centuries, Europeans endured a particularly terrible plague of "witch" burning. At the same time, due to the recent invention of mechanical movable type and the printing press, the continent witnessed an unprecedented surge in book publishing and literacy. The clash of irrational and rational forces led to confrontations with some of the time's most prominent institutions, especially the Roman Catholic Church, as Europeans' advancing ability to read and interpret the Bible themselves gave rise to the Protestant Reformation.

In a similar way, Judge Burnett's decision to allow cameras into his court just as the Internet was beginning to flourish would have ramifications that no one at the time could have predicted. Seeing *Paradise Lost* changed Jason, but he had no Internet connection. What mattered was that the film also affected countless others, and they did have Internet access—and the Web provided them with a means to discuss and examine what they'd seen. Now, as large numbers of Americans became able to see some trials for themselves, they became more informed about legal processes and more willing to criticize perceived abuses. The case of the West Memphis Three, in particular, led many to think that prosecutors in it had crossed a line by evoking fear over reason and emotions over evidence. Some saw in the result a version of "justice" they could not abide.

Those who reacted were not Don Quixotes, tilting at abstractions. They had families to support, careers to nurture, and plenty to do with their lives beyond line up in various ways to support three prisoners in Arkansas. Most assumed there were innocent men and women in prison—probably even on death row. They understood that these men and women, like the West Memphis Three, probably also hoped to somehow be freed. And they knew that most of these innocent but faceless prisoners would live until they died in prison. That's how it goes. Not every injustice can be righted.

But where, against all odds, cameras had recorded what many considered a court-sanctioned crime, many found they simply could not turn their backs. *Paradise Lost* galvanized tens, then hundreds, then thousands. They responded in large ways and small.[97] Media fostered interest. Interest fostered money. And the combinations of media, interest, and money fostered new attorneys and new investigations. Together, they represented—at least, for Jason, Damien and Jessie—a basis for new hope.

Now music folded into the mix. During the dark times at Varner, and now at Grimes, Jason had found it comforting to remember that Metallica, the band he liked so much, had contributed its music to the film *Paradise Lost*. It was phenomenally encouraging for him to think that people with as much going on as Metallica would take time to care about his case and lend their hands—and a few guitars. What Jason did not know was that, by 2000, more musicians were stepping up to support him, Damien, and Jessie—kids who, many performers came to believe, were convicted partly based on their tastes in music. Some viewers may have jeered at the part in *Paradise Lost* when Fogleman told the jury that there wasn't anything wrong with heavy metal music "in and of itself." But many musicians were shocked to hear a prosecutor attempt to link some of their fans to murders by mentioning heavy metal.

One of those outraged musicians was Eddie Daly. Like Jason, as a kid, he had wanted—really wanted—to be a heavy metal musician. By 1996, when *Paradise Lost* came out, Daly had adopted the stage name Eddie Spaghetti, moved to Seattle, and was heading a band called the Supersuckers. Jason had never heard of him.

But Daly knew of Jason. *Paradise Lost* had struck a deep chord in Daly. He hated what the film represented. "No one is really safe from this kind of persecution," he said. "You might think that it would never happen in America, but it does. Granted, there are millions of other cases that are probably worthy of our attention, but you can't go after all of them . . . But maybe we can at least get these kids out of jail."[98]

A couple of years later, Daly was talking to another Seattle musician, Eddie Vedder, the front man for Pearl Jam, when somehow the West Memphis case came up. Daly recalled that he and Vedder ended up speaking about the case for hours. Vedder, who had already become both informed and concerned about it, told Daly that the Arkansas Supreme Court had affirmed the convictions, that Echols still faced execution, and that Baldwin and Misskelley, then in their twenties, remained in prison for life. Daly decided to act. As he put it, he knew he was "no Eddie Vedder," with records selling in the millions. Nevertheless, he could "do something."

Daly and his crew decided to bring like-minded musicians together on a CD to help raise money to investigate the Arkansas case further.[99] "It seemed to us that the injustices stemmed from the music these kids were listening to, and the solution may come from that," Daly said. "We knew it would be a lot of work, that putting together a record like this would be very time-consuming, but we decided we needed to assume that responsibility." Daly visited the prisoners in Arkansas. "I was struck by how funny and smart Baldwin is," he told a reporter. "In [the documentary], he was an awkward age—gawky and scared. And now he's educating himself. He's an algebra tutor at the prison. He looks like a college student. And he's got a lot of friends there who believe in his innocence."[100]

Though Jason was grateful, he had never heard of—much less, actually heard—most of the musicians featured on the compilation CD titled *Free the West Memphis 3*. Fans, however, particularly those on the west coast, recognized some of the biggest singer-songwriters and punk rock bands at the start of the new century. The Supersuckers, Tom Waits, Steve Earle, Jello Biafra, Kelley Deal, Zeke, Mark Lanegan, and the groups Rocket from the Crypt, Joe Strummer and the Long Beach Dub All-Stars, Murder City Devils, Nashville Pussy, The John Doe Thing, and Killing Joke all contributed cuts.[101] So did Vedder, without Pearl Jam.

Biafra explained his decision as, "It could happen to me. It could happen to you." Waits said, "In our system of justice, the best client for a lawyer is a scared millionaire. The worst thing in our criminal justice system is to be broke or different."

"I know I was born and I know that I'll die, the in-between is mine."

~ Eddie Vedder

Few at the time knew how deeply Vedder had taken that belief to heart. Here's how he once explained his response to *Paradise Lost* and the research he did after seeing it: "There is a lot of evidence to suggest that they weren't involved, and it's worth saying there was no real evidence to support the fact that they were involved or guilty. It seems like a case of discrimination, but not necessarily against color or sexual preference. It's more like against adolescence and ones that may look a little different."[102]

If prisoners had been allowed contact with prisoners at other units, and if Jason and Damien could have kept in touch, Jason might have known that Damien's wife, Lorri, had gotten to know Vedder personally, and Pearl Jam's front man was contributing more than music to the cause of freeing the West Memphis Three. Vedder was contributing money, and he planned to contribute more, but as a businessman, he wanted to approach the case with something like a business plan. Growing awareness of the Arkansas case resulted in contributions, large and small, that went both directly to Lorri on behalf of Damien and to the men as a group, via a fund established by the folks behind WM3.org. But realistically, Vedder wanted to know, how could the men be freed? Realizing that high-powered legal work would be crucial, he needed to understand what was possible, given the constraints of law—and what was not.

In the late 1990s, Vedder asked John Philipsborn, a prominent San Francisco attorney experienced in trial and appellate work, to take a look at the status of all three cases and propose a starting point. Philipsborn accepted the job without charge. He said that as he examined Damien's case, he and Vedder began working closely with Lorri to calculate how much money would need to be reaised "because there was a lot of material that hadn't been looked at very well." As a result of those discussions, Philipsborn said, Vedder offered to help financially "on an ad hoc basis."

One of the first things the musician did was to invite all the defense attorneys currently involved in the case to come to Seattle to see if a coherent strategy could be devised. Philipsborn said the question underlying the meeting was, "Would it be possible to raise funds in a concerted way to get lawyers and experts to take a concentrated look at this case?"

The group gathered on May 14, 2000, at the Sorrento Hotel in Seattle. Vedder and Lorri were there. The attorneys present included Stidham, who now represented Jessie for free; Edward Mallett of Houston, who was representing Damien; and Steve Bright, a death penalty expert and executive director of the Southern Center for Human Rights, who was also helping Damien. Philipsborn attended, of course, and he had invited Michael Burt, the chief trial lawyer for San Francisco's public defender's office.[103] According to a memo from that meeting, Burt, a nationally known death penalty litigator, had been recruited specifically "to broach the subject of DNA testing."

Few outside the room knew the meeting was taking place. In the weeks that followed, Philipsborn recalled, "I made recommendations about the sorts of lawyers that would be needed, the sorts of activities that should be undertaken. I wrote to Dan Stidham and got his files, and I wrote some motions about impounding evidence."

But the truth was that the three cases, which had looked disorganized enough at trial, had deteriorated further since then. The fact that Jessie still had Stidham, his trial lawyer, working on his behalf stood out as an oddity itself. Jason had no one. And though Damien's lawyer had already argued on his behalf before the Arkansas Supreme Court, Philipsborn said, "It wasn't clear even to Ed Mallett that he was well situated as a post-conviction lawyer in the Echols case." Though Mallett was president of the National Association of Criminal Defense Lawyers, Philipsborn explained, he was not a post-conviction lawyer.

"He essentially got volunteered to help in the Echols effort, but after the Rule 37 ruling, Damien was on his way to federal court, and it was fairly clear to us with experience that the case was not properly poised to go into federal court. There were a number of issues that needed to be addressed."

Changes within Damien's team presented another complication. After Damien took Mallett off his case, he and Lorri recruited attorneys Joe Margulies of Northwestern University and Rob Owen of the University of Texas to represent him. As the west-coast lawyers tried to sort out the Arkansas mess, they stepped back and took a look at what had happened legally so far.

Back at the time of the murders, the police had arrested the men as a group, based on Jessie's confession. In essence, the three were tried separately because Jessie's trial was severed and because Jason's attorney opted not to cooperate with Damien's, as he considered the two defendants' cases antagonistic. All three entered separate prisons, and now all faced different issues. Damien had to fight his death sentence and had attorneys helping him do that. Jessie still had Stidham's support, but Stidham alone could not help him overcome his confession. And Jason, a tag-along to the case who'd still been sentenced to life, lacked even an attorney.

In terms of attack, the cases looked different. But the overview at the Sorento Hotel led to a new strategy. Yes, each man's case raised unique challenges. But the murders were a singular event. And since the film and creation of the website, the West Memphis Three had become a singular entity. It became clear that a simultaneous fight should be launched on behalf of all three and that, though individual pleadings would differ, new investigative information should be shared, as it would benefit all. For the first time since Burnett ordered that Jessie be tried alone, the lawyers decided, as Philipsborn put it, "that the three cases would rise or fall as a group."

Philipsborn contacted the three Arkansas prisoners. By the end of 2000, Jason had been without an attorney for the better part of five years. Then, he got a call from California. He recalled, "John Philipsborn told me he'd been hired by an anonymous donor to hire an attorney for me." He added: "John was not allowed to say who the donor was, and I always respected that. I figured, whenever it was meant for me to know, I would know. Eventually, I ended up hearing from somebody that it was Eddie Vedder, but I certainly never mentioned it to anybody." From that point on, Philipsborn kept in touch with Jason, apprising him of developments as the new legal campaign progressed.

Philipsborn explained that the plan called for each of the three inmates to be represented by an attorney from outside Arkansas, along with one from inside the state. While the lead attorney for Jason had not yet been chosen, Philipsborn asked Blake Hendrix, a well-established Little Rock criminal defense lawyer, to go to the Grimes Unit and introduce himself to Jason. "I liked Blake instantly," Jason said. "He told me that he believed in me and that, if I gave him the job, he'd do his best to see that I got out."

San Francisco attorney Michael Burt, who was at the Sorento meeting, agreed to represent Jessie. In Arkansas, Jeff Rosenzweig, a prominent criminal defense and appellate lawyer, signed on for Jessie as well. But who would take the lead in Jason's case? The plan, from the time of the Sorento meeting on, had been for Philipsborn to coordinate the teams' development and strategies regarding evidence, but that he would not represent any of the prisoners himself. After getting to know Philipsborn, however, Jason asked Philipsborn to be his lead attorney. "The degree of professionalism and dedication that John was exhibiting made me want him as my attorney, and when I saw his credentials, they made me want him even more," Jason said. "When I met Blake, I said I'd like for John to be my other attorney, and Blake said, 'I think that's the best idea I've ever heard.'" To Jason's relief, Philipsborn agreed, and for the first time since 1996, when the Arkansas Supreme Court rejected his direct appeal, Jason had a team of attorneys working to see him freed.

Eventually, Philipsborn traveled from San Francisco to Newport, Arkansas, to meet Jason in person. By then, the two already felt they knew each other. Jason appreciated the way that, even before they met, Philipsborn gave him information, included him in his team's discussions and asked his opinions. For instance, because he'd been kept virtually in the dark by his trial attorneys, Jason had never seen a copy of Jessie's confession. Portions of it had been reported in newspapers, on TV, and in *Paradise Lost*. Now, Philipsborn sent him a transcript. It was like seeing *Paradise Lost* again, only this time in perfect detail.

That was just one of the ways Jason found Philipsborn and Hendrix to be different from his trial attorneys. "John and Blake both had a lot more experience than Paul and Robin did at the time," he said. "Anything the state put forth—they didn't accept it on its face. They double-checked everything. John, he doesn't just go after one thing. He goes after everything. He doesn't exclude anything, no matter how small or large. He doesn't become fixated on any one aspect of a case. He's got to figure out the hows, the whys—every single detail about anything."

The teams hired separate investigators.[104] "There was some concern expressed that a number of death penalty issues had not been perfected in Damien's case," Philipsborn said; "the sort of normal litigation you would expect to see had not been completed. There were large areas of need that pertained to all three, and as we transitioned into the early 2000s, the consensus was there had to be additional work in all three cases. That led to negotiations to see all of the evidence and to hire criminalists because by then, we had been provided with some very generous donations by Pearl Jam and Henry Rollins and others, whom I presume that Lorri was dealing with separately."

The attorneys Philipsborn assembled, along with those Damien and Lorri brought to the table, all knew that, nationally, a potential game-changer was afoot in the form of forensic technologies, and Philipsborn, an expert in those technologies, wanted to be ready to use them. Despite images projected by television programs such as CSI, which premiered in 2000, the fact remained—and still does remain—that most police departments, crime labs, and states have been slow to adopt long-recommended practices for better use of the forensic sciences.[105] Nevertheless, interest in DNA for crime-solving, which had emerged in the 1980s, was being reflected in laws by the 1990s.

In 1994—the same year Jason, Jessie and Damien were tried—New York had passed a law allowing prisoners to seek post-conviction relief if they could present new scientific evidence that was not available at the time of their trials. Other states had followed, and now, as Philipsborn was rounding up attorneys to serve as new teams for the West Memphis Three, an Arkansas state senator was preparing a similar bill for his state. Within months, the Arkansas legislature would pass the bill "to accommodate the advent of new technologies enhancing the ability to analyze scientific evidence." Though few, if any, realized it at the time, passage of Arkansas's Act 1780, which allowed post-conviction DNA testing, loosened a critical bolt in the tight sealed West Memphis case, as well as in many future cases of wrongful conviction. Yet challenges under the new law still would not be easy. In order to take advantage of this historic opportunity, a lot of work had to be done—and money had to be raised.

Over the many months that followed, the legal teams quietly sent criminalists, investigators, and DNA experts to Arkansas. Jason now learned that Ford had not hired an investigator in preparation for his trial and had even rejected the offer of Memphis private investigator Ron Lax to assist, without charge, in his defense. It was stunning for Jason to realize how unprepared his attorneys had been with regard to evidence as he'd gone on trial for his life. By contrast, he said, his new attorneys "tried to get every little piece of evidence tested, as soon as they got the money to pay for it."

The specialists discovered that, though Lax's files weren't perfect, overall, his records stood out as the most comprehensive of any in the investigation. In comparison, the police department's records were a shambles. One of the criminalists noted that some physical evidence at the department that needed further scientific tests had not been "stored in a manner consistent with current scientific standards."[106] Even attorneys' case records were problematic. Stidham readily turned over everything he had, but Damien's lead trial attorney, Val Price, at first balked at providing the new teams with his files. Ford cooperated, but his files were sparse, to say the least.

Overall, Philipsborn said, "There was a great deal of stuff missing. There was no forensic science material there. Nothing you would have expected to have been obtained from the medical examiner.

No DNA. No serology work. No notes of criminalists. No notebooks. None of the hundreds of pages you would have expected had been gotten." Thus began the lengthy process of negotiating with state officials to obtain materials, particularly from the state crime lab—materials the new teams believed the defense attorneys should have gathered in 1993.

Hearing Philipsborn describe how much work had not been done confirmed what Jason had suspected after his trial: that he'd been prosecuted, convicted, and sentenced based on nothing of substance. It appeared that no one—neither his defense counsel nor the prosecutors—had acted with due diligence or demanded scientific investigation.

Though the attorneys were not being paid, this other work was expensive, and everyone knew that, if DNA tests had to be conducted, the costs would rise exponentially. Supporters who were not celebrities contributed what they could towards these efforts by way of the WM3.org website. Some contributed five or ten dollars a month for years. A Little Rock man committed to sending whatever return he got on his taxes every year until the men were freed. Generous as those gifts were, they could not approach the amount of money that would be needed to fight the legal battle ahead.

HBO's release in 2000 of a second documentary about the case, *Paradise Lost 2: Revelations*, helped considerably. After the show aired, the founders of WM3.org reported receiving almost eight thousand emails from newly intrigued viewers. HBO also devoted several nights to airing the original film, along with the sequel, and this time, viewers who wanted to look further into the case had several places to go on the Internet. Since the founders of WM3.org were featured in the second film talking about the site, they expected a strong response. What they got was overwhelming.

"On the night the show premiered, we each received thousands of emails," Sauls said. "I think the reason is that a lot of people are really moved by this story, and they want to connect with people who are involved—because they already felt connected." Bakken, who managed the site, said that, before PL2 was shown, the site received between one hundred to two hundred hits per day. In the two weeks when the cable channel showed the film, that number jumped to more than seventy three hundred per day. Pashley added that the site had shipped out more than five hundred T-shirts that read "Free the West Memphis Three." On March 20, 2000, Yahoo named the WM3 site its pick of the week.[107]

On June 9, the website received another spike when, while accepting a trophy at the MTV movie awards, South Park co-creator Trey Parker exclaimed, "Free the West Memphis Three!", Another came a month later when Access Hollywood showed an interview with Parker and his partner, Matt Stone. Parker was wearing one of the support fund's black T-shirts imprinted with the WM3 site's URL.

For the website's founders, work on the case became like a second job. "When I get up in the morning, I'm working on this case," Sauls said. "And before I go to bed at night, I'm working on this case. Sometimes I have to remind myself to do some 'work-work' so I can make money to keep going." By now, the HBO filmmakers and the website organizers understood that they'd become a thorn in the side of certain Arkansas officials who dismissed the media activity as uninformed, outside agitation. Gitchell complained, for instance, "People have been swayed by a slanted film and celebrities." The activists dismissed the officials. "They say we're Hollywood people sticking our noses where they don't belong," Sauls said. "But what happened in Arkansas is a threat to justice everywhere. It sounds corny, but that's what I believe."[108]

"Always remember that the future comes one day at a time."
~ Dean Acheson

For supporters, all this activity looked promising. But that promise seemed only to agitate Arkansas. An unexpected light had been directed onto its legal system, and suddenly people from all over were criticizing what they'd seen. Such exposure to outside scrutiny was new to Arkansas judges and lawyers. For years, the legal profession's response was no response. The case was simply not mentioned in public.

That could not be said about conditions at Grimes. There, the situation remained bad enough that inmates took the unusual step of reporting them to media. Michael Haddigan reported for the *Arkansas Times* that the paper received "a score of inmate letters . . . complaining of beatings at the hands of guards assigned temporarily to Newport from a Wackenhut prison in Louisiana." When Haddigan investigated, he wrote, guards and employees confirmed the mistreatment of inmates, though most employees spoke off-the-record. One guard, however, Joe Tagliaboschi, an ex-Marine, was willing to be quoted by name. He said the beatings were common knowledge throughout the men's prison. "They were vicious," Tagliaboschi said of the Louisiana guards. "They just didn't treat the inmates like human beings."[109]

On April 22, 2001, Jason turned twenty-four at that prison. By then, he'd heard about an encyclopedia named Wikipedia that had just appeared online, though he hadn't seen it, of course. Such a thing was hard to fathom. Though Jason worked on computers at Grimes, he was cut off from its great connectivity. Sites such as Wikipedia, along with so much of the technological revolution, belonged to the fast-changing world outside. It was digital, new and exciting—and as out-of-reach to him as driving a car, going on a date, or pulling on a pair of jeans.

The upside of his birthday was that he got a visit from the girl he loved. Seeing her was always good. And he received a lot of birthday cards. Some supporters added money to his prison account, but most simply offered their friendship, along with words of hope.[110] For the most part, though, his sense of the passage of time was just that every day dragged. When asked how he would describe his life to someone who'd had a more normal entry into adulthood, he said: "Go to your sixteenth birthday, and take everything that happened after that. Push it all aside, and replace it with prison memories." He now had eight years of such memories—some stamped onto his body.

One night at Grimes Jason awoke to discover that someone had broken into the locker under his bed. Jason told the barracks guard that he'd been robbed, but the officer did nothing. "So being the hothead that I was," he recalled, "I went into the dayroom and started knocking things over, like big stacks of plastic chairs. I yelled, 'All right, you bitches, you're going to wake up!' I went over to the first rack and yelled, 'This is a shakedown!' Then I went to the second rack, and lo and behold, I saw a bunch of my stuff there. I said to the guy, 'All right, you and I are going to the shower and we're going to fight.' The officers couldn't see you in there, and you could, so actually it was a cage match too."

Was the guy bigger than Jason?

"Oh, yeah. Yeah. Yeah," he said. "Most people were bigger than me. We called him 'Bird' and he probably had forty or fifty pounds on me. I remember he was a little bit taller than me and he had a lot more reach. He told me later on that he used to box."

Jason got the worst of Bird's reach. "He put a big gash under my eye and meat came out, like a piece of hamburger meat, just hanging there. It was about the size of the end of your pinky digit. I thought my eye was put out there for a minute. A thin layer of blood covered my eyeball and congealed, and I couldn't see. But the blood cleared in a minute or so. And, of course, half my upper front tooth was knocked out. So, yeah, he kicked my butt. Prison is very schoolyard."

Jason did not go to the infirmary for stitches. "I couldn't tell them I was in a fight," he said, "or they would have put me in the hole because I started it." Instead, he showed up for work at the school. "Ms. Moon and the rest were all, like, 'Oh, my God,' because I looked a mess, with a tooth half-gone, and a busted tongue and meat hanging out of my face."

The immediate consequence of the fight was that Bird returned most of what he'd stolen. "He gave it to me," Jason recalled. "He said, 'You fought for it. You can have it.'" Once his face had healed, however, the broken tooth had to be addressed. The unit's dentist told Jason that he was only authorized to pull what remained of the tooth. But here, Jason got lucky. Because of the wound on the face of victim Stevie Branch that some now believed was a human bite mark, dental impressions had been taken of Jason's mouth when he still had all his teeth. Because those impressions existed, the dentist, who also had a private practice, was kind enough to make Jason a new false tooth that matched the one he'd lost. For Jason, the fight amounted to little more than a footnote to memories that included monstrous things like the beating at Varner and the gassing at Grimes. Still, in addition to several others, he'd always carry a scar under his right eye, along with his false front tooth.

Prison was leaving its marks on Jason. That couldn't be helped. But he tried not to let the place distort him or give it the upper hand by allowing it to reshape him into someone he did not want to become. With the exception of confidences shared with his girlfriend and a few people he considered "golden," he kept his own counsel as he had since the night of his arrest. Now, however, he had the comfort of counsel from the outside. In confidential letters and phone calls, Philipsborn was letting him know all that was going on legally on behalf of himself and his friends in prison. In 2001, that was a lot.

After the Arkansas Supreme Court affirmed Damien's conviction, new attorneys had filed a Rule 37 petition for him, and Burnett had denied the petition. Now, in the spring of 2001, Damien's even newer attorneys argued before the state Supreme Court that Burnett erred in denying that petition because he had not provided written reasons to support his denial, as Arkansas law requires.[111] A month later, the Supreme Court surprised many observers by handing Damien's attorneys their first victory—however minor—in the case. They agreed that Burnett had failed to explain his reasons for denying Damien's Rule 37 petition, as required, and sent the case back to him with orders to do so.[112] Even at that, however, the high court took pains to stress the narrowness of its ruling, noting that all of Damien's other claims "are considered abandoned." Finally, on July 30, Burnett issued his written findings, explaining why he did not believe that Damien's trial attorneys had been legally ineffective: his ruling repeated almost verbatim the arguments the attorney general had submitted, and the high court accepted them without dissent.[113]

Jessie was running into similar obstacles. Stidham had filed a motion to preserve evidence in the case and had amended his Rule 37 petition, noting that, "since Mr. Misskelley's convictions, DNA and other forensic testing have advanced considerably." But the attorney general's office resisted those arguments too, claiming that Jessie had "failed to assert or establish any basis to believe that such testing would lead to any exculpable evidence." That argument, articulated here for the first time, hinted at what would become the biggest battle in the case since the trials. It would come down to a battle over evidence and, especially in light of the new DNA law, how much—or how little—the courts should consider.

Jason understood that his case, like Jessie's, was "all about Rule 37." Thanks to Stidham's intervention, Jason's petition had been filed in a timely manner. Now, with Philipsborn and Hendrix on board, work on it could proceed. Philipsborn filed a motion "to preserve evidence and for access to evidence for testing." Jason said, "We can look at Dan Stidham's petition like the catalyst. It was like the starter yeast. Then John came on and put in all the rest of the ingredients to keep it going."

Yet irony seasoned the fermentation. Rule 37 procedures focused on the conduct of a petitioner's trial attorneys. Now that his own efforts in that regard were ramping up, Jason learned that one of his two lawyers back then, Robin Wadley, had recently been disbarred for unethical practices. Those practices had nothing to do with Jason's case, and Jason realized that, compared to Ford's, Wadley's role had been pretty limited. Still, the juxtaposition of events presented yet another of the many peculiarities in this case that could drive a person crazy if he considered them for too long. Jason refused to dwell on them.

Because Damien was sentenced to death, his case was expedited at every level. That—and the fact that he'd had attorneys all along, due to the severity of his sentence—partly explains why, in 2001, when Jessie's and Jason's Rule 37 petitions had still seen little action, Damien's had already been heard—and denied—by Judge Burnett. Damien's attorneys faced a complex situation, feeling themselves poised to bring his case to a federal court but constrained by requirements that, before doing that, they had to exhaust every state-level remedy possible. Knowing that the exercise almost certainly would mean little but further delay, they dutifully filed the required petition to bring Damien's case back again before Judge Burnett, arguing that Damien was being illegally held.

Jason felt sorry for Damien having to go through such discouraging legal contortions. While little was happening with his own case, Jason did not begrudge any of the time, energy, and money that were pouring into Damien's. After all, only Damien had been sentenced to death. Everyone involved in the process now—the inmates, their attorneys, and the attorneys working for the state's attorney general—understood that the strictures of law would dictate a different legal approach for each of the men. They also understood that, if Damien's lawyers could unravel the prosecutors' case against him, it would be hard for the state to hold onto its cases against Jason and Jessie.

Besides the lift Jason got from the legal activity stirring in 2001, he could see on the prison's television that something at least as vibrant was happening—not in court, but outside the courthouse. In March, when lawyers for Damien and for the state were presenting their oral arguments about Damien's Rule 37 petition before the Arkansas Supreme Court, about a hundred supporters of the West Memphis Three stood side-by-side in front of the building. News reporters from the Little Rock and Memphis markets noted how unusual it was to see such a show of support at any oral argument, much less one held for convicted child-killers.

The men and women standing in front of the Supreme Court building held a long strip of postcards, linked in plastic sleeves. They explained that founders of the website WM3.org had organized the event and that the postcards had been sent by people from throughout the United States and around the world who also supported the men but couldn't be present. Sauls told a reporter that the peaceful demonstration was intended to raise an alarm about the case inside Arkansas, in hopes that officials and ordinary citizens there would take time to examine the police reports and the trial transcripts that were now online, and to delve "deeper into the justice system and look at things for themselves."

Grove Pashley, a professional photographer who also helped organize the event, recalled collecting and putting together the thousands of postcards displayed that day. "It made me so proud to see dozens upon dozens of WM3 supporters unfurling this banner in public around the Arkansas State Supreme Court building and the Arkansas Capitol," he said. "Images like that re-enforced our hope that one day the system would right this wrong!"

For the first time in history, it was becoming possible for citizens near and far to take a "deeper" look into the justice system, thanks to the Internet. The West Memphis case would demonstrate how far an interested public was willing to go to research a case, find official documents, and put them online so that people could decide for themselves what had and had not occurred, and who or what made sense—or didn't. The demonstration outside the Arkansas Supreme Court attempted to combine the power of new media with the old tactic of direct action to target a state's judiciary. Where it would lead—if anywhere—no one knew. One thing that was becoming clear, however, was that more and more ordinary people shared the feeling that Jason's former teacher, Sally Ware, expressed in an open letter she'd sent to regional media. "I believe a young man has been in prison for eight years for a crime he did not commit," Ware wrote. "I cannot stand by and be silent."

While Sauls, Pashley, Bakken and Fancher were in Arkansas for the courthouse event, they took time to visit Damien, Jessie and Jason in prison. They found Jason, at twenty-four, looking relaxed and comfortable in his frayed white uniform. He greeted them like the old friends they now were. He told them about his job managing the school's database on a computer; about the college courses he was taking in anthropology, accounting and American politics ("to see what our government is built on"); and about how, in his time off, he liked to play computer games like Chess Master, Quake and Sonic.

The Californians, in turn, plied him with questions.

Jason, how has prison changed you?

"I'm not as naïve as I was," he said. "It's made me more reflective on things I should be proud of and enjoy, things like freedom. I don't take things for granted. I know you've got to love life, enjoy it—embrace it while you've got it." He added, "Most people my age, if they go to college, they party. They have fun. They don't stop and think as much."

Do you have any hard feelings?

"I used to. But as I've grown and matured, I've come to understand that hard feelings don't get you anywhere."

How do you feel about the justice system, about law enforcement?

"They're underpaid and overworked. There's a lot of pressure put on these people—so much pressure that, to get the pressure off, they might make the wrong decision."

So what do you think is the real reason you're here?

"The real reason? Someone had to pay the price. I know I didn't do it, and that's the main matter. They shouldn't be content just to say we did."

Then what about the jury?

"I understand what people thought. I used to think that way too. To me, a 'suspect' meant 'that's who done it.'"

Jason's tone was cheerful, upbeat and confident. While he and his visitors understood that they faced an almost impossible legal challenge, they spoke as though success was practically a sure thing. They spoke about "when," not "if," Jason got out.

"Jason, would you speak, like, on college campuses when you get out?"

Jason, one of the quietest guys in prison, nodded. It was easy to recall all the delusions he'd had about the justice system at the time of his arrest: beliefs that had been stripped from him, one by one in the months that followed. Since entering prison, he'd been stripped of another: the belief that courts routinely corrected trial errors through systems of post-conviction appeals. He now knew how rarely true that was—and that, if corrections were made, they were brought about only by powerful lawyering against a powerfully entrenched state, usually with the help of significant amounts of money and generally occurring many years late. He had only to look around him, at the men serving long sentences in near anonymity, to be reminded of how coming from nothing made the chances of such miracles remote.

"I would definitely speak," he answered. "This is happening all over America. It's not just here. I've had this experience, and it shouldn't go to waste."[114]

To Jason, visits like that were more than breaks in the monotony; they were priceless. The Californians cherished the visits as well, despite the toll they took. "We had a lot of difficult times over the years," Sauls would recall, "but in my memories, the feeling that we all had when we were told that the visit was over and we watched the guards taking our friends back into the bowels of the prison while we all walked back to the parking lot and our rental car were among the most depressing.

"We were free to decide where to go at that point. Lunch? Back to the hotel? Maybe we could go visit a friend or plan a dinner for that evening. We imagined that our friends in prison were taken back to their cells or barracks to an unimaginably frustrating half-life in a concrete box. We never left those prisons without tears in our eyes and that stunned silence that always came when the spell is broken. We would sometimes get so involved in conversations that we'd forget where we were; we were simply visiting with a friend. But then, they were hauled back into their nightmare, and the prison staff was holding the doors and gates open for us to leave and go back to our relatively wonderful lives—back home to our loved ones and families and our comfortable houses."

The case dragged on, the Californians kept traveling to Arkansas, and the partings never got easier. "I think the most difficult times were when we felt so helpless to get these young men out of those prisons," Sauls said. "Leaving them behind again and again. Walking away from them over and over and still not feeling like enough progress was being made. Watching the years pass and holding those bad thoughts in the backs of our minds . . . what if they NEVER get out? What if Damien is executed? How will we deal with that? What will actually happen if they schedule an execution and we have to watch as they take him and kill him? It was difficult to even bring ourselves to consider that idea, but once in a while it would come up. Psychologically those were the most difficult times for us. Feeling helpless, and then trying to imagine that, if we felt so depressed and helpless, how must our friends in prison feel?"

As the summer of 2001 drew near, the phenomenon of artists and ordinary citizens joining forces to call attention to a perceived injustice in a small state in America's Mid-South became a story on National Public Radio. That June, Neda Ulaby reported, "Activists around the country are organizing rallies and concerts this weekend to benefit the three young Arkansas inmates known as the West Memphis Three." With music of the band L7's *Boys in Black* in the background, she played a voice-over from Paradise Lost in which Griffis, the self-described occult expert, could be heard testifying about having "personally observed people wearing black fingernails."[115]

By the end of that summer, Jason was itching to move again—anywhere. He just wanted to be somewhere that wasn't Grimes, where he'd lived now for three and a half years. In the summer of 2001, the state decided to end its experiment with private prison management. Control of the Grimes Unit was transferred back to the Arkansas Department of Correction. Jason decided to take that opportunity to request a move.

He could trace most of the reason for his unrest to the officer who'd harassed him since his arrival at Grimes. When the state took over the prison, that officer got a job with the state and stayed on. "I figured I was tired of messing with him," Jason said. "He'd cut my visitation time short for no reason. He intercepted mail I wrote on the computer, even though I had permission to type it and print it out. And everybody was afraid of him. He was a captain, and the staff was intimidated too. They didn't want to stand up for me against him, so I decided I was just through with it."

CHAPTER SIX

VARNER II

August 1, 1998 - October 7, 2005

Prisoners wanting to relocate are not given a lot of options. On September 11, 2001, Jason was back at Varner, working the morning shift in the staff's dining room, when Al Qaeda operatives hijacked four airplanes to attack the United States. "There was all these rumors about what was going to be happening with inmates," Jason recalled. "A lot of guys had this fantasy that the state was going to give them this opportunity to get out of prison to fight. Others thought that the government was going to declare martial law and execute everybody to make space for prisoners of war. And some of the staff talked up the same rumors. It was a very weird time."

Jason had returned to Varner, where Jessie already lived, just seven weeks before the terrorist attack. "It was not one of my better decisions," he later reflected. "I should have stayed at Grimes. But when you're in there, you want to get out so bad, you think you'll do anything just for a change. What you're seeking is release, but once you get to where you've been transferred, you're like, 'Oh, yeah. It's just another prison.'

The problem was that Varner never had been "just another prison." It was huge to begin with, packed with young offenders, many violent—and now it was expanding. In response to the nation's War on Drugs, the federal government had offered states unprecedented amounts of money to build ultra-high-security "supermax" prisons. The deal would cost the states little—at least, on the front end. Arkansas officials, like their counterparts in many other states, jumped at the chance for federal money. They opted to build their new Supermax Unit adjacent to the maximum-security one at Varner. Inmates did much of the construction. Jason was there to watch the isolation cell blocks go up.

When the Supermax Unit was complete, Damien and the other death row prisoners, who until then had been held at another unit under more moderate conditions, were now moved to the Supermax's more severe isolation. Though the Supermax was a separate brick building, connected to Varner by a tightly barred corridor, the move meant that Jason, Jessie, and Damien were now living on the same prison compound, closer to each other than they'd been at any time since their arrests.

Existence of the Supermax changed conditions at Varner. The sudden availability of hundreds of adjacent isolation cells meant that Varner prisoners could be transferred into them for a wider array of infractions. "With the Supermax, everything got harsher," Jason said. "More rules were put into effect, which meant there were more opportunities to get in trouble. The police were able to start enforcing all kinds of rules, including those regulating the length of inmates' hair, how they shaved, and general grooming. When I first went to prison, it was hard to get put in the hole. Even when I got that disciplinary for having the twenty-five cents and the Motrin, I never spent a single day in the hole. If that had happened after the Supermax opened, I'd have done that whole, thirty day punitive in the hole."[116]

On the other hand—and maybe because of the tougher administration—life at Varner was not as bad for Jason as when he'd first entered there, six and a half years before. For one thing, he was by now a seasoned inmate. For another, he had the comfort this time of knowing that he was not legally alone. True to his word, Philipsborn was keeping him apprised of everything happening in his case. Through Philipsborn, Jason knew that Barry Scheck, the famous New York lawyer who had founded the Innocence Project, was working "behind the scenes" to examine the possibility of using DNA evidence on the men's behalf.

News like that helped Jason keep his spirits buoyed. So did the volume of letters he continued to receive. People wrote explaining how they'd learned about his case through "boards" and "chat rooms" on the Internet—meeting places that Jason found hard to comprehend. Some correspondents let Jason know that, while most of those involved with the case on the Internet seemed to believe he was innocent, a few sites did exist to argue for the convicted men's guilt. People reported that John Mark Byers and Todd Moore, parents of two of the victims, had posted angry messages there.

All the Internet activity—pro and con—was hard to grasp for someone who'd never so much as held a cell phone. Jason had heard, for instance, that one non-supporter, or "non" in the case's new lingo, had created a website containing dozens of documents from the investigation and trials. At the time, nobody knew—least of all, Jason—that the fledgling archive of West Memphis case documents would become the largest repository of records relating to a criminal case on the Internet. It would be years before Jason would learn that the site was developed by a man his own age, who ran it from his apartment in Denmark.

> "There is one question, Inspector Callahan: Why do they call
> you 'Dirty Harry'?"
>
> ~ Harry Julian Fink

Like so many, Christian Hansen had become fascinated with the case when he saw the first *Paradise Lost* documentary. That was in 1998, while Jason was at Grimes. In the three years that followed, Hansen read everything he could find about the investigation and trials. Hansen understood supporters' arguments that there was no physical evidence linking Jessie, Damien and Jason to the murders. But he remained troubled by the knowledge that Jessie had confessed to the murders, not once but twice, after his conviction. (The first time was as sheriff's deputies were driving Jessie to prison; the second occurred on Feb. 17, 1994, with Davis and Stidham present.) Those confessions made it hard for Hansen—and many others—to accept the notion that the teenagers were innocent.

However, Hansen was unlike many others drawn to the case. He was keenly interested in facts and willing to separate them from the many layers of emotion that had imbued the case since the murders.

He lurked in chat rooms, reading what was said there, but he preferred to look at unbiased source materials. For a number of very rational reasons, for example, he wished that the West Memphis police had recorded Jessie's entire interrogation.

Hansen was not a lawyer, a college graduate, or what in the U.S. would be called a white-collar worker. Single, he lived in Aarhus, Denmark's second-largest city, where he'd grown up, graduated from high school, and worked in manufacturing. He'd gotten his first computer, a Commodore 64, at the age of thirteen—three years before the West Memphis murders. Having studied English in school and polished it with TV, movies, and the Internet, he had almost mastered the language by the time Jason returned to Varner. By then, Hansen was running the website "Callahan.8k.com," which was posting an increasing number of documents about the West Memphis case. Supporters of the WM3 and non-supporters alike were beginning to recognize "Callahan" as a vast and neutral online "reference room" for the case, even though few knew who was running the site or why it had that unusual name.

The answer was simple. Hansen had become a fan of American actor Clint Eastwood long before he saw *Paradise Lost*. Because of that, an Internet friend had nicknamed him "Callahan," after Eastwood's character in Dirty Harry. So when Hansen created his own website, he named it "Callahan.8k." At first, Hansen said, he devoted just some of his posts on the site to "the whodunit and motive aspects" of true crime, including the West Memphis case. But as his interest in law expanded, he realized that no other case intrigued him like the one from Arkansas did. When another non-supporter took down a document archive he'd begun about the case, Hansen thought it was "unfortunate that people no longer had access to the documents," so he uploaded the material to his own site. Eventually Hansen devoted the entire site to the West Memphis case and Callahan.8k became the most complete online resource for case-related documents.

"There were enough websites expressing opinions," he said, "so it was only fitting that this would be the 'Switzerland' of the West Memphis Three cyberland." He added that if he'd known that he would soon remove his other content and devote the site exclusively to documents from the West Memphis case, "I might have given it a different name."

In the United States, the website WM3.org was keeping supporters apprised of the latest case developments, to the extent that those could be known. And by the end of 2001, Jason had settled back into life at Varner, where he saw Jessie every now and then, though briefly. "I'd like to talk to him to see what he sees and hears and where he stands on things," Jason said at the time. But in their regimented environment, chats like that were not possible.

By November, Jason had served his mandatory kitchen time and again earned a position of responsibility. He became a disciplinary clerk, which put him in charge of keeping records on everyone who'd gotten into trouble. The job didn't compare to the one as school clerk that he'd left behind at Grimes; on the other hand, Varner offered some benefits that Grimes didn't. For example, Varner had a chapter of the Jaycees—the American Junior Chamber of Commerce—that prisoners with a good record could join.[117] Jason became a proud member. The group was allowed to hold fundraisers and sell sandwiches to raise money to rent movies that inmates wouldn't otherwise see. Twice a year, the Jaycees got to spend some of their proceeds on a "banquet," to which they could invite their families. In December 2001, Jason was in charge of the event.

He looked forward to it, relishing the thought of eating catfish again with his mother, as they'd done so often on the dock at Lakeshore. His girlfriend was going to pick up his mom, who no longer had a car, so the two could come together. Jason wanted both of them to "see that even though I am in prison, I am doing as well as can be and I have people who love and support me." But seeing his mom was crushing; she seemed to be "just hanging on by a thread." Her mother's brother—Jason's Uncle Hubert—had died. And Jason's brother Matt had been seriously injured in a car wreck, so that he now had a hard time walking. By comparison, it almost looked like Jason, in prison, was living the middle-class life of a young, suburban American. His girlfriend, who'd stuck with him since they both were 16, was entering her last semester of college—

and applying to law schools. Jason himself was continuing to take whatever college classes he could. Here he was, heading one of the prison Jaycees' most important committees, and in his spare time, he was privately studying finance and investments, with books provided by supportive friends.

"I don't want to get out and be that sixteen-year-old kid I once was," he said. "I want to keep up." He knew "to stay away from credit cards," and how "mutual funds are a safer investment and a higher yield," and that now was "the best time to buy stocks." He wished he could "get out right now and just buy a bunch of stocks while it's low, and just keep buying stocks every month," because he didn't want his kids "to live in a trailer park." Yet, how could he talk about such dreams and ambitions that night at the banquet? Life in the trailer park had come to the prison to visit, reviving his best—and worst—memories.

After everyone left, Jason had time to reflect in his bunk. His downfall had brought on his family's. After the murder victims and their families, he, Damien and Jessie had become victims—and then there'd been so many more. "We might have lived in a trailer park, but we were moving up," Jason said. "My mom had gotten her GED. We'd gotten out of the grip of my stepdad. Me and my brothers were all in school. I was about to get my first job. Our trailer was ours because my grandmother had left it to us. We had a lot of belief in America." Now his family was torn apart, tattered and struggling—and he was just another data point in America's burgeoning gulag.[118]

Month after monotonous month passed, and often in such quiet hours, that caustic question why ricocheted through his brain. Jason knew that Paul Ford had fought for him in the pretrial hearings. But then, he'd only called one witness at trial. Why? He wondered if Ford had concluded his case was hopeless. "It was a no-win situation with Burnett," Jason reflected. "It was hard to fight against Judge Burnett and the prosecutor too." By now, Jason had come to believe that Burnett "knew from the get-go that he wasn't going to let us win this case. He didn't want the publicity to be that his court was the one that let the killers go."

Yet in the stillness, Jason would also think: "I wonder if he knows that we are innocent. Does he really believe we did it? Or does he wonder?" He wrestled with the same questions with regard to Fogleman and Davis too, because of the way they'd dealt with Michael Carson. Again and again, he asked himself: "Did they really believe what Carson said I did to one of those children?"

Many people could not. This author's critical book, *Devil's Knot*, was published in 2002, the second year of Jason's second stint at Varner. [119] Soon after, Elizabeth Fowler, a Hollywood producer, optioned it for film. Later Fowler said of that decision, "When I first read *Devil's Knot* in 2003, our country was in the middle of a national discussion about the Patriot Act after 9/11. I was struck by the parallels of the manipulation of communal fear resulting in a willingness to rush to judgment and to sacrifice due process. I was also struck by the notion that, after the initial terror had calmed, *Devil's Knot* became a story about the power of the people—that when our deliberately designed governmental system of 'checks and balances' repeatedly failed with a flat refusal to admit any errors with this case, it was the citizenry who rose up and through websites, documentaries, books and both on-the-ground and virtual movements cried 'foul.'"

In Arkansas, however, confidence in the courts prevailed—though with a few exceptions. A trio of women who saw no evidence of the men's guilt printed flyers, staged concerts, and organized rallies in support of the West Memphis Three. A college instructor offered the case to her writing classes as an exercise in critical thinking. A few criminal justice teachers discussed the case in class. But most schools, and especially state institutions, avoided mention of the local case that was drawing international attention.

Jason knew that most Arkansans believed the worst about him, if only because they saw him and Jessie as pawns of the demonic Damien. He sensed that some of the ministers who came to the prisons where he was held regarded him as something of a prize—a bona fide Satanist in need of salvation. Some inmates tried to redeem him too. But Jason rebuffed attempts to convert him and chose not to attend chapel. Though there was much about the world he did not understand, and much about his case in particular, he felt complete in silence and solitude. Others were welcome to believe as they wished. He was glad that chapel was there for them. Personally, though, he said, "I worship God. I don't need to go down there."

That did not mean that faith for Jason was easy, especially since there were so many kinds of faith. Take the faith that the families of the murdered children had placed in the police, the prosecutors and the courts. Jason had experienced enough powerlessness himself to understand how powerless those parents must have felt as they buried their children. He had struggled for answers, and he knew that they had struggled too. He knew how comforting faith in official action could be—because he'd held onto such faith too. Lying there, he also thought that, like those parents, he knew what it was like to be torn from people you love.

But now, he knew that while he did not want to live without faith and hope, life demanded more. Blind trust was not enough. And pain was not a sufficient reason to set reason aside. "If my child were murdered," he reflected, "I would stop at nothing to find out who did this to him. No matter how much it hurt, I would make sure that the police got the one who was guilty of the crime. I would make sure they did their job. I would not let them pull some ace out of the hole—a rabbit out of the hat—and just accept it because they are the police, and I want so much to believe they have found someone that I can hate and unleash all the pain, anger, suffering and grief that have been caused by my loss."

Jason kept such thoughts to himself, but some supporters were not so reserved. In March 2002, Henry Rollins wrote about the West Memphis Three in his newsletter to fans, "They were incarcerated through ignorance and a blindness that is as infuriating as it is horrifying . . . These three are innocent, and to stand for the kind of insanity that convicted them is to align oneself with all that is bad." He added, "I know that this is not the only case of innocent people in prison, and I am not trying to imply that this is the only case like this that should be addressed. But it's there, glaring in your face, obscenely flaunting its ignorance and hatred. You can't let this kind of thing happen on your watch and call yourself free."

Similar questions disturbed those outside the prison who'd become interested in the case. Some, like Hansen in Denmark, found Jessie's confessions persuasive, though much about the case remained troubling. Others, convinced of the WM3's innocence, wondered whether regional religious biases had played a part in the verdicts, or if the police had directed attention to the teens to spare someone else, or if the judge and the prosecutors had been in league to assure the convictions for reasons no one knew. For some, suspicions about the integrity of law enforcement in the area were heightened in 2002 when it was reported that a handful of Crittenden County drug enforcement officers were indicted for skimming money from drivers passing through West Memphis on the city's two interstate highways.[120]

In 2002, Bartholomew Sullivan reported in *The Commercial Appeal* that the West Memphis Police Department's new chief, Robert H. Paudert, suspected illegal activity among some officers. Not knowing whom he could trust, Paudert had taken his concerns to the Federal Bureau of Investigation. Agents there understood he had reason for concern. For years, Crittenden County had opted not to participate in the state's network of county drug task forces, which shared all drug monies seized. Sullivan reported that, in 2000, Crittenden County's independent drug task force had seized $5.43 million on the highways that passed through West Memphis and Marion. That constituted more than half the total amount of drug money seized during that year in the entire state. In 2001, FBI agents conducted at least two sting operations. Those led to indictments the following year.[121]

As Sullivan reported, "It may have been the recent, sudden improvement in the livelihoods of some of the officers—fancy motorcycles, big houses—that made neighbors and fellow officers suspicious." Some of the flash points that caught investigators' attention were a sheriff's deputy who lived with his schoolteacher wife in a quarter-million-dollar house, two deputies who flew private airplanes, one who'd reportedly paid $18,953 in cash for a Harley-Davidson motorcycle, and another who was said to have paid for a $26,500 ski boat with $100 bills.

In July 2002, a federal grand jury indicted four narcotics officers, charging them with stealing money from suspected drug couriers. Two former sheriff's deputies and two men from the West Memphis Police Department were charged with having pocketed more than a half-million dollars. Three of those men, including West Memphis Police Inspector James Sudbury, a narcotics detective who had played a key role in the investigation into the 1993 murders, had been subjects of a probe that was still underway at the time of the murders. Sudbury was not indicted in 1993 or in 2002, though after the second investigation he was fired for violating policies regarding cash seizures.[122]

"Indeed," Sullivan wrote, "suspicion about misuse of the drug war tactic that's supposed to drain the profits from illegal drug dealing is an old story in Crittenden County. An Arkansas State Police investigation in the early 1990s turned up some wrongdoing involving seized evidence and sloppy recordkeeping by an earlier version of Crittenden County's drug task force. At the time, a few wrists were slapped, including those of two of the three recently fired West Memphis police officers and a sheriff's deputy . . . But Prosecuting Attorney Brent Davis elected not to file charges in 1993, records indicate."

Yet it was almost as though the indictments and the history they represented had unfolded in a vacuum. Except for Sullivan, nobody mentioned Davis's role in allowing the "highway robbery" to continue. By 2002, Fogleman had become a respected circuit judge. And Judge David Burnett was being heaped with honors. In March 2002, the Arkansas Supreme Court named him chair of its Committee on Criminal Practice, and at the end of the year he was elected president of the Arkansas Judicial Council, a prestigious group made up of all the state's judges, including those on the state's court of appeals and Supreme Court. "That 2002 election was a big deal for me," Burnett told an interviewer. "Being recognized by my peers was an extraordinary compliment."[123]

It seemed to Jason that, the more the West Memphis trials were criticized from outside Arkansas, the more the legal establishment within the state supported them. It looked like a strange gap was developing between people who saw the case as a cause for alarm and a legal community that saw nothing extraordinary in it. Didn't there need to be some common understanding between the public and the courts? Sometimes, Jason thought that his case surely would collapse of its own absurdity. But then, he had only to look around himself—at the gray cinderblock walls, the bars outside, the police and the electrified fence—to remember how wrong he'd been to believe for so long that absurdity could not prevail.

With so much mystifying about the past and so much to long for ahead, Jason kept sane by focusing on the present: on his work, girlfriend, letters and Hacky Sack. At night, even when his reveries looped back to his trial, he'd never lie awake long. Drowsily, he'd think, "It was like playing Mike Tyson's punch out on Nintendo. The courts are Iron Mike and I am Little Mac. But someone unplugs my controller from the game console and Little Mac gets knocked out. One! Two! Three! You're out! That's it. Game over."

> "Anyone who has the power to make you believe
> absurdities has the power to make you commit injustices."
> ~ *Voltaire*

Near the end of 2002, officials at Varner moved Jessie into the barracks where Jason lived. Jason said he was glad because Jessie had struggled in prison, fighting a lot, and Jason hoped that now he could "help keep him out of trouble." He wished he could have been there for Jessie when the West Memphis police asked to interview him. As Jason now saw it, "The police were not going to let Jessie out of that interrogation room until one of three things happened: (1) Jessie's father makes the police let him out, stating, 'Enough is enough; as you can plainly see, my son does not know anything about these things'; (2) an attorney arrives and makes the officers let Jessie go; or (3) Jessie agrees with their views and just gives in to their overpowering and aggressive tactics."

He elaborated, "I do not know where Jessie's father was during all this mess, and, obviously, Jessie did not have an attorney. So poor Jessie knows only that telling the truth to these people is not working.

He's been in the interrogation room for hours. How long does it take to answer a few questions? How many times did Jessie tell the police the truth that they refused to accept? How did the police show Jessie their dissatisfaction with his truthful answers? How did it make Jessie feel to be saying what he knows to be right and yet having the 'good guys' not believe in him and absolutely refuse the truth? One cannot imagine how torn Jessie must have been feeling after hours of their calculated and ruthless tactics, knowing that he was telling them the truth and yet still they refused to accept it.

"I bet he was wishing for someone with morals and a sense of decency to come into that room to make it all stop, to say, 'Hey, Jessie, sorry to put you through this mess. We know you are telling the truth. Here, we'll call your father to come and get you so that you can go home and live your simple but peaceful and pleasant life.' And everything would have been okay. But, no. These strangers, who now are extremely hostile to Jessie, who refuse all the true answers, will not let him go, and no one is coming to let him go home. What can Jessie do but agree with them?"

For Jason, Jessie's slide from resistance to compliance was as understandable as heat melting ice. He'd felt that heat—that pressure—himself. He'd experienced the cajoling, the refusals, and even the life-saving enticements. No. Not for a minute could Jason blame Jessie for his collapse. It was too easy for Jason to put himself in Jessie's place.

"Jessie never wants to hurt anyone or disagree with people or make anyone mad at him," Jason said. He begins to think, 'It is just words.' If he just agrees with them, they will let him go home. They have, after hours of interrogation, made it plainly evident, even to Jessie, that they are not going to accept anything from his mouth but what they want to hear, so that they can wrap this case up and get everyone off of their backs. So what does Jessie do, being the good guy that he is? What can he do? What could anyone do in that position, but begin to agree with them. Meet them halfway in the lies, and if he gets it wrong, don't worry, they are now heading in the right direction. They are his friends now, so they help him out if he gets some of the answers wrong. It is like a difficult test, except that the 'instructors' are walking him through with each question and if his answers are wrong, they'll supply the facts.

"Jessie still knows it is wrong, but at least at the immediate moment, some of the stress that these people have caused him is being lifted by him answering the questions the way that they want him to. That is the way I think that day went down for Jessie. He had no choice. They only recorded what they wanted to. They never allowed anyone who had Jessie's better interest into that room."

That was Jason's subjective assessment. He had no way of knowing, as he contemplated Jessie's experience, that at almost the same time, a college professor in Puerto Rico was also reviewing Jessie's session with the West Memphis police—but from an objective point of view. Dr. Martin D. Hill, who taught pharmacology, had seen *Paradise Lost*, checked out <u>WM3.org</u>, and become intrigued by the amount of information increasingly available on the Internet. He began to scrutinize parts of the case that he found particularly "mind-boggling." Jessie's confession was one of those.[124] Hill wanted to see if he could find new information embedded in the parts of Jessie's interrogation the police had recorded. He said he wanted to "ponder the deep question: 'How can you tell when someone is saying nothing?'"

Taking an academic approach to that question, Hill searched the transcripts for key words, noting when they were spoken and by whom. In a study he later published in a scientific journal, Hill concluded that Jessie had provided "none of the key, specific, verifiable details" of the crime, that "the police were the source of nearly all of the substantive information" regarding it, and, further, that the information that Jessie himself supplied was "contradictory" and "incorrect."[125]

Jason did not know about Hill's study, and it would have changed nothing if he had. Reports of a different kind dominated the news that spring of 2003: the explosion of America's space shuttle Columbia and the U.S.-led invasion of Iraq. At Varner, the big news for Jason was a job change. Jason was moved to work as a clerk in the prison's law library. It was an intellectually demanding job that required speed, computer skills, and the ability to communicate about law with inmates who often knew little about it beyond that they'd been convicted. Jason welcomed the challenge.

He worked in the library from seven in the morning to forty-thirty in the afternoon, and again, from seven to ten in the evening. While a free-world employee ran the library, clerks like Jason were expected to fill stacks of requests for books submitted by inmates. When inmates brought in handwritten legal motions they wanted submitted to the courts, the clerks had to type them. Jason worked nonstop, looking up cases on the library's Gateway computer and running off copies for inmates on the little dot-matrix printer.

"I worked my butt off in there," he said. "That was the most hard-working job there was. You had the Supermax just opening up, and the death-row population moving into it. There were statutes and court rules to learn. I learned all about LexisNexis, a database of law, there. It gives you connections to court rules, statutes, journals—anything related to law, state and federal. I was getting a crash course in legal research, without instruction or guidance."

He reflected, "I wouldn't say I was educated, really, but I was working with what I had access to. I learned how to make a search phrase to look up certain terms. I'd type up a legal brief description and index it for the guys or print it out for the guys in lockdown. After a while, I devised a cheat sheet for myself. I set up a hyperlink, saved it, and when I needed it, I could pop it up, and it would take me straight to LexisNexis."

Jason's system worked, at least within the limits of his position. "Guys come in," he said, "and they don't have any idea where to begin researching their case. So the first thing I tell them is, 'Hey, I'm not a lawyer. And I can't be a lawyer. I'm definitely not your attorney. I would love to work magic for you, but you've got to be your own lawyer or find a lawyer.' A lot of times, I would type letters to attorneys for them. But I was always very clear on how I could help and how I couldn't."

What he could do was explain how legal processes were supposed to work. He'd talk inmates through their direct appeals, Rule 37 petitions, and *coram nobis* petitions—filings asking a court to correct a previous error "of the most fundamental character."

(Courts can respond by issuing writs of error *coram nobis* in order to "achieve justice" where "no other remedy" is available—but they are extremely rare.) Jason understood that, but rarely offered such disheartening information, preferring to direct prisoners to the statutes and the most relevant or authoritative references for each point they wanted to raise. Thus informed, the inmates could start requesting the resources they wanted by name. But there was always a grim tenor to the work. Though prisons are required to provide law libraries, Jason privately knew how much of the work he saw prisoners doing there would almost certainly prove futile.

"Most people didn't have a clue about the law in any way, shape, form, or fashion," he said. "And the more they would file and get rejected, the more hopeless they would feel. I never saw anyone get some relief. No. It's a tough system, and the majority of those guys were not innocent. They were just trying to get better deals or something. Some people, like me, would think, 'I've got a slam-dunk case,' but the law is basically a whole bunch of opinions, and people's opinions are as multitudinous as there are people, and it's very hard to get judges' attention to reflect on their opinions."

Every delusion about law Jason had entertained at sixteen was long gone. He understood full well the magnitude of the job his current lawyers faced. Once a person was convicted, the obstacles to a rehearing were huge, no matter how rational the need for one might appear. "You have everything you need for relief," he said, "innocence and everything that proves that. And you think that the law is like a computer program or a combination lock. You get all these things that are necessary and it works. But it's not like that. They can just shut you down and refuse to listen or even to give you a reason why your petition has been denied. It's not like there's a recipe that works all the time. It's like you'd get a recipe for baking a cake, but a thousand times out of a thousand and one, it doesn't bake."

In addition, Jason knew, the recipe for his own case was more complicated than most. The state's theory of the case was that he, Damien and Jessie had murdered the children together, yet each of the inmates' cases presented different challenges. Jessie's lawyers had to tackle his confession. Damien's had to fight against death.

And Jason's lawyers, ironically, had to get a court to consider the distinctive factors pointing to his innocence. And all of this had to be accomplished despite the state Supreme Court's findings that Jessie had confessed to the police and that "there was evidence from which the jury could reasonably find that both defendants [Echols and Baldwin] said they killed the children."[126]

The teams of attorneys Philipsborn formed produced a high-octane mix of legal minds and egos engaged in a high-stakes effort. By 2003, when Jason was working in the law library, he was aware that tensions had arisen among the attorneys, especially over strategies and timing. He anchored his confidence in Philipsborn. "John's belief is that you don't get into the ballgame if you can't control the football," he explained. "He's not going to get in there without everything he needs. John plays for the long game. He had no faith in Burnett, but he knew you've got to get everything you want to get in before the lower courts so it will be there for the higher court. He never speculated about how long the process might be, but I held out hope."

When asked how he'd managed to hang onto that hope, knowing what he did now about the law, Jason said he'd chosen to develop a positive attitude as a child, "being around people who were always complaining about things." He said, "They were too busy complaining to see the good things, and I tried not to be that person. Regardless of what's going on, there's some good in it too, even if it's just your ability to do pushups in isolation—because there's some people who can't do pushups. Not that you turn a blind eye on what's going on. But at the same time, you don't want to spend so much energy focusing on the hard stuff that you don't let yourself find happiness."

As a result, in addition to hope, Jason embraced gratitude and patience. He knew how rare it was for someone in his situation—especially someone without money serving a sentence of life instead of death—to have an attorney. He appreciated Lorri Davis, Eddie Vedder, all the musicians, and all the supporters who'd made contributions, large and small, to the WM3.org website. He wished he could thank them all, and he considered it his role to keep faith with them. "I definitely wanted to be free—immediately," he said.

"But then, I also knew I didn't want to do all this work and go into a retrial because we were hasty and get the same result as before. So I was always thinking, 'If it means staying here a little longer and getting things right, that's what I want, rather than blowing all my chances because we didn't get all the work done correctly.'"

When Tom Quinn, Philipsborn's investigator, visited, Jason offered what he could—mostly, he said, by "rehashing" his alibi and providing the names of people he'd encountered in the county jail. Beyond that, he kept up with his case through Philipsborn and his own research in the library. "John would always send me the rough drafts of the motions he was going to submit, copies of letters he would send to the state, and copies of emails. If John had a phone conversation with Fogleman about the case, he would always follow it up with a letter to me about what they talked about, so there was a record of their conversations."

When Quinn later returned to the prison, he brought messages for Jason from several of the people he'd already interviewed. Among them were Sally Ware, Jason's former teacher; Joyce Cureton, his former jailer; and some kids Jason had known in school. "They all said, like, motivational things they wanted me to know because they knew Mr. Quinn would be seeing me," Jason said. Quinn also reported on his visit to the West Memphis Police Department, where he'd checked out for the attorneys how evidence was being preserved.

The attorneys wanted a lot of physical evidence retested. Jason recalled: "The state said, 'You can't have everything tested.' So, instead of fighting for everything, the attorneys broke the evidence into groups of what they thought was most important, less important, and so on. They said, 'Let's get an approved group going, and while that's being done, we'll fight them on the other stuff.'"

This was groundbreaking work in Arkansas. Requests to retest evidence in the West Memphis case would require one of the first applications of the state's new law allowing scientific testing that was not available at the time of the prisoners' trial. State officials opposed many requests for retesting on the grounds that they were not likely to provide exculpatory information. "I still don't understand the state's argument," Jason said. "It's not like the state was going to have to pay for it—even though the statute allows for the state to fund it. Our case was extraordinary in that a lot of people heard about it and were willing to fund the tests." In fact, the state's attorneys dug in, and battles to find out where some evidence was kept, what items could be retested, and what laboratory would conduct the tests would continue for almost three years.[127]

Jason had long ago learned to live with his disappointments with Paul Ford at his trial, but now he learned that Philipsborn had found reasons of his own to be dismayed. Ford, it turned out, had never personally checked any of the information provided by the state's crime lab. Philipsborn believed attorneys had an obligation not to accept any of the state's science at face value. So now, for the first time, investigators working for Jason were reviewing the crime lab's work. While doing that, they discovered in Ford's file a note that had never come to light before.

Its importance was hard to determine. The note was simply a brief message jotted down by someone at the crime lab on January 5, 1994—exactly two weeks before the start of Jessie's trial. It stated that Fogleman had called about the "three West Memphis boys" and that he wanted to know "about overlays in re to weapon." The note added that Fogleman had said it was "fine" to bill his office "for the photos." But that was all there was to it. Though the investigators went to the crime lab and examined all the records there, they found nothing that appeared to relate to the note: no transparencies, no record of a return call to Fogleman, and nothing about "overlays of a weapon."[128]

The discovery raised several questions. Crime labs frequently make acetate transparencies of weapons—knives, especially—in attempts to match them with markings left on a body. But nobody at either Jessie's trial or at Damien and Jason's had mentioned—much less produced—transparencies of a weapon from the crime lab. Yet at Damien and Jason's trial, Fogleman had repeatedly suggested that the knife found in the lake behind Jason's house caused the injuries to Christopher Byers. And in his closing remarks to the jury, Fogleman had used a knife and a grapefruit to physically demonstrate to the jury the mark that the so-called "lake knife" had made, while pointing out the similarities between those marks and the wounds on Christopher. It was an unscientific, unorthodox—and critics have said, unethical—demonstration.

Now the question loomed: Had the crime lab, in fact, made transparencies, or overlays, of the lake knife, as it appeared Fogleman presumed? If so, what happened to them? Were they not introduced at trial because they did not match the victim's wounds? If so, who made that decision? And if the lab did not make transparencies of that knife or some other weapon, what was Fogleman referring to when he called? And why were there no other records—in the prosecutor's, defense attorneys' or crime lab's files—that mentioned "overlays of a weapon"?

The memo was tantalizing because, if the crime lab had made transparencies of any weapon related to the case, the prosecutors were required by law to supply them to the defense. But, while no one could dispute the memo's existence, no one could explain it, either. It would remain a mystery while Jason's team continued its deeper probe. The one point the memo did make clear was that its discovery came years too late. Had any of the six trial attorneys examined the case records as Philipsborn now did, they would have found the memo, and if it had been introduced at trial, someone from the state would have had to explain it.

Years after the discovery, Philipsborn said, "While it's certainly possible that discussions of the transparency slipped the mind of someone on the prosecution team, it seems to me that the existence of paperwork addressing the transparency is an important issue. Of course, had it been raised at trial, one of the possible 'outs' for the prosecutors is that they were not addressing the knife in question in connection with the transparency. But if that were the case, Dr. Peretti would have been able to give them that out." As it was, the question was never raised, and Peretti never addressed it.[129]

> "Few people are capable of expressing with equanimity opinions which differ from that of their social environment."
> ~ Albert Einstein

Meanwhile, Jason understood why most of the legal activity playing out in court focused on Damien. All the attorneys had filed multiple motions to preserve evidence. But, while Jessie's and Jason's teams were working behind the scenes, Damien's lawyers were also fighting before the Arkansas Supreme Court. In October 2003, Damien's attorneys and lawyers from the state attorney general's office stood before that court, offering oral arguments as to whether or not Damien should be granted a new hearing on the evidence in his case.

The court wasted little time. Before the month was out, it issued two rulings that stung Damien: the first denied his petition for a writ of error *coram nobis*; the second simply affirmed Burnett's reasons for denying Damien's Rule 37 petition. Explaining its agreement with Burnett, the court addressed one of the most troublesome questions of Damien's case: whether or not his mental health at the time of his trial was good enough to enable him to assist in his own defense, as the law required. In Damien's petition for a writ of error *coram nobis*, his attorneys had argued that it was not. When they denied that petition, the justices wrote:

"Echols's first ground for relief is his claim that he was incompetent at the time of his trial, in February and March 1994. He relies upon the affidavits of Dr. George W. Woods, dated February 9, 2001, and May 15, 2001, wherein Dr. Woods concluded that Echols was incompetent at the time of his trial, based upon his review of Echols's prior mental-health records, the trial transcript, video tapes of Echols's testimony, and interviews with Echols conducted in December 2000. Echols asserts that he has only recently been made aware of the extent of the mental problems that he was facing at the time of trial, and that his illness actually prevented him from being aware of his incompetency. He further claims that before and during his trial, he was administered drugs without his consent."

The Supreme Court ruled that it was too late for Damien's attorneys to raise these arguments. "The exhibits submitted with Echols's petition and the records from his direct appeal demonstrate that the defense team was aware of Echols's history of mental treatments at the time of trial," the Court ruled. "For example, the report compiled by defense investigator Glori Shettles, which is contained in the trial record, reveals the extent of Echols's mental treatments at the East Arkansas Regional Mental Health Center (1992-93), St. Vincent's Hospital of Portland, Oregon (1992), and Charter Hospital of Little Rock (June and September 1992). Indeed, an entire volume of the record from his trial is devoted to the records from the foregoing treatment centers, as well as documents submitted by Echols to the Social Security Administration (SSA) for the purpose of obtaining disability payments. These are largely the same records that Echols now relies on to support his petition for a writ of error *coram nobis*."

Jason knew from his many correspondents that for thousands of supporters, interest in Damien's mental health, state of mind, intellectual pursuits, and tastes in art had formed the core of their case. It seemed forever ago that he and Damien had sat on the dock at Lakeshore dreaming of a life beyond the trailer park. Well, they had gotten out, he chuckled. And now, Damien was famous, as it seemed he'd somehow expected to be, and because of Damien's charisma, and the woman he'd married, he, Jason and Jessie all had good attorneys. By the time the Arkansas Supreme Court rejected Damien's petition, it was clear that he practically had developed a cult following, though nothing like the one Griffis had suspected.

Many who'd watched *Paradise Lost* had not seen Damien as a mentally disturbed teenager, but as a sweet, smart, Goth kid in a region largely unprepared for the idea that a person could be Goth and not somehow dangerous. Others had a decidedly different reaction, more than one remarking online, "You only have to look at him to know he's guilty." For better or worse, Damien aroused something in people. It was something close to fear, and Fogleman latched onto it. Jason could not imagine Fogleman trying to sell the jury on the idea that Jessie had once led anything, much less a Satanic cult. And Jason doubted that Fogleman would have dared to point to him and say, "There's not a soul in there." But Damien was different. At trial, Fogleman had been able to persuade jurors Damien was, in fact, the soulless leader of a Satanic cult, and when the jurors sentenced Damien to death, they compounded his charisma.

Its strength could be seen in 2003, when a couple donated space at their art gallery in Los Angeles for an exhibit featuring works about the case. The event was called "Cruel and Unusual." About twenty nationally known artists, including Grove Pashley, one of the founders of WM3.org., contributed works to raise funds for the case. Jello Biafra gave a spoken word performance denouncing the death penalty. Actor Winona Ryder addressed an opening night crowd estimated at more than four thousand gathered in a parking area adjacent to the gallery. "We believe a terrible injustice happened ten years ago," she said at the microphone. "an injustice that involved six young lives. Three are dead. Three are holed up in prison for crimes that we and millions across America believe they did not commit." She added, "We would like to see Damien, Jason and Jessie given new trials—this time based on concrete evidence, actual facts, and substance—instead of rumors, prejudice, superstition, and what amounts to a modern-day witch hunt. We would like to see a real proper investigation to determine who really did kill those children."[130]

At around the same time, Rollins, the spoken-word artist who had been supporting the men for so long, told a Utah newspaper: "The only thing separating these guys from a life of incarceration or death is the will of good people to do the right thing. At this point, that's all. The state of Arkansas will not pay for the [DNA] testing. God will not pay for the testing. It's just down to you, me, and anyone who gives a damn."

On Dec. 31, 2003, the Supersuckers performed at a club called Slim's in San Francisco. A young woman named Anje Vela, who booked bands in the area, attended. Later that night, she went to the band's website, where she saw a banner for the West Memphis Three. That led her to the website of Henry Rollins. "I stayed up into the early hours of the morning reading all the court documents online," Vela said. "I then ordered *Devil's Knot*, and that's when I was ready." Vela said that what she learned about the case accumulated until a day when, "all these pieces somehow caused a little revolt within." She began looking for ways to enlist musicians for the two-pronged effort to raise awareness about the case and funds for the legal work.

> "It seldom happens that any felicity comes so pure as not to be tempered and allayed by some mixture of sorrow."
>
> ~ *Miguel de Cervantes*

At Varner, Jason reunited with his old friend Smitty. He even helped Smitty find romance. One of the women who wrote to Jason had let him know that she was a fan of the Dallas Cowboys. "When she'd write to me, it was always 'Dallas-Cowboys this' and 'Dallas-Cowboys that.' Well, Smitty was always talking about the Dallas Cowboys too. So I wrote to the woman and said, 'I tell you what. Why don't you talk to each other?'" The two connected, love blossomed, and when Smitty got paroled, they married. Jason remained friends with both.

But 2003 ended in misery. In June, he'd passed the ten-year mark since his arrest. He'd just suffered a long bout of the flu. He'd felt the Supreme Court's rebuke to Damien as "a drastic blow." He was unhappy with what he called "the momentum" of his own defense and was thinking about asking the governor to grant him executive clemency, an act that until then had been unthinkable because it would mean begging forgiveness for the crime he had not committed. "I am considering this option," he said, "because I see how slow Burnett is going to be about things, and I know how slow the whole court system is, and honestly, I am sick of it. I just want to go home and this is the quickest way I can see to get things done."

This was Jason in despair. His girlfriend argued that what he had in mind was a bad idea. He hadn't mentioned it yet to his attorneys. "But," he complained, "they aren't the ones behind bars." He was sick, bitter, discouraged—lower than he'd been in jail, during his trial, or at any time so far in prison. But the real issue was not the flu or his case. The problem was with his heart, which was breaking. When he felt a little better, he said that he and his girlfriend were "in the midst of a 'crisis' and that he'd "just been plain old-fashioned blue."

Maintaining a romance during a life sentence in prison sucked. And a social life limited to a few thousand male prisoners left a lot to be desired too. It didn't help that 2004 was the year that Mark Zuckerberg began writing the code for a new website he called 'Thefacebook'. The Internet was becoming increasingly personal and speeding the concept of social networking. But not for prisoners. While Jason hungered for the technology that was empowering his generation, he could not get his hands on it. He could use computers for work but not to connect to the wonderful Internet. In the spring of 2004, when Jason turned twenty-seven, other twenty-somethings were connecting online—and even discussing him there—while most of his interactions were with a few free-world prison employees, the other white-suited inmates, and his watchful, key-jangling guards.

Yet, almost imperceptibly, the air around the case was changing. Part of that change could be felt at the University of Arkansas at Little Rock's Bowen School of Law, where students invited Judge John Fogleman to discuss how he'd prosecuted the West Memphis case.[131] Instead, Fogleman prosecuted *Devil's Knot*, a book of more than four hundred pages, that included four hundred and thirty endnotes. Displaying pages from the book on a projector, he said he'd found seven factual mistakes in it. The book stated that Fogleman had been a juvenile judge; in fact, he had been a juvenile prosecutor (as Jason well knew). The book claimed that Fogleman's father had served on the Marion school board; that should have been his grandfather. It stated that Fogleman's father had served as president of the Arkansas Bar Association, but again, that was the wrong Fogleman; his uncle had been the ABA president. The book also reported incorrectly that, after Jason's arrest, he'd been given a dental x-ray.[132] In addition, Fogleman said he'd found errors in the captions of some of the book's photos. While none of those mistakes was damning per se, if you put them all together, Fogleman told his audience, you had a book with little truth in it. Fogleman said that such "sloppy" reporting demonstrated the author's "lack of concern for accuracy," and that her book, therefore, "should not be relied on at all."[133]

The attack was basic trial strategy for discrediting a witness, the witness here being *Devil's Knot*. Demonstrate some inaccuracies and generalize to plant doubt about the accuracy of every word. But if the technique worked with jurors, law students proved tougher. When Fogleman accepted questions, two of them asked him to address aspects of the case that were "more substantive" than the faults he'd found in the book. His response was to belittle criticisms he'd heard about the police investigation, his prosecution of the case, and the judge's handling of the trials, describing them as "nonsense" and as examples of "how the West Memphis Three's supporters mislead." Fogleman concluded his talk by assuring the audience that he'd had personal experience with Damien Echols prior to the murders and he had found him to be "weird."

The same month that Fogleman spoke in Little Rock, a friend sent Jason a copy of the *Arkansas Times*, in which Damien's wife, Lorri Davis, spoke publicly for the first time about her marriage. Because of Damien's recent setbacks in court, she said she felt "compelled" to try to explain why she loved him. "I see how he has been portrayed in the media, and I understand that the perception of him here in this state is still, largely, that he is, first of all, guilty and that he's also evil and scary. And I see that, with some very, very important exceptions, he is still portrayed that way. I want to try to change that. I cannot just sit back any longer and not speak out for him." She also explained the work she was doing on Damien's behalf. "I'm his voice," Davis said. "Because of where he is, he doesn't have one. I work with his attorneys. I help raise funds for the three cases. I work with people who want to help in any way they can. I'm working to get the truth out. And it will come out."[134]

For Jason, however, the year that began as "blue" in January had turned utterly bleak by April. The eight-year friendship-turned-love that he'd shared with the girl-turned-woman from Little Rock was definitely, dismally, finally over. He was in prison for life. She was 24 and free. And in her free world, she had met someone else. Intellectually, Jason understood. She could not be expected to share his entombment. But understanding did nothing to keep his heart from breaking.

Jason quit being the model prisoner, the good guy who worked in the library, the inmate who could be counted on to counsel more troubled souls. "It was emotionally difficult," he would later say mildly. Then less mildly: "For a little while, it pissed me off. I'd had this attitude that if I did good and obeyed all the rules, I'd get through this and we'd be okay. But that's not what happened." He smoked weed recklessly. "It's pretty easy to find in there," he said. "Usually, there's a few people who get it regularly. I usually paid five or ten dollars for a joint. It just depended. I did it every now and then, but this time I just did it with a negative frame of mind and bad attitude. I really think it was my negativity that invited negativity. I just fell into this 'woe is me' mode, like it didn't matter what I did, just like me getting out didn't hinge on whether I'd really killed anyone or not. It was a weird frame of mind for me."

Predictably, Jason was caught and sentenced to thirty days in punitive isolation—the hole. He was knocked back to Class 4 status and lost his job in the law library. But by the summer's end, he was doing better. "Whereas earlier, I was literally despairing," he said, "now I've regained composure, set a goal, formulated a plan to get there and am on my way." He'd been released from solitary a few days earlier but would remain on punitive status, without commissary, telephone, or visitation privileges for another week. He intended to rebound, first by enlisting in the prison's boot camp program. "It is very rigorous and strict—however it will permit me to regain my Class I-C status sixty days quicker than if I went through the hoe squad. Also, once completed, I will regain a modicum of respect from the prison administration. My former employer, Mrs. Williams, has promised my job back as soon as I graduate. Mostly though, I am doing this to regain some of my own respect for myself. I do not like excuses and refrain from using them. However, I did just that—I made up excuses to break rules, feel sorry for myself, and do things I just do not do, and for that I am paying the price."

In that dark year of 2004, Jason's wish for his twenty-seventh birthday—after the impossible one of a prompt release—was that Metallica would come to see him and, while they were there, put on a concert at Varner. It was an absurd thought: getting the Arkansas Department of Correction to allow a famous heavy metal band to perform in a maximum-security prison. At times, though, it seemed that it would be easier to get Metallica into Varner than to get three innocent men out.

Strangely, it may have been Judge Burnett who gave Jason his best birthday present that year, when he approved requests for new tests of certain evidence. Almost since the time Philipsborn had taken over coordination of the three defense teams, he and Michael Burt of Jessie's team, in consultation with Barry Scheck of the Innocence Project, had been negotiating with Prosecuting Attorney Brent Davis to have a long list of items from the crime scene tested—and, in some cases, retested. After a lot of "wrangling," Philipsborn said, the sides settled on two lists of items to be submitted to Burnett. Because of the DNA law enacted three years earlier, in 2001, Burnett signed two orders—on Feb. 20 and June 2, 2004—authorizing the transfer of more than eighty items from the Arkansas crime lab to an independent laboratory equipped for DNA testing.[135] Burnett noted: "...the parties have agreed that biological material found on the...evidence has the scientific potential to produce new...evidence which may be materially relevant to the defendants'/petitioners' assertions of actual innocence..."

Now, for the first time since the arrests eleven years earlier, there was a chance of finding new evidence and bringing it to court. Burnett's order was exact. It spelled out who would conduct the tests (the Bode Technology Group in Springfield, Virginia), who would pay for them (the defendants), how the chain of custody would be preserved, and precisely what items were to be tested. Among those items were "one package containing ligatures from wrists to legs, right and left of victim Moore"; "two dark Caucasian hairs removed from Branch"; a "hair found on Byers' body"; a "Negroid hair removed from a white sheet"; and a "Kershaw folding knife." The order noted that the state reserved the right "to object to the relevance of any results of testing," while the inmates reserved the right "to litigate the legal and scientific validity of any of the state's objections."

Jason knew that the law operated on its own, sedate sense of time. He paid for hope with patience. Fortunately, news from Philipsborn kept him encouraged. For example, Jason knew in 2004, that Tom Quinn, the San Francisco investigator, was spending months in Arkansas, knocking on doors and asking delicate questions. While Jason watched news of funeral arrangements for former President Ronald Reagan in June of that year, Quinn was in Jonesboro, talking to Danny Williams, the counselor who had written the sorrowful letter to Jason about how he feared he'd inadvertently given Michael Carson some of the information which Carson had used against Jason, presumably in hopes of receiving favors in return when it came to his own prosecution.

Quinn asked Williams if he would describe his encounter with Davis in a sworn affidavit, and Williams agreed. As Williams had written in his letter to Jason, he said he'd been "shocked" when he'd learned that Carson, a counseling client of his, planned to testify against Jason. Fearing that he'd inadvertently given Carson the information he planned to use against Jason, Williams had contacted Paul Ford, expecting that Ford would call him to offer testimony that would discredit Carson.

Instead, Williams said in his affidavit, shortly after he spoke with Ford, a law enforcement officer came to his house "with some form of paperwork" which Williams "took to be either an order or subpoena." It was a demand that he meet with Brent Davis. Williams told Quinn that he was taken aback by the formality of the summons, since he and Davis knew each other through work and a phone call would have sufficed.

The formality continued when Williams met with Davis, and the prosecutor told him he wanted to take a sworn statement from him and then recorded "some" of the interview that followed. Williams found it disturbing that Davis, who had some influence over Williams' job, asked him why he had contacted the defense lawyer. Williams said Davis "explained his concerns" about his having done that and that Davis "seemed upset" and apparently felt that Williams was "out of line" for offering to testify "that Michael Carson was not telling the truth about how he had received information about the West Memphis murder case."

The other surprise awaiting Williams came at Jason's trial. While Carson did take the stand and describe hearing Jason say that he and Damien had killed the three West Memphis children, "sucked blood from a penis," and "played with the balls," Ford never called William to testify—something Williams said he could not understand.

Williams told Quinn that he heard later that Ford said he did not call him as a witness because he was changing his statements about Carson and Ford therefore considered him an unreliable witness.

But Williams said that was not true and that "at no time" did he "recall having done that." Williams said emphatically, "I would have testified truthfully, and would have set forth the evidence" he'd related to Quinn.

The affidavit raised troubling questions for Jason. He could understand Ford not wanting to call a witness who might say one thing in private but change his testimony when called to the stand. That would only look bad. But here was Williams saying under oath that he had no intention of changing his testimony. Furthermore, the law required, that if Davis recorded an interview with Williams, the prosecutor was required to provide the tape—or a transcript of it—to Ford. If Ford had that tape or transcript of sworn statements Williams had made to Davis regarding Carson's credibility, Ford could have used them to challenge any changes Williams may have attempted to make at the trial. So why had Ford not called him?

Jason found it hard to fathom the significance of Williams' affidavit. He found it especially troubling that Williams stated, "I was concerned that Mr. Davis was upset with me. Our professional relationship was such that he could have contacted me informally about the matter, and asked me to talk to him. He chose to have a law enforcement officer come to my house . . ."

Since his trial, Jason had directed many of his thoughts at Fogleman. Now he considered Davis. Williams told Quinn that he needed to maintain good relations with county officials to keep his job. From the affidavit, it appeared that Davis had used police power, along with his own position as chief prosecutor, to intimidate a witness. And not just any witness. Williams was the one witness whose testimony could have damaged the credibility of Michael Carson, the only person prosecutors had found to offer substantial evidence against Jason.

Yet, Jason thought, if Davis had indeed attempted to intimidate Williams, the tactic would not have been new. Jason recalled his teacher Sally Ware telling him that she had wanted to testify about Jason's character, but that her principal had told her that to do so would violate student-teacher confidentiality and could be grounds for firing. It reminded him of Mrs. Cureton at the jail, who'd also wanted to testify for Jason but who'd gotten an order from her boss, the sheriff, to get out of town so she could not be served with a subpoena. "This was not an isolated event," Jason said. "This was a pattern, a way of doing business."

It didn't even take knowledge of such nasty details for others to detect an unsavory whiff to the legal "business" in Arkansas. In the fall of 2004, the Canadian publisher Arsenal Pulp Press, released a book titled *The Last Pentacle of the Sun: Writings in Support of the West Memphis Three*. It was a collection of writings, fiction and non-fiction, that touched on the crimes and convictions.[136] For Jason, the attention from a foreign publisher was gratifying—another sign of how far concern about Arkansas justice had spread. And in October, a cover story in the *Arkansas Times* raised another concern.

Victoria Hutcheson told Little Rock writer Tim Hackler that her testimony about witches and occult activities at Jessie's trial had been a "complete fabrication." Hutcheson claimed that West Memphis police detectives told her what to say, threatening that if she did not testify as instructed they could take away her son, Aaron, and implicate her in the slayings.[137]

Jason remembered Hutcheson from the only time he'd actually seen her: a strange encounter that took place between the murders and his arrest. He remembered Jessie showing up unexpectedly at his house, explaining at the door that a friend of his in Highland Trailer Park wanted to meet Damien. In fact, Jessie said, she was outside right then, waiting in a truck. Damien was at Jason's house, and at Jessie's request, he'd gone out and gotten into the truck with Jessie and the woman. "They went to her house," Jason said. "That's where she tried to entrap him."

While Jason was surprised by Hutcheson's reappearance ten years after the trials, Jessie's attorney was not. Stidham, now a district judge, told Hackler, "Vicki Hutcheson's testimony was crucial to the prosecution because it was the only real corroboration that they had for Misskelley's ridiculous statement to the police. Even though she did not testify in the next trial of Echols and Baldwin just two weeks after Misskelley's trial, everyone on the jury in Jonesboro knew about Misskelley's statement and Hutcheson's testimony." Stidham said, "Hutcheson's recantation of her trial testimony was "not all that shocking" to him because he had always believed she was lying, but that, "The real shocking thing to me about her recantation is the level of misconduct on the part of the West Memphis police. It obviously knew no boundaries."

Hutcheson told Hackler that, at the time of the trials, she was desperate and willing to go along with a scenario about Damien driving her to an "esbat" or witches' orgy that Jerry Driver had dreamed up. "Every word of it was a lie," she said. Since then, she'd been to prison four times on drug and hot-check charges. She was still on parole when interviewed by Hackler. When he asked why she was refuting her testimony now, she credited a prison ministry:" I learned in order for God to forgive me, I had to clear my conscience."[138]

Mike Allen, the former detective who helped recover the victims' bodies, was now the police department's assistant chief. He told Hackler, "It appears that Vicki Hutcheson is trying to get her fifteen minutes of fame." He questioned why it had taken her more than eleven years to come forward with her claim of police coercion. The only other observation Allen had to offer was that "The case gets more bizarre every day."

That was one of the few points upon which everyone involved could agree. By now, Damien and Lorri had changed legal teams again, opting to hire Dennis Riordan and Donald Horgan, two prominent San Francisco trial and appellate attorneys.[139] Damien's legal position had become so complex that they found themselves in the unusual position of not even knowing which court—state or federal—they should now be addressing. On Oct. 28, 2004, Horgan, attorney Theresa Gibbons, also of San Francisco, and attorney Deborah R. Sallings of Little Rock, filed pleadings on behalf of Damien in both the Arkansas Supreme Court and the U.S. District Court in Little Rock. On the first page of each, in bold type, was the required notice: "THIS IS A CAPITAL CASE."

The motion filed with the state Supreme Court—a mere six pages, plus exhibits—argued that the high court should reverse its ruling affirming Damien's conviction because of the case's "extraordinary circumstances." Those, the attorneys explained, were the discoveries recently made during interviews with Damien and Jason's jurors.

"Nothing is so firmly believed as what is least known."
~ Michel de Montaigne

Investigators for all three of the men in prison had been digging into what had gone on during the juries' deliberations. In speaking with jurors from Damien and Jason's trial, they learned that one juror's knowledge of Jessie's conviction had played a "large part" in his decision. Without that, the juror said, he'd found the evidence against the defendants thin.[140]

Another juror stated under oath that she too knew Jessie had already been found guilty. She told Quinn that she'd kept a set of "good notes" during both the trial and deliberations—and that those notes, which she provided to Quinn, clearly reflected consideration of Jessie's conviction. "In my view," she said in her affidavit, "based on my own background and beliefs, Damien Echols seemed to me to be Satan walking alive."

Yet another juror reported that being on the Echols-Baldwin jury "spooked the hell" out of him and that he'd "never felt so scared." According to Quinn, this juror had said, "He couldn't sleep at night and 'felt he could hear noises outside and would look out the window.' His fear was the result of the talk of those kids being part of a cult, and looking into the audience and seeing the victims' families and the families of the accused. The accused had their families there as well as friends, some dressed in black with straight black hair and cult symbols."

This same juror told Quinn that he feared that, if the jury voted for guilt, "some of those people who were free on the street might seek revenge and kill him." Quinn wrote that, although the juror said he was never personally threatened, "he felt that something could happen to him." Quinn reported that, "Since the kids on trial were not afraid to kill, [the juror] said he thought, 'maybe they had friends or were part of a cult that was capable of killing.'" Later in the interview, the juror reported that he'd seen "a girl in the gallery with black lipstick, black hair, the gothic look." Quinn quoted the juror as telling him that, "When he looked into the gallery, where Echols' people were sitting, he saw those kinds of people and thought, 'They're going to kill me.'"

To Philipsborn and the other attorneys, this was important stuff, especially the information that the jurors had considered Jessie's statements to police and his conviction at Damien and Jason's trial. Those matters had tainted Jason and Damien's trial, in violation of the U.S. Constitution. The attorneys' sense that this single matter could lead a court to require new trials for the men was reinforced when investigators discovered lists of "pros" and "cons" that had been created by the jury on flip boards during the 1994 trial. The sheets clearly showed Jessie's statements as weighing against Damien and Jason. These pages, along with the jurors' statements, were submitted under seal to the state Supreme Court. Damien's attorneys argued that, in light of them, the jurors "considered collectively, must be found ... to have been biased against the defendants."[141]

But as far as the Arkansas Supreme Court was concerned, this was old ground already covered. It lost little time in denying the motion. For one thing, the high court ruled, Damien was late in asking. "It has been more than ten years since Echols's conviction," the justices said. "This fact clearly demonstrates that Echols did not exercise due diligence in bringing his claims to light—especially in view of the fact that the point on which he relies (the jury's alleged consideration of Misskelley's confession) was known to the court, the prosecutor, and to Echols's defense team at the time of trial."

The Arkansas Supreme Court further explained, "In his memorandum brief, he [Damien] points out that, during trial, the trial court denied his motion for a mistrial when one of the police witnesses inadvertently mentioned Misskelley's statement. At that time, the court [Judge Burnett] stated, 'I suggest ... that there isn't a soul up on that jury or in this courtroom that doesn't know Mr. Misskelley gave a statement.' Thus, Echols should have been aware from the time of his trial and conviction of the possibility that the jury might have been aware of and considered this extraneous information."

That response surprised none of the appellate attorneys. The state of Arkansas had been telling them in every way it could that it was through with this case. For that reason, Damien's lawyers had simultaneously gone to federal court with their petition for a writ of *habeas corpus*. The roots of this kind of appeal trace back almost eight hundred years, to when sheriffs in England's countryside put people in jail and kings decided that they had a right to know why the physical body, or corpus, of a person was being held. In the mid-1700s, William Blackstone, an English judge, put it this way: "The King is at all times entitled to have an account, why the liberty of any of his subjects is restrained, wherever that restraint may be inflicted."[142] In modern times, the writ has evolved into a legal action that requires a person under arrest to be brought before a judge to ensure that the prisoner can be released if the arresting agency cannot show that it has sufficient cause or evidence to hold him. The principle is that the state may not "have the body" (*habeas corpus*) of an innocent person. Damien's state petition for a writ of *habeas corpus* had been denied. Now he was bringing that petition to a federal court.

Damien's federal petition argued that the Arkansas Supreme Court was wrong in rejecting the claim that Damien's (and Jason's) trial had become unconstitutional when the jury considered information about Jessie's confession, and that the state's high court had wrongly rejected Damien's Rule 37 petition, citing failures by his trial attorneys. Because the state Supreme Court had dispensed with those two issues for the final time, the petition said, Damien now had the right to ask the federal court to review the constitutionality of his trial.

But Damien's federal petition was complicated by the fact that Burnett had approved the DNA testing of materials found with the bodies, and those tests were still being conducted. A federal judge had to consider that the DNA test results remained an open question before the Arkansas courts. For that reason, Damien's lawyers asked the federal court either to grant the writ of *habeas corpus* or to hold it in abeyance until Arkansas issued its final ruling regarding the forensic tests.[143]

And so another Christmas came and went. Another new year began. In February 2005, the video-sharing website YouTube.com was launched. By the end of the year, it would have more than one hundred million views per day—none, of course, by Jason. Technology, even of the stupidest kind, could move at the speed of light, but legal matters concerning an individual's life and liberty moved at the speed of a horse-drawn wagon. A month after YouTube's launch, Arkansas's attorney general asked the federal court to dismiss Damien's *habeas corpus* petition because the state DNA matters had not yet been resolved.[144] "One can only speculate to what extent the results of the DNA testing will affect the case," Attorney General Mike Beebe wrote, "and, potentially, given the already-lengthy history of this case, those matters could be litigated in state court for years to come."[145]

In August 2005, U.S. District Judge William R. Wilson, Jr. disagreed with the attorney general. He ordered that Damien's petition be held in abeyance in federal court until all claims concerning any DNA evidence were exhausted at the state level, adding that he expected the DNA claims to be pursued in state court "with diligence."[146]

With Judge Wilson's ruling holding the federal petition in abeyance, Damien's attorneys felt that they had good ground on which to move forward. Citizens' concern and digital connectivity were affecting changes. Without being able to foresee what impact they might have, new media were, nonetheless, confronting old legal processes. Thanks to HBO's cameras at the trials, sites like WM3.org and Callahan8k.com, the recent startup of Facebook, the responsive generosity of countless supporters, and the work of out-of-state lawyers and investigators determined to prevail, the three inmates finally had been able to reach an agreement with Prosecuting Attorney Brent Davis to conduct basic DNA testing on materials found at the crime scene. Yes, there had been long delays in the process. Unforeseen problems had arisen. But by November 2005, it appeared that analysis of what one attorney called "a large body of 'unknowns'" would be completed by the end of the year.

The prisoners and their attorneys were excited by the possibility that the tests would conclusively establish their innocence. At the same time, they realized, as one of the lawyers put it, that, "given the mess that was made of the crime scene, the unsophisticated manner in which biological materials were preserved, and the passage of time," they could wind up with little new information. There was also the possibility that the tests would produce DNA profiles that could not be matched to any of the victims or the defendants. If that happened, the attorneys expected the state to argue that any foreign DNA could have been at the crime scene before the murders or brought there by searchers, investigators, or morgue workers. The hope was that identifiable DNA would be found, not in a body bag, but under one of the victim's fingernails, for example, where it would be hard to explain away. It was a gamble worth taking, but an expensive one. One of the attorneys said at the time that the DNA testing alone "cost the defense more than a million dollars."[147]

In June 2005, friends helped Damien publish an autobiography, *Almost Home: My Life Story, Vol. 1*.[148] On the last page, which he dated May 22, 2004, Damien reported that he had caught a glimpse of Jason, who was housed in the Varner Unit adjoining the Supermax. "The Jason sighting," as Damien called it, occurred while he and Lorri were having their weekly visit. "I looked up to see him about thirty feet away in the hallway, looking at me through the glass," Damien wrote. "He raised his hand and smiled, then he was gone, like a ghost."

By mid-2005, the *Arkansas Times* blogged that the West Memphis case had "spawned its own culture." The article noted that DVDs of the two HBO documentaries had just been released in the UK and that, in 2002, two years after Eddie Spaghetti produced his CD in support of the WM3, Henry Rollins had released another, this one called *Rise Above*. This benefit double CD was also a tribute to Rollins' former band, the influential punk rockers, Black Flag. It featured Iggy Pop, Rancid, Queens of the Stone Age, Slipknot and Chuck D. "I came up with the idea of doing an album's worth of Black Flag songs and getting all these cool singers in on the deal," Rollins told the paper. "I figured what could be better than to have none other than Chuck D. of Public Enemy kind of call out West Memphis, Arkansas, and put the place on the map?"[149]

Around the same time, supporters planned a Worldwide Awareness Day, with about fifty events scheduled in the US and abroad — including ones in Moscow and at a science base in Antarctica. Organizer Tammy Akin, an associate editor of the online magazine Punk Globe, told the *Boston Phoenix* that she'd talked to many people who'd heard of the case but who held the mistaken belief that the men had been freed long ago. "Then there's another whole generation of young people who have never heard of it, and then as soon as they hear of it, are just amazed," she said. "So many people who don't fit in where they're living can see that this could happen to them."[150]

Although Arkansas supporters arranged small Worldwide Awareness Day events at a half-dozen sites in the state, they were met, by and large, with resolute indifference by Arkansas's citizens and officials. At this point for Jason, however, a bit of official indifference would have been welcome. He liked working in the law library at Varner. But in the middle of 2005, shortly after Damien's book came out, he was abruptly "fired." What did it was that line on the last page of Damien's book, about how he and Jason has caught a fleeting glimpse of each other.

In Arkansas, prisoners on death row are not assigned Arkansas Department of Correction numbers like all other inmates because, legally, they are not sentenced to prison; they are sentenced to death. Therefore, the prison system is only holding them in "safe-keeping" for the counties from which they've been sentenced until the execution can be carried out. For that reason, the numbers assigned to death row prisoners all begin with "SK"—a designation some mistakenly believe stands for "state kill." Damien was SK931. Prisoners like Damien, held in safe-keeping or any other form of administrative segregation, are not allowed to have contact with each other, much less with inmates held in less restrictive conditions. As Jason explained, "When Damien put that in there about seeing me, for someone pretty high up, their number-one issue became, 'How did a general-population inmate and a safe-keeping inmate cross paths?'"

The encounter had been accidental. Not a word passed between them. But the incident, which had now been made public, proved an administrative embarrassment. Jason tried to explain that part of his job at the library was to type up legal requests for prisoners in the Supermax that his boss would pick up and deliver there the next day, but that, on the morning in question, she had asked Jason to make the delivery for her.

"She calls the library and says, 'I can't get away,'" he recalled. "Can you bring the cart to my office?' Well, her office was in the Supermax. Of course, there are riot gates all the way down there. She says, 'I'll call and get you cleared.' So I take the cart, and, sure enough, all the gates are opening for me, and I'm passing through. I finally get to the Varner Supermax Unit. I see Damien and Lorri in there. Lorri sees me and she taps Damien. He doesn't have his glasses on, so he puts them on. He looks up and waves. Then an officer says, 'Keep moving, Baldwin.' That's all there is to it. When I come back through, they're gone."

When Damien's book came out, an official in the prison system got a copy of it before Jason did. When he showed up for work at the library, he was fired. When he asked a captain why, the officer said, "Oh, I can't say," but added, "It wouldn't be anything to do with a book your friend wrote." Jason understood: "Death Row is not to have any contact with general population. And definitely not these two. But it happened. And now it was public." Action had to be taken, whether it made sense or not.

Losing the library job was a "big thing" to Jason. He remained unassigned to a new job for months. "At first I was upset about it," he said, "but then it began to feel like a perpetual summer vacation." Finally, he was assigned to a new barracks—as its janitor.

Jason looked for the bright side, even in the toilets. He was quick with the cleaning, which meant that, when he finished, he could help out on the recreation yard. In prison, that wasn't so bad. He'd gotten used to making the most of whatever situation he was handed. That was something he'd explained to Fay Lellios, a documentary filmmaker from California with whom Jason had corresponded. In 2005, Lellios flew to Arkansas for a visit, bringing along two cameras. Varner's warden allowed her to meet with Jason for three hours in his conference room. The result was an eight-minute film in which Jason discussed the role of writing in his prison life."[151]

"My name is Jason Baldwin," he said, straight into the camera. "I am a writer." Looking relaxed in his white uniform, he described himself as a "quiet and disciplined" person, someone who rarely spoke unless spoken to, and who felt "unrestrained" only when writing. He told Lellios that writing had become "like medicine" for him, allowing him to "purge" himself of emotions that otherwise could poison him. Writing made prison "bearable."

Jason said his first poem had been about Judge Burnett. "It was, like, 'Man, how could he not see? How could he not know that I'm innocent? Why would he not even listen?' The poem was, like, 'The gavel's bang couldn't hammer truth away.' It was real hard." Other poems, such as "I No Longer Face the Storm Alone," which Jason read for the film and from which Lellios took its title, expressed a sense of companionship that had helped him survive.

More conversationally, Jason described for Lellios the kind of pep talks he gave other inmates—and himself. "Everybody's got a unique situation," he said. "Everybody's got things in their life that they don't necessarily want to be going through or don't enjoy or don't like. But, man, we gotta stay strong, stay focused. And, if it knocks you down, get back up. Brush the dust off and keep going. 'Cuz you know, life is like that. It's great. It's wonderful. It's a blessing. It's a gift. I mean, you only live it once."

Jason had returned to Varner just weeks before a national tragedy: the terrorist attacks of September 11, 2001. Coincidentally, he would decide to leave three and a half years later, days after another national disaster. When Hurricane Katrina struck America's Gulf Coast on August 29, 2005, Jason was living in—and cleaning—Varner's Nineteen Barracks. And that's where he was a few days later, when, to his surprise, he was called to the unit's mental health office. "Mental health?" he thought. "I've never put in a request to see a mental health officer." He reported to the office with "a lot of trepidation."

"You know Shabazz?" the staffer asked. Yes, Jason knew Shabazz. The two had worked in the library together until Shabazz got reassigned to a medium-security unit known as "Little Tucker." The name distinguished the unit from the bigger maximum-security unit nearby, casually called "Tucker Max"—or "Big Tucker." Before leaving Varner, Shabazz had asked Jason, "If something works out, do you want me to try to get you over there?" Jason told him, "Yeah, sure. I'm into seeing new country."

Shabazz was as good as his word. He'd recommended Jason for a job as a habilitation counselor at Little Tucker. The mental health officer explained that, as a habilitation counselor, Jason would be expected to help "mentally challenged" inmates adapt to their time in prison. After hearing that he would be one of three counselors assigned to be available 24/7 for thirty inmates, some of whom were mentally retarded or schizophrenic, and that he'd be supervised by a licensed mental health worker, Jason said, "Yeah. Sure. I'm there."

"It was that old restless uneasiness," he explained, "the feeling that you're somewhere you don't want to be because where you want to be is home, but prison is where you are, and you're growing up in there. And then you hear about something that may be better. People say, 'Oh, man. You'll love it at Little Tucker.' So when something like that opens up, you're ready. Plus, it's a way to travel—as crazy as that sounds."

CHAPTER SEVEN

LITTLE TUCKER
October 8, 2005 - January 19, 2007

On October 5, 2005, Jason boarded a van—not for home—but for the fifty-minute ride north, across the Arkansas delta, from Varner, which held more than two thousand, five hundred inmates, to Little Tucker, which held about five hundred. Seeing it came as a shock. "In Varner," he said, "you have these giant, open barracks, with as many as fifty-six people living in them. Varner had more than two thousand inmates. There's a top tier, a middle tier, and a bottom tier, and this giant bullet-proof glass that goes up three stories. You'd have people climbing up on the bars, banging on the glass, making this crazy, jungle-like sound. It was constant, but you got used to it."

Besides being so much smaller, Little Tucker was old. From his stays at various prisons, Jason understood that each unit's floor plan reflected the philosophy of incarceration that was in vogue at the time it was built. But he'd never before been to a prison like this. Here, "there were these big, iron bars, and they opened cells with these old-fashioned keys." The prison reminded Jason of the one in the movie "Shawshank Redemption," and he found it amazing. "When you got in," he said, "they came and hung a light bulb in your room."

For fifty years, Arkansas's first prison, known as The Walls, actually occupied the site in downtown Little Rock where the state capitol now stands. When construction of the current state capitol began in 1899, its foundation was laid by inmates. As building progressed, inmates from The Walls were dispersed to two new prisons. One of those was built in 1916 on more than four thousand acres of rich farmland near the tiny town of Tucker. More than sixty years later, when a second, larger maximum-security unit was added to the property, that became known as "Tucker Max," and the old prison began to be called "Little Tucker." For decades, Little Tucker held Arkansas's death row and the state's electric chair. Between 1926 and 1948, the state executed one hundred and four prisoners there. In the 1970s, allegations that other inmates had been routinely tortured with an electric device known as the "Tucker telephone" led to investigations and court-ordered prison reforms."[152]

By the time Jason arrived in 2005, the place had earned a more placid reputation, especially compared to Varner's. The warden at Little Tucker was pretty "laid back," Jason said, and, as a counselor, Jason got to have his own room and an office with a TV, VCR, plants, and a computer—though with no Internet access, of course. It all came as a pleasant surprise, especially the way he was welcomed. "I walk in and I'm immediately surrounded by people," Jason said. "And I can tell that some of these guys, they're not altogether up to speed. These are the people I'm here to counsel. And they're happy I'm here. They're showing me around. They say, 'This is your cell! This is the counselor's cell!' Then, I look up on a balcony, and there's Shabazz waving at me."

At twenty-eight, Jason could tell that he had stepped into a new kind of prison experience—and maybe a new stage of his life. It was comforting to know that some DNA testing was underway at a laboratory that the attorneys for the prisoners and the state had agreed upon. Even so, battles about it continued. "A lot of items Brent Davis won't agree to allow us to test," Jason said in an interview at the time. As a result, Philipsborn prepared to argue in favor of the tests in court. That court, however, would be Burnett's, and, as Jason said ruefully, "We know how he rules."[153]

Supporters knew little about the battles for new scientific tests at the time, but the struggle represented a new front in the clash between the West Memphis Three and the state that had won their convictions. Rulings in the West Memphis case had already set several precedents in Arkansas law, and now, as attorneys for the state and the men in prison hammered out procedures for tests under the new DNA law, the case was moving into even newer legal territory. There was a time when Jason would have found it hard to believe that state officials who claimed to want "the truth" would resist acquiring new information that might lead to pertinent truth, especially if that truth showed someone had been wrongfully convicted. But that time had long since passed. He understood now that, in general, "justice" played out more like a football game than anything he'd been taught in civics. A win for the state was a win, and players on the state's side, including prosecutors and attorneys general, didn't like the idea of losing a trial after it had been won. While an NFL official might change a ruling after checking an instant replay, nothing like that happens in law. The state's attorneys general fought hard to keep their win, and if that meant working to keep new evidence from reaching a court, they considered that fight their job. Thus, a new state law allowing DNA tests, inmates seeking the tests, and supporters willing to pay for those tests did not mean that the tests would be conducted. Terminology had to be debated, evidence located, timelines established, shipments scheduled, and items prioritized—and every step of that process took time and time, and still more time.

While the testing issues played out in courts and laboratories, Jason adapted to Little Tucker. But more than his residence had changed. For years, he had been saying, "I want to go home." He didn't say that anymore. He knew "home" as he remembered it had vanished long ago. He was a man in his late twenties. "I don't even know where home is anymore," he said. "I just want to be free. I'll find a home."

Maybe it was easier to imagine a new home now that he had a new girlfriend. "She's a great girl," Jason said. "I just hope I can get out of this place soon to be with her." Yet the desire was tempered by caution. Quietly and indirectly—with neither blood nor beatings— prison had taught Jason its hardest lesson. "She's got it in her mind to wait on me as long as it takes," he said. "But I know what that can do to a girl if it becomes too long. I don't want that to happen again."

As always, he focused on his work. Though the counseling job had its perks, it was unrelenting. "You're like a doctor on-call," Jason said, "but it's 24/7, and some of these people had severe needs. You've got to make sure they take their meds—all their meds—and some of them were taking heavy psychotropic medicines. In a way, it was strange. I'd had all this history with mental illness, with my mom and Damien. And then, when I got to prison, they'd tried to force me onto medications. And now here I am, working in that industry, so to speak. I have a job working with people like that, and I have zero-to-no training."

"What I did have," he added, "was patience and good communication skills and kindness. Habilitation meant these men were in highly structured activities all through the day. All these guys had various degrees of mental deficiencies. There were always petty squabbles. For example, if we didn't vote ahead of time, there'd be squabbles about what they were going to watch on TV. Or somebody would take a puzzle piece and put it in his pocket and take it back to his cell, so somebody couldn't finish the puzzle. I was engaging them all the time. It was a madhouse, for lack of a better term."

Inmates and counselors alike tried to make the best of it. For Jason, friendships always helped, and one of his good friends during this time was another counselor he called Jibril. That was a Muslim name, related to the name Gabriel, that the inmate had adopted since coming to prison twenty years before. The prisoner's official name was Ronald Ward. Over time, Jason learned how much he and Jibril had in common. Both were from Crittenden County (Jason from Marion and Ward from West Memphis). Both were tried for triple-murders in Judge David' Burnett's court with Fogleman as their prosecutor. And both had been sentenced as teenagers (Ward at fifteen and Jason at sisteen) to serve life in prison (though Ward had initially been sentenced to death).

Jibril was seven years older than Jason, but both also considered themselves strong. Jason remembered one day, while everyone was waiting for lunch, he and Jibril sat down for a quick game of dominoes. They bet pushups. Jibril asked Jason how much he wanted to bet. Jason said, "Nothing less than fifty." Jibril laughed and countered, "A hundred a skunk." Hearing that, the men in the room gathered around.

"Well," Jason said, "I'm not the best at dominoes or any game that relies on chance starting off, so he ends up beating me and skunking me. So I'm down there doing pushups, and the guys are counting them out. I mean, I'm pretty good up to fifty, but after that my arms were shaking and Jibril had taken on the role of Major Payne from the movie.[154] Those last ones are taking a bit, but I got 'em. But while I was down there doing them, my glasses fell off, and he'd done picked them up. I'm like, groping around, 'Where are my glasses?' He's playing around with them. Everybody's laughing." Light moments like that helped ease the long wait for action on his case.

By the end of 2005, Bode Lab had completed its analysis of the first batch of agreed-upon items. As Jason, Damien and Jessie expected, none of the material tested could be traced to them. On the other hand, the tests had not produced what Philipsborn called "a home run." Some of the DNA material had come back categorized as "unknown": that is, it was not from the men in prison, it was not from the victims, and it could not be connected to anyone else associated with the case whose DNA was known.

Back in high school, before his arrest, Jason would have thought that scientific tests of crime scene evidence that didn't connect people in prison to the crime would have prompted an automatic review of the case. By now, however, he was much better educated in law. He did not need Philipsborn to explain how the attorney general's office would reason: that the absence of scientific evidence linking Damien, Jessie and him to the crime did not mean that they weren't there to commit it. "Absence of evidence," as has famously been said, "is not evidence of absence." The attorney general's office was dug-in on this case, and no mere "absence of evidence" proving the men's guilt was going to persuade it to reconsider.

With fledgling new investigations having been launched in several directions, a new and unlikely team quietly joined the effort on behalf of Damien. Earlier in 2005, filmmakers Peter Jackson and Fran Walsh of New Zealand, creators of the popular *Lord of the Rings* series, had watched the *Paradise Lost* documentaries. Like countless others, they were appalled. "I didn't have any understanding of how the American justice system worked," Jackson said, "because the

New Zealand system is based on British law. We don't have district prosecuting attorneys. There are no elections here for these sorts of roles or for judges. People work their way into these positions and earn them by appointments. And we have quite a good judicial review system here, for when things go wrong."

Walsh said she was equally surprised to learn what could happen in U.S. courts. "I was shocked when it became clear to me how much political power and political expediency played into 'justice' in America," she said. "We have corruption here, but it's not predicated on someone's political aspirations." Seeing the case as a "puzzle," Walsh dived into the online resources that had been developed by supporters and non-supporters alike, finding all of it "enormously helpful." She said she gradually began to "piece together what hadn't happened" regarding forensic experts and to wonder "why they weren't called in the first place." She also contacted Lorri Davis. The two became close friends.

That relationship made Damien's situation personal for Walsh. She said she felt overwhelmed to realize the odds against his release—how, in going back to state courts, he faced "everybody, in the end, who had a vested interest in maintaining a guilty verdict." Jackson was particularly amazed that so much of the post-conviction review kept returning to Judge Burnett. Nothing like that happened in New Zealand, he said, due to the belief there that a judge who'd already ruled on a case would have "things to protect." To Jackson, passing the review to a different judge or set of judges made sense.

"I have a great belief that everything comes back to human nature," he said. "It's all about the money. Money is the bottom line for just about everything: people have their jobs, their careers, their reputations, and usually families to support. They have everything to protect. Once you put guys in a position that they have to protect their basic livelihood, human nature is going to be to protect themselves and their positions, so you're putting these guys in a bad position to start."

In December 2005, when Jackson and Walsh were headed to New York for the premiere of their film *King Kong*, they arranged to meet Riordan and Davis there. The foursome spent a half-day in a hotel room discussing how the newcomers could help. Jackson said, "We didn't want to throw money into a pot. We saw a lot of areas that we thought needed to be investigated, but unless somebody was going to pay for them, it wasn't going to happen. We told Dennis, 'We think you guys should investigate X, Y and Z, and we're happy to cover the costs of that.'" The pair estimated that they paid for most of the DNA testing from then on.

They became, as they put it, "embedded" with Damien's attorneys. "We found that focusing on one defense team was going to be most effective," Jackson said. "Anything that helped Damien was going to help Jessie and Jason. It was going to be a three-for-one." He said he found it "interesting and a little horrifying that, in trying to overturn a conviction and present any evidence that the state would be willing to consider, you essentially have to do their job for them. You have to do the investigative work that they should have done." In a battle against a state, with state-paid investigators, attorneys, and a crime lab, Jackson said he felt the couple was simply "leveling the playing field" by contributing part of their fortune to offset costs of new investigations and testing for Damien.

Consequently, as 2005 ended, attorneys for the West Memphis Three were still sorting out their respective strategies. In early 2006, Philipsborn wrote to Lorri Davis,

"My view, having at one time essentially 'baby sat' all three cases and now having taken on Jason's matter, is that given the progress of Damien's case through the system, in the absence of a DNA 'home run,' it is more likely that one of the other cases will cause this case to get serious review. I say this not only out of loyalty to Jason, but rather because much of the focus to date has been on Damien— who, after all, did testify in his trial and who is viewed as the central character in the matter. My sense is that if there is some systemic concern that these convictions are rotten, it may be easier for that concern to surface in a case in which it can be said that the accused never had his say in court. That is why I am particularly sensitive, at this juncture, to not publicly tying Jason to the other cases."

Philipsborn continued: "Having noted this view, it is clear that Damien's case needs the focus of current attention, and it is also clear that Damien will be in the best position, initially, to offer a critique of the integrity of the state proceedings. He has an excellent team to assist him in doing that. The emphasis of current investigation, in my view, should be on: more alibi info if it is out there; the lack of relationship between Jessie, Jason and Damien at the time; the time of death and likely death scenario; the unreliability of the Misskelley version of events."[155]

Everyone understood that Damien's death sentence had already set him on a separate and faster legal track. Jason and Jessie, by contrast, still had not yet had their Rule 37 hearings, though, by now, Burnett had agreed to combine them. When that joint Rule 37 hearing was held, Jessie's lawyers would have to confront what the state called his confession. In assessing Jessie's situation, Philipsborn wrote that he was concerned about "the Misskelley statements, both before and after trial." The attorney expected that Jessie's lawyers would introduce better alibi evidence than Stidham brought forth at trial. "Like Jason, who was at school the day of and the day after the killings," Philipsborn wrote, "Jessie's post-killing routine did not change, which is extraordinary if you assume he was a mentally impaired, easily manipulated killer—which is essentially the theory espoused by the prosecutors."

Philipsborn intended to show that, while Ford could have presented a strong defense for Jason at trial, he had failed to call key witnesses. He'd "dropped the ball," Philipsborn wrote. "The jurors never found out how far it was from Jason's house to the crime scene. They were not shown the route that he would have had to follow to return there to catch the Thursday morning school bus. They were not told about the traffic density along the route of travel, or the opportunities (given the population density in his trailer park) for someone to have seen him, covered with mud, water and blood, skulking back home." In short, Philipsborn wrote, Jason's argument at his Rule 37 hearing would be that he "had a defense that was never put on."

Jason understood that, legally, his case was heating up. He also knew that, while he labored inside his prison helping inmates write their names or properly use the toilet, momentum about the case was building outside as well.

In the spring of 2006, Dr. Martin Hill, the professor in Puerto Rico who had earlier conducted the analysis of Jessie's statement to the police, took his interest in the prosecution a step further. Hill inaugurated jivepuppi.com, a website on which he attempted to synthesize the abundant information now available. "Being in science and being a skeptic have made me question rigorously the available evidence," he said. "I would have no problem with good evidence appearing against them. I would at last relax and say, 'Hmmm…. So that's what happened.'"

Instead, he said, he became a supporter of the West Memphis Three because of what he called "the deafening lack of good evidence against them . . . and the substantial evidence that points away from them." Hill would add to jivepuppi.com for years. Ultimately, he said, the work led him to "see the world differently—justice, police, honesty, dishonesty." It showed him "the power of self-delusion and how it seldom fades over time."[156]

The amount of information available on the Internet had grown immense. And there were even glimmers of change within Arkansas. Most notably, an instructor at a state university invited Stidham to speak.[157] The combination emboldened Jason to speak out personally about the state of affairs. In an open letter addressed to Gov. Mike Huckabee that was published in the *Arkansas Times*, he wrote: "You say you haven't seen proof of our innocence. I say that is possible, but only if you haven't searched."

A few weeks later, Jason again wrote to the paper, this time to address West Memphis Three supporters in Arkansas and around the world. "I know many of you over the past decade or so have literally inundated the governor's mansion with letters," he said. But, because no one else knew the extent of that support, Jason asked supporters to write to the governor yet again, this time addressing their letters to him at a post office box. There they would be collected and delivered to the capitol en masse on the second Worldwide Awareness Day ahead. "Today is my birthday," Jason wrote, "and I have but one wish. This is the last year of my twenties. I'll be a happy man indeed if I can spend just one day of it a free man."

On July 14, Worldwide Awareness Day, supporters in Arkansas laid out five hundred and fifty-two letters on the steps of the Arkansas capitol, all of which were sent in response to Jason's request. Some letters came from Little Rock, one from as far away as Paddington, Australia. Jason had asked supporters to write a brief statement on the outside of their envelopes so that their feelings about the case could be read without opening the governor's mail.

From Ireland: "These men were convicted on hearsay that snowballed out of control and this tragedy rolls on and on."

From Poland: "I used the case...with my eighteen-year-old students as an example of how justice can be violated in a democratic country."

From New York: "Is a 'confession' from a disabled and challenged youth enough 'evidence' in your state to ruin lives?"

From Oregon: "Guilt should be proven, not innocence."

About ten percent of the letters came from within Arkansas. One from Little Rock read, "If this is how a murder investigation is conducted in Arkansas, then I'm afraid to think of how many other innocent men and women are behind bars."

At the capitol, supporter Amanda Lamb spoke for many when she told a TV reporter, "I am very angry and frustrated that we can't get anyone in the state to address our concerns." A spokesman for the governor said that the letters would be delivered. Still, he reminded the crowd, the governor's powers were limited: this was a matter for the courts.

"I've had a wonderful time, but this wasn't it."

~ Groucho Marx

Jason's life at Little Tucker revolved around the inmates under his care. The man convicted of murdering three children was now responsible for tending to grown men who were cognitively, emotionally, and physically challenged. His days began with breakfast at 4 a.m., followed by a check to make sure that his "guys" had combed their hair, brushed their teeth, and washed their faces. A few men had suffered traumatic brain injuries. One, who'd had a stroke, had no short-term memory. Jason saw it as his job "to make their prison experience as easy on them as possible."

As for himself? He hadn't tasted a banana since his arrest twelve years before, but his Hacky Sack kick record had risen to four hundred and fifty. Jason carried on, trying to model the mantra he preached to his men: "Do what you can with what you've got where you're at."

In 2006, living by that mantra became easier. Life itself took on a glow. The "great girl" who'd entered Jason's life the year before wanted to marry him. Jason was—cautiously—thrilled. Even as he walked in his white uniform down the gray-painted halls of his prison, he felt different. He was twenty-nine, in love, and—almost as if he were living a normal, free-world life—he imagined himself a married man. Even though he was in prison, he wouldn't be alone. He'd have a wife who loved him and whom he could cherish. And, with all that was happening in his case—all the work of the lawyers and supporters—it seemed tantalizingly possible that he would one day actually get out—even if, at the time, he could not imagine how. He could fall asleep at night imagining freedom with a blissful twist: walking into the arms of his "great girl" to begin a new life together.

But day-to-day life left little room for dreams of any sort. Being a habilitation counselor proved to be more demanding than any clerk job he'd ever had; he was a twenty four-hour-a-day caregiver, who never got a day off. After more than a year of that, Jason was burned-out. "It was a great experience," he said, "but I was looking for a vacation, so when somebody said there was an opening for a clerk in the field security office, I was like, 'Oh, yeah. Field security!'"

Jason's old friend Mojo was already a clerk at Tucker's field security office. Late in the summer, when a job maintaining the office's database came open, Mojo recommended Jason for it. As Jason later reflected, "It was a weird job for an inmate." Since Tucker, like most Arkansas prisons, was also a massive farm, a sizeable part of its staff worked in the fields, overseeing a much larger number of inmate laborers who worked on the prison's hoe squads. The white-suited prisoners were usually guarded by armed sergeants on horseback. The sergeants' supervisors—the lieutenants, captains and majors—got to ride around in trucks. Except for the models of the trucks, the scene on any day could have come from an earlier century. Jason was told that his job at the field security office would be to keep track of work hours and payroll for all the staff. That would include tracking their sick leave and overtime, when they were in the fields or assigned to other duties due to weather, and whether they'd gotten the required training.

Jason knew he could handle the database work. He took the job. But he was almost knocked off his feet the first day he showed up for it. The field security office at Tucker was not attached to either his unit or the nearby maximum-security unit. Rather, it was a freestanding, house-sized building on the penitentiary grounds. "So, when I first get over there, I knock on the door. It's just like going up to somebody's house. Some guy inside says, 'Come in.' He sounds like my Uncle Hubert. I step in and there's a couch, a coffee table, a coffeemaker, and a big-screen TV. There's a ceiling fan and I see pictures on the walls! I'm coming in from the outside, so my eyes are adjusting to it. I look down and there are hardwood floors, polished a dark brown. It's surreal. I've been walking on nothing but concrete floors for years!"

To Jason, it was an alien environment. "It looked like it was picked up from outside the prison walls and put down inside the prison walls. It looked like home." But his intuition sounded a warning. "Right then, at that moment, when I first looked at it, I thought, 'This right here is not going to last long.'" The perception traced back to other losses—the guitar, his father, and even the opportunity to speak for himself at his trial. Instinct born of experience told Jason, "If it's too good to be true, something's going to derail it." Nevertheless, standing there in the doorway, facing a better form of imprisonment than he'd known since his arrest, Jason said: "I make the decision to accept it, and enjoy it, and experience it for as long as it will last— hoping maybe it will last until I'm released."

The romantic dreams and new work assignment weren't the only promising changes to occur that summer. Through his extensive grapevine, Jason had heard reports that Pam Hobbs, the mother of victim Stevie Branch, had found some knives in a box that belonged to her now ex-husband, Terry Hobbs, and that among the knives was one she believed had been in Stevie's pocket on the night he disappeared. By now, Pam Hobbs shared many of the doubts that had been cast on the convictions in her son's murder case. She no longer trusted the police investigation or the results of the trials. Instead of bringing the knives and the rest of the box's contents to police or prosecutors, she'd asked her sister to bring them to Jessie's lawyer, Dan Stidham.

Philipsborn regarded news of Pam's discovery with caution, if not skepticism. After all, it had occurred years after the murders and after the Hobbs' divorce. "It was a little hard to get to the bottom of her motives," he said. He told Jason that, instead of redirecting attention to the knives turned over to Stidham, he and the other attorneys preferred to stay focused on the ongoing forensic tests.[158] Jason agreed, partly because he trusted the work being done, and partly because he understood the risks of rushing to judge someone.

While Stidham held onto the knives, Elizabeth Fowler, in Hollywood, was turning her attention to Pam and Terry Hobbs. In early 2006, Dimension Films bought rights to the movie based on *Devil's Knot*. The studio hired screenwriters Scott Derrickson and Paul Boardman to write the screenplay. "There is already a dark tone to the material, but we are absolutely committed to only telling the truth, and not exaggerating to entertain," they told Variety in May. "We all understand the gravity, the high stakes of the situation."[159]

Hoping to ground the film on the family of one of the victims, Fowler offered Pam and Terry Hobbs $12,500 each for the rights to their respective accounts of the murders and trials. She also spoke with Ron Lax, the central figure in *Devil's Knot*, seeking his help in fleshing out what was known of the couple's background. Lax explained that the West Memphis police had scarcely investigated any of the victims' parents and that, regrettably, he had not investigated them either.[160]

In June 2006, shortly before Jason was assigned to the field security office, Lax had assigned an investigator from his company, Inquisitor, Inc., in Memphis, to conduct a background check on Stevie Branch's stepfather. The investigator turned up a history of encounters with police, including some domestic violence, but nothing that had put him in jail.[161] On Aug. 16, about two weeks after Jason got the field security job, screenwriters Derrickson and Boardman flew into Memphis from Los Angeles to review files at the West Memphis Police Department, and to get to know Lax in order to understand his personality, how he worked and how to portray him. The next day, Lax showed them around the neighborhood where the victim's families lived and the trailer parks that were home to the accused, and brought them to the ditch where the boys' bodies were found.

On Aug. 18, they met with and interviewed Pam and Terry Hobbs, who had accepted the deal with Dimension, at Terry's house in Memphis. The following morning, before flying back to LA, they had breakfast with Jerry Driver. For the next few months, the screenwriters maintained contact with Lax by phone and email. Lax told them he was preparing to interview Terry Hobbs but asked them not to inform either Pam or Terry of that, as investigators usually got better information if they showed up unannounced. The screenwriters told Lax where they'd located Hobbs.

Thus, by the end of 2006, the trials of the West Memphis Three were being scrutinized by professional investigators, academics, Hollywood writers, New York and New Zealand filmmakers and countless lay people online—from several angles, for many purposes. High school teachers were having students in advanced English classes compare Arthur Miller's account of the Salem witch trials in his play, *The Crucible*, with the account of the West Memphis trials detailed in *Devil's Knot*. Criminal justice teachers were using the case to illustrate investigative errors. A number of college graduates who'd learned of the case during the past decade went on to study law because of it.[162] A journalism graduate student who analyzed pretrial reporting on the case by the region's two biggest newspapers gave them generally high marks for fairness—except when it came to their reporting on what she called "occult rumors."

"Despite reporting the rumors of Satanic activity, and despite reporting confirmations that the police were pursuing the occult angle in their investigation," Holly Ballard wrote, "these newspapers never reported on evidence, or lack thereof, of a cult in the area where the boys' bodies were found. This missing element reflects an overall reluctance on the part of the police throughout the investigation to reveal information to the media." Though she noted that "no such evidence was ever reported by the police, the prosecution or the press any time before, during or since the trials," the papers had "clearly paint[ed] a picture of the triple-murder as a Satanic ritual slaying."[163]

Jason knew of Ballard's paper because she had first contacted him after reading *Devil's Knot*. He also knew that Jackson and Walsh were now involved in the case, not because they were working specifically for him, but because Philipsborn and Damien's lawyer, Dennis Riordan, had, as Jackson put it, "a good relationship." But, as with everything else Jason learned from his attorney, he told no one. Though he'd long ago outgrown the policy adopted at his arrest of not speaking unless spoken to, replacing it with savvy discretion, when it came to discussing his case—Jason simply didn't. He kept up with it and let his attorneys speak for him. Absolutism made the policy easy. And it freed Jason to focus on what had become, to his surprise, a remarkable time in prison.

"Oh, yeah," he said. "I was living life right then. A lot of good things were going on." His "two-year work week" as a habilitation counselor was behind him. Compared to that, his new job at the field security office seemed like a vacation. As soon as he'd transferred here, Jason's workload had lightened significantly. And now, with summer and the growing season over, work was even slower. The administrators there were an easy-going bunch; someone had even borrowed an electric guitar from the prison chapel that Jason could practice on when he'd finished his work on the computer. His legal hopes were higher than they'd been at any point since his conviction. And, to top off his happy outlook, he and his "great girl" had set a date to get married in January. For a guy serving life in prison, Jason, at twenty-nine, felt pretty darn good.

CHAPTER EIGHT

SUPERMAX

January 20, 2007 - June 25, 2007

The blow, when it came, landed a knockout. In a flash, the guitar, the field security job, the wedding, Jason's life at Little Tucker itself—all were gone. One minute, he was "living life." The next, he sat in a double-locked cell in Varner's Supermax Unit. For the umpteenth time in his young life, Jason was back in the hole, in "punitive isolation." This time, however, he was in something deeper—and darker—than even the terms "hole" and "punitive isolation" would suggest.

In Jason's last days at Little Tucker, while he was blissfully unaware, prison officials had gotten word that someone within the system was selling contraband computers. Internal affairs officers zeroed in on Little Tucker, particularly the field security office. On Jan. 19, 2007, officers burst in on the little building. In a scene reminiscent of the night of his arrest, almost fourteen years before, they ordered Jason and his co-worker to sit on a couch while they searched the place. Officers confiscated the guitar and several computers, including some on which illegal video games had been installed. They ordered Jason and the other inmates back to their barracks. They put Jason and one other man into a van headed to Varner.

But this time, Jason wasn't brought to the Varner Maximum Security Unit where he'd been twice before. From the sally port, guards led him to the Supermax Unit, where they confiscated everything Jason had except the clothes he was wearing. They took his books, radio, and Hacky Sack. They then led him to Isolation Block Four, where the guards placed him in Cell twelve. Jason knew these isolation cells here were harsher than those nearby on death row because there, at least, prisoners were allowed some possessions. This cell block was called "punitive" for a reason.

"Oh, yeah," Jason said. "It's super-restricted. Those cells don't have TVs. They don't have a shower, so you have to be taken out for that. You don't get deodorant. You don't get books. You can't have any of your property. They're like a cell with bars all around that's inside a bigger cell. You can't even reach the doorway. There's no window that looks outside. At 'lights-out,' at night, they pass out mattresses and they collect them in the morning, so during the day, you don't even have a mattress, just a concrete slab and a stainless steel toilet. It's like, if the prison was Dante's *Inferno*, punitive isolation is at the bottom. It's punitive and it is punishment. So you're just sitting in there all day. You can't even lay down in there and sleep your time away."

In prison, just as outside, there are rules to be followed before someone can be punished. Like police in the free world, prison officers are required to follow defined procedures. A person cannot be held indefinitely for questioning or on suspicion that they've done wrong. Policies require that an inmate be granted a hearing where evidence can be presented and his guilt or innocence judged before any form of punishment, such as isolation or loss of class, can be imposed.

But in January 2007, none of that happened to Jason. He was not charged with any rule violation. He was not granted a hearing. Officers simply questioned him about the computers, and when he did not tell them what they wanted to know, they put him in isolation in the hope of breaking his will.

This time, unlike when he was arrested and offered the deal by the prosecutors, Jason could have accommodated his interrogators without having to lie. Jason had known the moment he'd stepped into the field office that life there was too good to be true. The sofa, coffee table and big-screen TV—all those had been okay. But other amenities the office staff allowed, such as the guitar, were not. The guitar Jason was learning to play had been donated to the chapel, where it was surplus and not being used. Nevertheless, it was supposed to have stayed in the chapel. Being out of place made it contraband. But, while the guitar would have been problem enough, it was the computers with video games that had brought in internal affairs.

Jason saw quickly enough that the office staff was allowing things that weren't by-the-book. But that wasn't necessarily new. He'd encountered some form of laxity in every job he'd been given, going back to when staff at the school had left food to fatten him up. That had been illegal too, a violation of rules. But practically every supervisor in Jason's experience had offered some similar kindness. "It's just a human thing," he said, "when you're working close to people."

Jason put the guitar into that category—against the rules but causing no harm. He didn't learn about the more serious issues at the office until he'd been at the job for a while. He explained, "I get assigned to my state computer, and then I find out that my work partner also has this souped-up computer of his own. It has video games on it, and he says, 'Do you want one? I can make sure it happens.' He said he'd already had a few of these, over a span of many years. He'd gotten them, used them, and then, when he'd got a chance to upgrade, he'd sold his used one to some other inmate."

Jason was quick on the computers he used at work, but he'd been yearning to see what he could do with one that wasn't tied to a job. He was curious about the Internet, where he knew that minute details of his case were being discussed, but Internet access was out of the question. Games, however . . . It was 2007. Jason, closing in on thirty, hadn't played a computer game since 1993—eons ago in terms of technology. "Sure," he told his co-worker. Later, he would recall: "I had a bunch of video games and a program to help me learn the guitar and tune it."

All that was cool. Then, another line was crossed. Every now and then, his co-worker showed him they could get on the Internet. That was dangerous. "He'd get on and do something and then log off real fast," Jason said. "The server was, like, super-slow, so it wasn't like we were sitting there surfing. All I wanted to do was go to WM3.org and see all this stuff I'd been hearing about."

The fun lasted for about five months. Then, an inmate who had purchased a cast-off computer from Jason's co-worker got caught with it. "That's how the whole domino thing tipped over," Jason said.

A few questions, a few answers, and a few hours later, the department's internal affairs officers were searching the field security office.

Contraband is a plague in prisons. Some forms are tolerated, like prescription eyeglasses provided for prisoners by family members and friends. Alcohol, or cell-made hooch, while not tolerated, is common. Marijuana is so prevalent that an inmate once smuggled a joint out of a prison to a reporter, just to prove he could. Periodic shakedowns in prisons almost always turn up drugs. Those kinds of things are par for the course. Weapons top the list, as the most serious contraband. But just under weapons on the list are devices for electronic communication—cell phones and computers. Prison administrators don't want inmates communicating with victims, with homeboys back in the gang, with soft-hearted dupes they can rip off, or, especially, with other inmates. To administrators, control of communication inside a prison is as important as physical control. Yet, despite constant efforts to control black markets, they exist in all forms in most prisons.[164]

So the computers were a very big deal. On the day of the crackdown at the field security office, several inmates at Little Tucker were put into that unit's hole. Jason and his co-worker were the only two sent away to the oblivion of Varner Supermax Unit. "They were using punitive isolation as leverage," Jason said, "to try to make me give them information on staff members." An officer from internal affairs visited Jason regularly. "He'd say, 'Baldwin, I'm not mad at you. Shoot. If I was an inmate and somebody offered me a computer, I'd take it too. So I don't blame you a bit. I'm mad at the officers who let all this go on.' And, of course, he wants me to name them. But I'm, like, 'Shit. I can't help you with that.' I'm like, 'I know I was breaking the rules, so go ahead and punish me. Do what you need to do so we can move forward.' I didn't fight them; I was guilty. But I wasn't going to give them information. So I was just sitting. I was going to be hardheaded as long as they were going to be hardheaded. I thought they were going to keep me back there for the remainder of my time."

Three days after Jason was moved, a reporter who'd emailed the prison department to inquire was informed that, while Jason had been transferred to the Supermax, he had not been charged with a rule violation, nor had he been busted in class. "All that has happened is that some sort of investigation has been started," the spokesperson said, adding that Jason was being held on "investigative status." Later, Jason denied that report. He said that, in fact, he was never assigned to investigative status but, rather, was held under circumstances that fit none of the department's requirements. "They should have assigned me to investigative status," he said, "because then I would have been allowed to have my property, like Damien was allowed to have his. But that's not what they did." [165]

Before the shakedown at the field security office, the *Arkansas Times* reported that Jason planned to be married on Jan. 24, 2007, to a woman from Georgia. But, needless to say, prisoners in the hole aren't allowed to hold weddings. His intended was allowed occasional visits with him at the Supermax, however. The first of those, a bare week after his arrival, was especially remarkable because it brought together, not just Jason and his fiancée for the first time since his bust, but Damien and Lorri, as well.

Visits to men housed in the Supermax are held in a tightly controlled area walled with bars through which visitors and inmates can see who's visiting whom. Under certain circumstances, particularly when visitors are members of an inmate's family, they are allowed into the locked visitation cell with their loved one for what is called a "contact" visit.

Jason was allowed a contact visit with his girlfriend, and when they looked around, they saw Lorri there visiting Damien. All four were stunned. "We were like, 'Oh, my God, what's going on?'" Jason recalled. He estimated that he and Damien got to talk for ten to twenty minutes. It was enough time for Jason to explain that he was now at the Supermax too, that he and his girlfriend were going to be married, but that, "Obviously, I'm in trouble, so the wedding's been postponed." Damien laughed. "I think we'd been repressed for so long," Jason said, "Damien thought it was funny." At first, the woman visited Jason "quite often," he said, but as his weeks in solitary confinement turned into months, she "just drifted away."

According to regulations, Jason should have had a hearing at the end of his first thirty days in the hole, before that time could be extended. But as his sojourn in punitive isolation had never gone according to policy anyway, that date in mid-February came and went without a hearing or anything else to mark Jason's ambiguous status. Officers investigating the computer affair told him point blank that he could be released if he talked. Because he wouldn't, he remained without television, books, natural light, or the simple comfort of a mat on his concrete slab during the daytime, with no end in sight. Yet, because all inmates are required to be allowed contact with their attorneys, Jason was kept informed about the activity in Memphis.

Another drama—this one at the heart of Jason's case—was unfolding across the Mississippi River, one hundred fifty miles away in Memphis. By the end of January 2007, the DNA testing was almost complete. Analysts continued to review some data, and some non-DNA evidence still remained to be evaluated, but the results already in hand provided information that Damien's attorney, Dennis Riordan, publicly predicted would "shed significant light on the case." The tests, he said, had revealed the profile of an "unknown" person associated with the murders. As the attorneys arranged to meet with prosecutor Brent Davis to discuss the new scientific evidence in advance of planned court action, Ron Lax turned his attention to Terry Hobbs.

On Saturday, February 24th, Lax and one of his investigators, Rachael Geiser, drove unannounced to Hobbs's house. According to the six-page report Geiser dictated two days later, "Terry was sleeping when we arrived, as he told us he had returned from the casinos in Tunica, Mississippi, at approximately 5:00 A.M. We arrived a little after 9:00 A.M. He did invite us into his home, where we spoke in the living room. When we arrived, Terry asked us to wait for a minute while he disappeared to put in his false teeth. He did joke that his false teeth "have nothing to do with the bite marks."

Geiser continued, "While Terry was putting in his false teeth, I did notice a very large cigarette ashtray lying on the table in front of me, at which time I confiscated two cigarette butts." She wrote that the butts would be forwarded to attorneys. So too would be a tape-recording of the "conversation with Terry" that she and Lax conducted. She noted that Hobbs had "seemed more than willing" to answer their questions.[166]

By the time Lax and Geiser visited with Hobbs, the prison department reported that at least nineteen inmates had been punished as a result of the computer-smuggling probe at Tucker, and that eleven employees had either resigned or been fired.[167] The department did not report the extent or irregular circumstances of Jason's confinement. He occupied a cell in a "limbo that seemed to stretch out forever." Still, he saw his punishment plainly: it was the price he had to pay, first, for knowingly violating rules and taking risks back at the field security office, and second, for refusing to help the state in its investigation, which seemed to be ongoing.

On March 14, as the end of Jason's second thirty-day stint in punitive approached, the *Times* contacted the prison spokesman again to ask about Jason's status. It had not changed, the official reported; he had not been charged with a rule violation and he had not been reduced in class. This time, however, his time in the hole was not arbitrarily extended. On March 16, Jason was taken from his cell-within-a-cell and placed into another one at the Supermax—one that resembled those on death row, in that it had a shower and TV, and he got back his books and possessions. Now, he was told, he was being held in "administrative confinement." Three weeks later, Jason observed his thirtieth birthday—his fourteenth birthday behind bars.

Though "administrative confinement" is still isolation, Jason's condition certainly eased. He received the birthday cards that committed supporters sent, grateful, as always, for the encouragement. A few of his correspondents reported the interesting news that was percolating out of Marion and Jonesboro: Burnett was making it widely known that he would not run for re-election as judge, but planned instead to campaign for a seat in the Arkansas Senate; and Brent Davis, the longtime prosecuting attorney, had announced his intention to campaign for Burnett's vacated seat on the bench.

"Nobody made a greater mistake than he who did nothing
because he could do only a little."

~ *Edmund Burke*

As interest in the West Memphis case continued to spread,
people around the world were now turning regularly to sites such
as WM3.org, jivepuppi.com, and Callahan.8k.com to learn more.
Of those sites, WM3.org and jivepuppi.com both pronounced their
beliefs in the men's innocence. Only Callahan.8k.com remained a
neutral archive. But, while Christian Hansen had started that site
believing the men to be guilty, the material he'd gathered on his
own website had by now convinced him otherwise.

Since 2001, when Hansen began putting West Memphis case-
related documents online from his apartment in Denmark, he had
received help in the forms of legwork, posting work and donations
from a few committed fans. One of those, who asked to be identified
only as Greg, was a computer programmer in Arkansas who'd
grown up near West Memphis. When Hansen notified supporters
in 2004 that he was no longer interested in keeping up his site, Greg
took it over, paying for it and adding to the archive with the help
of other supporters. Eventually, Hansen resumed his duties as the
site's webmaster, though Greg remained involved. When asked how
he viewed the site's importance, he responded modestly, "I consider
it somewhat important, in that both sides of the controversy have
complimented it;" then added, "Callahan is more fair than the trials
the WM3 received."

In 2007, the year Jason went to the Supermax, another important
contributor joined the Callahan effort. Monte Walker was a thirty-
seven year old single dad living in Flintville, Tennessee. He had a
business degree in marketing, and worked in transportation and
agriculture. He was also, he said, "one of those people that recorded
and watched the entire O.J. Simpson trial" and became "interested
in true crime and the justice system" from that point on.

By the spring of 2007, Walker had seen the West Memphis
documentaries, read the books, and finished reading the entire
Callahan website, except the pleadings section. "I had been

under the impression that all of the evidence files were on the site," he said. He emailed Hansen to let him know how much he appreciated Callahan and to ask if there was any way he could help. Walker said, "That started a chain of correspondence from which I learned that only a fraction—maybe fifty percent—of the case file was online. With as much fulfillment as I had received from Callahan, it was an easy decision to get involved and 'complete' the case documents section."

That summer, Walker put together a team of a half-dozen people to help him copy the entire file on the case at the West Memphis Police Department. It took about a year for the team to copy thousands of documents. Years later, Walker said he believed, "The real story behind Callahan's is two-fold. First, Christian lives in Denmark, and from there has worked hard to provide us all with case information. And second, that so many people volunteered to acquire documents or contribute to Callahan in some way (as noted in the site's Credits section).

Simultaneously to Walker's work, momentum in the case was beginning to build in Arkansas. Stidham was invited to speak about it at the state's largest school, the University of Arkansas at Fayetteville, near the same time that plans were announced to hold a rally called "Standing for Justice: A Show of Solidarity among WM3 Supporters" in Marion, on the lawn of the Crittenden County Courthouse. The event, scheduled for June 2, 2007, would coincide with the fifth Worldwide Awareness Day on behalf of the West Memphis Three.

Arkansas supporters approached the date with some apprehension. The county judge, who was informed in advance, told organizers that he was "notifying the local law enforcement agencies . . . just in case any incidents were to get out of hand." A discreet police presence was evident, but the event proceeded peacefully. Approximately sixty people attended. They came from more than a dozen Arkansas cities and towns, from states as near as Tennessee and Mississippi and as far away as Delaware, Arizona, Illinois, Florida, Pennsylvania, Colorado, North Carolina, New Jersey, Wisconsin, and California.

They stood in a circle holding hands in silence while a bell tolled once a minute fourteen times. Each ring of the bell—each minuted—

represented an entire year that Damien, Jason, and Jessie had already spent in prison. Three white roses represented the murdered children. The circle included the handful of women who'd organized the state's earliest rallies: the Green Party's candidate for U.S. Senate, the university instructor who'd been the first to bring the case into her classroom, a Nashville criminal justice teacher and students, the grad student who'd analyzed the case's pretrial publicity, and other devoted supporters, including Jessie Misskelley's father. [168]

It's safe to say that no one at that early June event had the slightest notion of how much pressure was now bearing down on Terry Hobbs, across the river in Memphis. On May 18, Lax and Geiser had attempted to interview Hobbs again at his house, but neighbors told them that Hobbs had moved. According to Lax's report, the women said Hobbs told them that he was "very sad" because of his wife, his children, and "the children in West Memphis."

Yet Lax was able to locate Hobbs, and the following day, two Saturdays before the rally in Marion, Hobbs met with the investigator at Inquisitor's office in Memphis. Lax reported, "Since he had just left work (he reports he is working at a lumber company in West Memphis), his dirty clothing was understandable, but he looked tired and ill kempt. He had not shaved in two or three days, and he appeared as a man under a great deal of pressure; however, his conversation was upbeat."

Hoping to collect additional DNA samples, Lax offered Hobbs coffee, soft drinks and water, all of which he declined. He had also placed an ashtray on the table, in anticipation of Hobbs smoking, but he never did.

Lax wrote, "After Hobbs spoke about his recent downward turn of circumstances, I told him there was additional trouble for him that had recently been discovered. I explained that a hair had been found under the ligatures that bound Michael Moore and that the hair had been sent for testing. He immediately commented that he was aware that additional testing had been done, which he thought was long overdue. I then told him that DNA had been isolated from the hair, and we wanted to collect DNA samples from all of the family members and of others who had access to the crime scene so we could eliminate individuals. At this time I asked him if he would be willing to provide us with DNA samples. He immediately stated that he would want to talk to D.A. Brent Davis first.

"After additional conversation, I told him that the DNA from the hair did not match the DNA profile of Damien, Jason or Jessie, nor did it match the DNA profile of Stevie, Chris or Michael. Hobbs' immediate response was, 'Who does it match?' When I hesitated, he urged me to tell him. I told him that the DNA profile matched his. He did not appear surprised or shocked and commented that it was wrong. I told him the science was not wrong, and he then stated that Michael Moore had been in his house, and the hair could have been transferred. I pointed out that we did not know whose shoelaces had been used to tie up each of the boys, but the hair had been found in the knot of one of the ligatures."

As this point, Geiser, who participated in the interview, invited Hobbs to smoke. Hobbs laughed and commented that the investigators just wanted his DNA and that they could probably get it from the sweat or skin particles he was leaving on the table. In fact, Geiser did take a swab from the table after Hobbs left, and the sample was forwarded to the attorneys.

Lax's report continued, "He then asked if we wanted a hair sample. I told him a hair sample, blood, or a cheek swab. He again commented that he wanted to talk to Brent Davis prior to agreeing to provide a DNA sample. At no point did he become angry, antagonistic or even belligerent. He maintained a very cool and calm demeanor throughout our meeting.

"Hobbs informed us that he had spoken to Brent Davis earlier in the week, but when we asked for what purpose, he was vague, stating, 'Just some things that have come up.' During this conversation, he said Davis had told him and other family members in the past that 'they' were going to be responsible for the reversal of this case if they kept talking. I asked if Davis was aware that we interviewed him in February, and he said that he was and that Davis had told him he should not talk to us."

But other people were more willing to talk. Within the next several weeks, Geiser spoke to Hobb's first wife, with whom he'd lived for a time in Hot Springs, Arkansas, and with Mildred French, a woman in Hot Springs who reported being assaulted by Hobbs. The picture that emerged from the interviews was one of a man, in the decade before the West Memphis murders, who had beaten his first wife bloody and broken into a neighbor's home, where he'd grabbed her from behind as she'd stepped naked from the shower.[169]

> "A man has to live with himself, and he should see to it that he always has good company."
> ~ Charles Evans Hughes

The finding of hair traced to Hobbs in the ligatures could not be dismissed. On June 19, 2007, the same day that Geiser interviewed French, an officer at the West Memphis Police Department interviewed Pam Hobbs about her ex-husband. Lt. Ken Mitchell opened the questioning by telling Pam that police understood she might have some new information about the case and that they were there at the request of prosecutor Brent Davis.

Pam Hobbs told Mitchell that she had married Stevie's father, Steve Branch, and had subsequently gotten divorced. She married Terry Hobbs in 1986, and they had a daughter, Amanda, together. During the recorded interview, Pam matter-of-factly outlined events on the day that Stevie disappeared, and how he was not home at around 4:50 p.m., as he'd been told to be, when she had to leave for work. But she seemed to become upset when describing how she did not know until the end of her shift, at nine that night, that Stevie was still not home. She said that, when Terry came to pick her up at the Catfish Island restaurant where she worked, he'd gone directly to a pay phone inside, and she didn't know whom he was calling. Instead, it was her four-year-old daughter Amanda, not Terry, who had told her, "Momma, we can't find him." When Terry returned, he told Pam that he had gone inside to call the police to report Stevie missing.

Mitchell asked what information Pam had that made her think Terry might have had something to do with the children's deaths.

According to a police transcript of the interview, Pam told Mitchell that she'd had an extramarital affair in January 1993, and that Terry had caught her in the kitchen kissing the man. "Terry walked in and he beat the guy up and all that stuff," she said. "But he doesn't really appear to be angry enough at me that he wants to divorce me or anything like that, you know, everything is gone be all right. We gonna go on with our marriage and stuff."

Ten years later, however, she said, Terry had "set a trash bag out on the carport and said that that was my clothes and that's what I could take with me . . . Terry had taken every stitch of clothing that I had. I don't know if he cut it with a knife or if he cut it with a box cutter or what. But the clothing that he had in that trash bag to give me—and this was even down to my bras and underwear—they were cut." Pam said she was reminded that Terry had told her in the beginning of their marriage, "I don't get mad, I get even."

Lt. Mitchell asked about the items that Pam's sister had brought to Stidham sometime after Pam and Terry's divorce in 2004. Pam said that when she and her sister, Jo Lynn, started moving things, they found a collection of twelve to thirteen knives, which Jo Lynn took home with her. When Jo Lynn examined the knives, Pam said, she found among them a pocket knife that their father had given to Stevie. "Stevie carried it with him all the time," she said. "He would have had it with him that day. It was in Terry's knife collection and we was wondering why in the heck is this knife here, because the family didn't give it to him."

Pam also said that they found a strongbox in the top of their closet that belonged to Terry, which he kept locked. She said that, when her brother-in-law had pried it open, they found a dental partial that Terry had worn, "a little bitty necklace that had a penny on the end of it, and the year was 1984; that was the year Stevie was born. And I think he had maybe a marble or something like that, and that's all was in that strong box."[170]

Two days later, on June 21, Terry Hobbs came to the police department to be interviewed by Mitchell. Terry explained that, though the family had a phone at their home, he did not call the police to report Stevie missing until he picked up Pam at the restaurant because he thought he "had mentioned that to Dana"—the mother of Michael Moore. The interview covered Terry's account of the night the boys disappeared, the day the bodies were found, and the couple's life thereafter. He said Pam's sister had planted the drugs for which he'd been arrested in Memphis.

Mitchell showed him a photo of what he said looked like "some partial dentures." Hobbs identified the partial as his and said that Pam and her sister had taken it. Mitchell next showed Terry photos of knives, and Hobbs said, "They're mine." He explained that he did not remember where he'd gotten most of them, "'cause a lot of time I would find 'em on the ground somewhere and just pick 'em up and put 'em in a little box or something like that."

Mitchell then showed Hobbs a photo of two items, one of which was a pocket knife, that Hobbs said he did not recall. Mitchell asked if Hobbs remembered Stevie having a knife at all. Terry said that, "his granddaddy may have given him one. It's possible. I can't say yes or no, though."[171]

By the time of that interview, at the end of June, Jason had spent a total of five months in solitary confinement at the Supermax Unit. He thought about Terry Hobbs occasionally, but speculation about who had actually killed the children had never struck him as productive. To the contrary, as he put it, "Any time I hear of someone being accused of something, I immediately start looking for that element of doubt. I don't start looking for ways of justifying the idea that that person is guilty."

Instead, his thoughts mostly looped back to his first stint in solitary confinement, at the jail, after his arrest. He remembered how hard he'd held onto the seemingly logical belief that officials were collecting physical and biological evidence from him because they had collected other physical and biological evidence with which they were going to compare it. Surely, he'd thought, that was why investigators had, not once but twice, taken fingerprints, handprints, footprints, hair, saliva, blood and writing samples from him.

Throughout those long months at the Craighead County Detention Center, Jason had trusted that scientific comparisons would exclude him as the murderer. But then came the shock at his trial when the prosecutors did not introduce a single piece of biological evidence. In fact, the only physical evidence they ever claimed linked him to the crime at all was a solitary fiber found on the victims—a fiber that they argued could have come from Jason's home.

Jason recalled begging Ford to tell him why—"Why had the state taken all that stuff if there was nothing to compare it to?"—and Ford saying he didn't know. Jason remembered Ford saying, "Their story was that there was nothing to compare it to." Though Jason had thought that made no sense, he'd felt "just swept along for the ride."

Now, some things did make sense. Now, Jason knew for certain that the state had possessed biological evidence from the crime scene all along. He knew that testing of that evidence was now complete. And he knew that those tests had, as expected, excluded him, Jessie and Damien.

He understood that the tests did not establish anyone else as the murderer. But disappointing as that was, what amazed him most was the deeper understanding as to why his prosecutors had not introduced any biological evidence at his trial: it would have undermined their case.

"Finally!" he thought. One of the most perplexing pieces of his fourteen-year puzzle had snapped into place. "There was biological evidence! The state had it before the trial! The state had it all along! And they didn't use it."

Philipsborn was careful to warn Jason that, because of the uncertain results, a difficult and perhaps long fight lay ahead. Jason accepted that. With no end to his "administrative confinement" in sight, he remained polite, stoic and patient, at peace with himself and his thoughts. When he found out that the hair of Terry Hobbs had been found inside the knots binding Michael Moore, he tried not to make much of it, though it did seem to him "a damning place to have a hair."

So much had changed in fourteen years—for the West Memphis Police Department, Jerry Driver, Vickie Hutchison, Melissa Byers, the Hobbses, Fogleman, Davis, Burnett, and even Robin Wadley, his trial lawyer who'd been disbarred. Citizens around the world—and including a fair number in Arkansas now—were calling the trials an injustice. Yet, in a more immediate sense, nothing at all had changed. At thirty, Jason sat locked in an isolation cell, just as he'd sat for months after his arrest at sixteen. Now, as then, though, he held onto hope, occasionally even allowing himself to envision what it would be like to be freed. Once, he committed that dream to paper, in a poem titled "We Emerged."

We emerged
        with skin
                pale as the tombs we were condemned in
as soft as mom's prayers

Our hands
        float past
                our faces
                        carrying
                                more than our dreams
could have imagined
as they wave away the memories that would anchor them as surely
as the steel Smith & Wesson cuffs we were just let out of

I open my mouth with a smile
Not sure if I could bear
        To go
                Back
                        In.

The price of such dreams was steep: the certainty, as each dissolved, that the cuffs remained in place: that he was still—as always—"In." He was grown now. He'd come of age in a hard way: as a convicted child-killer in prison. Yet through it all, he had not lost hope. He believed that the day would come when all the effort pouring into this case would bear fruit, when the state would admit he was innocent, and an honest investigation into the murders would finally occur.

On June 25, 2007, guards came to Jason's cell to tell him to gather his belongings. He was being moved again, back to Tucker, though this time he'd go straight into another isolation cell there, at the complex's Maximum Security Unit. On the drive, the van in which Jason sat cuffed and shackled passed close by the Diagnostic Unit in Pine Bluff, where he had entered the system and where the department's hospital was located. Jason did not know it, but inside that hospital, a thirty-seven year old inmate from West Memphis lay dying. Ronald Ward—Jason's friend, Jibril—would die there four days later.

Back in 1985, when Burnett sentenced Ward to death, the judge told a newspaper, "The tragedy in the Ronald Ward story is he's a victim of a society that allowed him to live in a situation where he had no guidance or control. But Attila the Hun probably had unfortunate circumstances, too. One purpose of our system is to protect and exact retribution."[172]

Ward died of natural causes. But so far, just during Jason's time in prison, states in the U.S. had executed more than nine hundred prisoners—twenty-two in Arkansas alone. By the time Jason moved back to Tucker, opposition to the death penalty was growing, and that year, two more states would join the sixteen that had already outlawed the practice. And, though it was too late for Jibril, Jason, and Jessie, another, less well known movement—this one to abolish the practice of sentencing juveniles to life in prison—had also begun.

Jason entered yet another prison, unsure of almost everything—except himself. He knew what he would and would not do and how much he could survive. He saw how cynicism and sham had perverted his trial. He knew that the "West Memphis Three" had supporters who recognized that too and that, because of them, he, Damien and Jessie eventually would "emerge" from the "tombs" to which they'd been "condemned." Yet, for all that, there was a way in which he remained as naïve as he'd been at sixteen.

Jason still expected that when the key turned and a court set him free, it would be because reason and evidence had prevailed at last. For all he'd experienced of cruelty and cunning—the deaths, the deceits, the deals—Arkansas inmate #103335 could not have fathomed the depths to which officials would yet go to keep him—and the truth of the murders—buried.

1   This trilogy uses endnotes because stories, like investigations, are multi-layered.

2   In 1977 I was a green reporter, a mom with two kids in school, and a member of Amnesty International, an organization that opposes the death penalty "in all cases and under all circumstances." That year, only sixteen countries had abolished the death penalty, though as I write this, thirty years later, that number has risen to ninety. The United States is still not among them.

3   In "Carl Albert Collins v. State of Arkansas," No. CR75-110, Mar. 7, 1977, Chief Justice Fogleman also found that "death by electrocution is not unconstitutionally cruel."

4   Courts have traditionally accorded juveniles some kinds of special treatment, though standards have been haphazard. During the 1980s and 1990s, many states, including Arkansas, enacted legislation that allowed juveniles to be "transferred" to adult status for trial under particular circumstances and according to different procedures. Arkansas is one of fifteen states that allows prosecutors to decide to charge a juvenile as an adult, though, if contested, the transfer must be approved by a judge. "Trying Juveniles as Adults: An Analysis of State Transfer Laws and Reporting," U.S. Department of Justice Office of Juvenile Justice and Delinquency Prevention, Sept. 2011. https://www.ncjrs.gov/pdffiles1/ojjdp/232434.pdf. For a brief history of courts' treatment of juveniles, see: http://www.pbs.org/wgbh/pages/frontline/shows/juvenile/stats/childadult.html.

5   The Foglemans in Crittenden County likely trace back to a German family named Vogelmann, members of which emigrated to North America in the mid-1700s. A branch of the family that spells its name 'Fogelman' is prominent across the river, in Memphis, Tennessee, particularly in real estate. Their name shows up in the Fogelman College of Business

and Economics at the University of Memphis and the city's Fogelman YMCA. Avron B. Fogelman, a Memphis real estate developer, was a former part-owner of the major league Kansas City Royals baseball team and several Memphis-based sports teams.

6   Mississippi History Now: http://mshistory.k12.ms.us/ articles/319/surviving-the-worst-the-wreck-of-the-sultana.

7   *Memphis Argus*, April 28, 1865.

8   The official number of dead from the *RMS Titanic* is 1,502. Small markers in Jefferson Davis Park in Memphis and in Knoxville, Tennessee, commemorate the *Sultana* explosion.

9   *Arkansas Democrat-Gazette*, April 25, 1999

10   As reported by Seth Blomeley in the *Arkansas Democrat-Gazette's* profiles of Fogelman and his opponent, Courtney Henry, in their 2010 campaigns for the Arkansas Supreme Court.

11   The public defender, Thomas B. Montgomery, said he is ethically barred from speaking about the case and that, because it was a juvenile case, records from it have likely been destroyed.

12   Jason's mother, recalled that she had to pay part of the court-ordered restitution every month, "And if I didn't pay on it every month, they would send my kids to a juvenile home." It was her understanding that she was paying for damages to the window of a car that had been shot out with a BB gun.

13   "15-Year-Old Death Row Inmate Says He's 'Still Scared' of Dying," by David Speer, Associated Press, Oct. 11, 1985, http://www.apnewsarchive.com/1985/15-Year-Old-Death-Row-Inmate-Says-He-s-Still-Scared-of-Dying/id-798e9 c622ddadb70eceea37d20def176. The Supreme Court's opinion:. http://opinions.aoc.arkansas.gov/weblink8/0/ doc/94303/Electronic.aspx. The court's criticism of Burnett notwithstanding, Arkansas judges the following year voted him the state's Trial Judge of the Year.

14   Here, the defendant, David Strobbe, was charged with murdering a woman near West Memphis by running her over with a car. The jury found Strobbe guilty and sentenced

him to life in prison. But when Strobbe appealed, the
state Supreme Court found serious error with Fogleman's
prosecution. The "critical evidence" withheld from Strobbe's
attorneys was nothing less than information that the state's
key witness, who had offered eye-witness testimony against
Strobbe, had himself participated in the murder. "The state
knew its case rested primarily on this one witness," wrote the
high court's new chief justice, "and they represented that he
was merely there—that he only saw the crime." The Supreme
Court further noted that the district's chief prosecuting
attorney claimed he was not personally aware of that fact at
Strobbe's trial because his deputy, "Mr. Fogleman, apparently
had not thought it significant enough to tell him." One justice
concurred with stronger language. "I agree the decision must
be reversed," he wrote, "but in my opinion the error consisted
of officers of the state misrepresenting the truth, not merely
remaining silent." David T. Strobbe v. State of Arkansas, No.
CR 87-143, June 20, 1988. (http://opinions.aoc.arkansas.gov/
weblink8/0/doc/94691/Electronic.aspx) Years later, Fogleman
told a reporter that he'd been embarrassed by that ruling. "I
learned a very, very valuable lesson," he said. "From that point
on, if there was anything—just about anything—I provided it
to the defense." (Center for Public Integrity, Mar. 8, 2004.)

15 Center for Public Integrity report, 2004; http://www.
magnacartanews.greatnow.com/Arkansas_Prosecutorial_
Misconduct.html

16 Damien, born Dec. 11, 1974, was the oldest of the three. Jessie,
born July 10, 1975, was six months younger. Jason, born April
11, 1977, was a year and ten months younger than Jessie and
two years and four months younger than Damien.

17 Jason's mother, is adamant that she did not throw a knife
into the lake. In an online exchange in 2013, she wrote that,
". . . for anyone saying I threw a knife in the lake is wrong... I
didn't allow my children to have knives, and when Jason got
a knife a year earlier he accidentally threw it way out in the
middle of the lake . . . my children had no knives at the time

of the murder of those three children!" However, in Jason's
Rule 37 hearing on Aug. 14, 2009, Joseph Samuel Dwyer, a
friend of Jason's, testified: "I remember the scuba diver who
found a knife in the lake. I also remember that it was Jason's
mother who threw the knife in the lake. She did not want
him to have any knives. She had found one and she threw
it out there out of anger." These statements correspond with
recollections of Jason's brother Matt, as related in a letter
to me dated Mar. 15, 2013. In a Petition for a Writ of Error
Coram Nobis filed in 2008, Jason's attorneys told the court
that "post-conviction investigation has revealed that at least
two witnesses [Domini Teer and Garrett Schwarting] told
police that they were aware that a large knife was thrown
into the lake before the murders. Also, one of the officers
has indicated the officers were given precise directions on
where to find the knife."

18 In 2001, Fogleman recalled, "I started working as a deputy
prosecutor in 1983. I was also the juvenile prosecutor, and
I think I'd had encounters with all three of the defendants. I
think all that came into the trials, at least in the hearing to
transfer the case to juvenile court. I think Jason had only been
there one time, maybe. It may have been a felony. But it wasn't
anything of a violent nature. And Jessie, to be honest, I can't
remember. I'm pretty sure I'd had dealings with Jessie as well.
And, of course, Damien had been in there a time or two, and
he was different. In his attitude and the things he was accused
of. They all had a little twist to them. 'Bizarre' may not be
the right word, but he was definitely outside the norm. His
attitude was the only thing that stands out really in my mind.
Probably when he was in juvenile court—it was probably
close to 10 years ago, it may have been after he had come back
from Oregon, he'd gotten into trouble, I think. I remember
him coming into court, and I remember the way he just
turned and looked at me, and it wasn't evil, it wasn't laughing,
it wasn't sad, it was just blank. There wasn't anything there. I
commented to somebody at the time, the way his eyes were

and how empty they seemed. At that point, I just thought it was odd, and even as a prosecutor who'd dealt with a lot of things, it was odd and a little unnerving. Most of the juveniles we deal with are typical kids from poor economic circumstances, where crime is basically a way of life for them. Their families have been involved in the criminal justice system for years. You get a certain arrogance with them. For some who come in, it's obvious, just from their appearance, that they won't ever be back; they're scared. But Damien's attitude was different from anybody's I'd ever experienced before. And frankly, he didn't stand out from anybody else in my mind up until that point."

19   Arrest report, Nov. 15, 1992. http://callahan.8k.com/images/ jasonb/baldwin_prior_arrest.JPG

20   Statement signed by Lt. James Sudbury, date unknown. In the statement, Sudbury wrote that: "On the day after the bodies of the three boys were found I had a conversation with Steve Jones, a Juvenile Officer for Crittenden County, Arkansas. In our conversation, I found that Steve and I shared the same opinion that the murders appeared to have overtones of a cult sacrifice." The statement described a visit Jones and Sudbury paid to Damien's house, the Polaroid photo taken of him and the officer's observation of "a tattoo on his chest of a five pointed star or pentagram…"

21   Jason's mother, recalled that, "When they came to my house that night, they brought Jessie's so-called confession and a search warrant listing what kind of items they were looking for;" that the warrant mentioned "different colored fabrics," specifically red, blue and green; that they also searched for "waxy material" and "some kind of cult-related items"; that they "took a blue rug out of my bathroom"; that "they took all of Jason's rock t-shirts that were black, even though they weren't supposed to be looking for black"; that police said the shirts were taken because they were "cult-related"; and that they stayed "for a good hour and a half, going through things." Jason's brother Matt wrote that he was staying at a

friend's house the night Jason was arrested, sleeping in the back yard in a makeshift tent. "We decided to go for a walk. We noticed a lot of police cars go by. By the time we reached Domini's home, we noticed a swat-like team with automatic weaponry all over her property, even on top of their home. I began to fear the worst. They had been badgering my friend Damien for a month, and I had heard all the rumors the cops, probation officers, and prosecutor had been spreading." Matt said he asked his friend's father to escort him home. "Upon arrival I see all these cops with guns. One cop in particular says to me, 'We arrested your brother for those kids' murders.' And I told him my brother didn't do it. I cried. I went in and saw my brother's room being ransacked. That night was one of the worst nights of my life."

22 Before questioning Jessie, police had taken a confusing statement from members of a family known as the Hollingsworths, part of which included the claim that on the night the boys disappeared they'd seen Damien and his girlfriend walking near the site where the bodies were later discovered. Police also had a statement from William Jones, an eighteen year-old who lived in Lakeshore Trailer Park, in which Jones said Damien had confessed committing the murders to him. Jones later recanted that statement.

23 Jessie's questioning began at ten in the morning and ended after 5 p.m. Many of Jessie's statements contradicted each other. The contents of the two recorded parts of the interview illuminate the start of the case and what would become its trajectory. At one point a detective told Jessie, "You mentioned earlier … this cult thing…" The word "cult" would be mentioned fifteen times in the course of those two recordings, but the first time it is mentioned, it is spoken by a detective. Jessie referred twice to "when we had that cult," each time in exactly those words. The other twelve times the word is heard on the tapes, it is spoken by a detective. As evidence, the recorded snippets of Jessie's interview were far from perfect. But compared to anything else the police

had developed so far, they stood out as monumental. The detectives held a hurried conference with Fogleman outside the room where Jessie sat waiting to be sent home. The prosecutor decided that Jessie's statements constituted sufficient cause to arrest him and to find and arrest Damien and Jason. In an unusual move, the judge who signed arrest warrants for all three teenagers ordered that the warrants remain sealed. As a result, when detectives announced at a press conference the next morning that the killers had been apprehended, the public had no idea how thin the police case was. Several issues relating to Jessie's confession were raised in his direct appeal. The Arkansas Supreme Court dismissed them all, though it noted that playing the tape recording of a child's voice saying, "Nobody knows what happened but me," came "perilously close" to overbearing the teenager's free will. http://opinions.aoc.arkansas.gov/weblink8/0/doc/167688/ Electronic.aspx

24   Det. Ridge later told Jason's mother that Jason had refused to talk to the police.

25   In Arkansas, juveniles in police custody must initiate any request for a lawyer. Even a parent present at the station cannot insist that an attorney be allowed in with a juvenile who's being questioned if the juvenile himself has not exercised his right to an attorney.

26   Jason was making a common mistake, thinking the tests were meant to exclude him if he was innocent. In fact, the samples were ordered as part of the state's attempt to build its case.

27   Jason, Damien and Jessie appeared before William P. Rainey, a West Memphis municipal judge. Hours earlier, Rainey had authorized the arrests of the three and issued search warrants for their homes. When questioned later about the unusual nighttime searches, Rainey testified that he'd been told by Chief Detective Gary Gitchell and Det. Bryn Ridge of the city's police department that there existed a "close relationship between the alleged perpetrators;" that there was evidence that "possibly could be removed or destroyed" if not gathered

immediately; "that you had three parties who had been in close contact with each other and would be very available to converse with each other, and the overall circumstances of the type of crime that this was, the obvious violent nature of it." Rainey said he had found "the totality" of the information Gitchell and Ridge reported to him about what Jessie had said during questioning "very credible."

28 Newspapers did not report where Jason, Damien and Jessie were being held. I doubt many reporters knew; I certainly didn't. But I was intrigued by how much remained unknown about this case, especially since no one even knew what the arrest warrants contained. Three weeks after the three teens were jailed, I wrote my first column about the case in the weekly *Arkansas Times*. Like other reporters, I recounted rumors about the accused. They'd been noticed at the local skating rink, I wrote, "not because of any trouble they caused, but because of Echols' distinctive style of dress, black with a long overcoat." I'd interviewed several West Memphis residents soon after the arrests, when *The Commercial Appeal* in Memphis published excerpts from Jessie's statements to police on its front page. "Now," I wrote, "only a few speak of the defendants as human.... Instead, the killings' Satanic overtones, the victims' age, and the reported brutalities drive the crimes to a deeper place in the psyche, a place resistant to natural explanations, where religion and emotion converge."

29 The length of time Jason was held without contacting his family is uncertain. His mother recollected that she was not told Jason's whereabouts for about four days. "Paul Ford kept telling me he was in Jonesboro, and I kept going to Jonesboro," she said, "And they would tell me he wasn't there. They kept lying to me. Finally, Paul Ford called me and told me they were setting up a phone call or visit for me." Matt Baldwin recalled: "I brought his iguana Ozzy there on one occasion." Matt said, that when his mom "ended up having a nervous breakdown" and being hospitalized, it was "one of the saddest things [he'd] ever seen anyone go through;" that when he

returned to school after the arrests, "I had friends that would ask me if my brother had murdered those children;" that "I was in constant defense of my brother and friends;" that "I stopped doing my work in school" and "started listening to music during class, and "the teachers wouldn't even pass out work to me,"; and that he was in school with Fogleman's son. "I sat right next to him in science class. I never talked to him, though. I thought of talking to him to send messages to his dad, like, 'Hey, lay off my brother, you know he's innocent. Drop the case. What's the matter with you?'"

30   Davis and Fogleman, both now judges, declined to be interviewed for this book.

31   In a tape-recorded author interview with Fogleman on April 23, 2001, when he was asked if he had concerns that someone might have planted the knife, Fogleman said that, as far as he was aware, no one knew that the search was to be conducted but the police: "It crossed my mind that there was a possibility that if the word got out that we were going to do this search, that somebody, say the 'real murderer' could have gone out and planted it, but then it occurred to me, they would have had to know, not just that we were going to look, but when we were going to do it." It is clear, however, that many people knew of the search in advance, as reporters from several media were at the lake, recording images of the diver emerging with a knife.

32   Jason's mother, Gail Grinnell ,said, "Ford did talk to Hubert. My uncle gave a statement and Ford recorded it."

33   In an author interview on July 3, 2012, Joyce Cureton said that she had worked at the detention center since 1988; that Jason was kept in lockdown—"where we can have visual of them, like if they're on suicide watch"—in the jail's hospital room for about a week; that Craighead County Sheriff Larry Emisom "said he wanted him in there and to never let him out except for a shower"; that Jason was kept confined "twenty four hours a day, not able to get out into the day room, where tables and TV and everything was"; that "you can't

treat a juvenile the way you do an adult;" that "it would have
been illegal for me to keep him in constant lockdown"; that
she moved Jason to a cell from which he could at least see the
TV; that "Emisom backed down when I moved Jason because
he knew I'd been trained in the juvenile;" that she realized
soon after Jason's arrival that he was neither a suicide risk or
a threat; that "It didn't take me but about a week to see that
all that was a crop of bull, so I started letting Jason out of his
room;" that as she got to know Jason, "What I saw in him
was a little boy in a place where he didn't need to be"; that
"You couldn't keep from caring about him; all of the girls that
worked for me cared about Jason because he was one of these
kids that never gave you any trouble, never back talked you—
everything was 'Yes, Ma'am,' 'May I please?'—he was just so
well mannered"; that "He just wasn't the kid that they had
portrayed him to be"; and that after one has run a juvenile jail
for years, "it don't take you long to figure out if a kid is rotten,
or if he's a good kid, or a spoiled kid, or what have you."

34   "To Die For," *SMUG Magazine*, Sept./Oct. 2000.

35   Email from Joe Berlinger, Nov. 29, 2012: "When we arrived
     is an important distinction to me because we spent eight
     months embedding ourselves in the community and really
     getting almost unprecedented access to all sides, which is
     much stronger reporting/documentary filmmaking than just
     showing up for the trials ... The achievement of *Paradise
     Lost* is those first eight months, not simply the recording of
     a trial which anyone could have done, but what we actually
     achieved during the eight months prior to the trial is to me
     the real success of the film. And, I think this distinction
     of when we arrived is also very important for the history
     [because] it wasn't just Judge Burnett's decision... He told
     us that his decision was going to be based on the approval
     (of cameras in the courtroom) of ALL parties, so we had to
     convince ALL SIX defense lawyers, BOTH prosecutors and
     ALL SIX FAMILIES. That is a very tall order and was only
     possible because we spent those first eight months prior to

the trial in West Memphis building strong relationships with ALL parties."

36 This case arose just as Arkansas was changing its system for paying public defenders in capital cases from the counties' responsibility to the state's. As a result, none of the defense attorneys was paid for his work on the case until well after the trials, and they had no money for investigations. Attorneys representing the defendants have said that they accepted stipends from the filmmakers on their clients' behalf, to pay for investigations and expert witnesses.

37 Years later, in 2005, investigator Thomas Quinn interviewed Jones, who mentioned the visit to Jason. Quinn swore an affidavit stating that Jones said he'd told Jason during the visit that he believed he was innocent and that he'd offered his assistance.

38 Arkansas's Second Judicial District is comprised of six counties in the northeast corner of the state. Judge Burnett had the discretion of working from any courthouse in the district. Judicial proceedings in the West Memphis case were held in Marion, the county seat of Crittenden County in the southernmost part of the district, where West Memphis is located; in Jonesboro, the seat of Craighead County, where the district prosecutor's office is headquartered; and in Corning, home to one of the two courthouses that serve Clay County, the county farthest north.

39 Merriam-Webster defines "trial" as "a formal meeting in a court in which evidence about crimes, disagreements, etc., is presented to a judge and often a jury so that decisions can be made according to the law." Dictionary.com defines "trial" as "the determination of a person's guilt or innocence by due process of law." And *Black's Law Dictionary* defines "trial" as "a judicial examination and determination of issues between parties to action, whether they be issues of law or of fact, before a court that has jurisdiction." Jason might have been surprised to learn that few definitions of the word "trial" contain the word "truth."

40 "Prosecutor realizes he has his hands full," by Bartholomew Sullivan, *Memphis Commercial Appeal*, Jan. 16, 1994. http://westmemphisthreediscussion.yuku.com/topic/2729#. UhvMJhbvwb0

41 Jessie was convicted on two counts of second-degree murder and one count of first-degree murder. His attorney, Dan Stidham, wrote a synopsis of Misskelley's case that was posted on the website WM3.org. In that he wrote: "We learned, after the trial, that the first vote the jury took in the jury room was eight for conviction, four for acquittal. Despite the limitation the court imposed on us, we were able to convince four jurors he was innocent. We only needed one strong-willed juror for a hung jury and ultimate mistrial, which would have been the next best thing to an acquittal. The eight wore down the four, however, and they reached a compromise verdict. Although we didn't get an acquittal, we were fortunate enough to avoid a capital murder conviction, and thus the death penalty."

42 The state Supreme Court would later note that the case against Jessie rested almost entirely on his recorded statements to police; there was no other evidence of substance against him. Yet Jessie's statements alone had been enough to convince the jury. It had not mattered that Jessie's lawyer, Dan Stidham, had argued that the boy's mixed-up statements constituted a "false confession." The term was relatively new at the time, and though Stidham presented a reputable expert to testify that people do sometimes confess to crimes they did not commit, the jury found that hard to believe.

43 T.J. Williams, interviewed at his home in Corning, Mar. 24, 2012. The population of Corning, about an hour and a half north of West Memphis, is about thirty four hundred and ninety seven percent white. Williams grew up there and did factory work. He described himself as a "sports nut" who, though not religious, believed in his "own little way." Before the trial, he said he'd seen news of the murders on CNN and heard "gossip" at his factory about "all the boys being sexually abused, Satanic worship and stuff." The

murders occurred on his daughter's fifth birthday and his two sons were younger. Williams said the fact that the victims were children had "no effect" on him, though he did worry before the arrests, "Could they [the killers] be coming here to Corning?" This was Williams' third time on a jury and he took the role seriously. "Oh, my gosh," he said, "you've got somebody's life in your hands. You don't look forward to doing anything like that, but I wouldn't try to get out of it, either." He said the duty was stressful and that he was nervous going into it, "because it's such a big thing." As the jury was being selected, he said he realized that he had "an advantage because all I watch is sports." Most of what he'd heard of the case had come "just from people talking." He said he knew most of the other jurors. "We all came from the same cut," he said. "Most of us went to school together." What follows are other excerpts from the interview, arranged by topic. On Burnett: "I'd say he was stern, pretty much my-way-or-no-way." On Jessie's attorney, Dan Stidham: "He was doing the best he could, but he didn't have much to work with; it looked like he was new at it." On Prosecutor Davis: "He kinda scared me because he was really hard and direct. He looked right at you. He wasn't messing around. He knew his job. He got to the point. He didn't walk around it." On Fogleman: "He was very charismatic. You liked him right away. A lot of times when he was talking to the jury, it felt like he was talking to me. He made a lot of eye-contact and I liked that. Between him and Davis, I got the feeling that he was in charge. He did most of the talking to us, and he did most of the questioning." On Jessie: "Seeing Jessie brought in with his bullet-proof vest, all shackled up, like you see on TV, and here it was in real life, it was a thrill. Jessie's lawyer kept saying Jessie was mentally challenged . . . but he said he knew the difference between right and wrong. [Jessie's age] did not really matter. You know right from wrong. You know when you're doing something wrong when you're four years old or younger. You're taught it. Yeah, he was slow, probably not as smart as everybody else, but he did know. To me, the doctor saying he knew right from wrong was what mattered most. I would have liked to see him get up there [to testify]. I'm not saying it would have changed anything, but it might have. [Seeing Jessie at the defense table] keeping his head down made me feel like he was ashamed. He didn't want to be there no more. There were a few times, when they were talking about specific stuff, he looked like, if he could have, he would have crawled under the table." On his alibi: "I felt a lot of people were lying about where he was at and stuff. His alibi had him in all these places at the same time, and towards the end of the trial, his side had all these people saying he was wrestling. The last guy the prosecutor brought in was the guy who rented the ring, and it was the week before [that Jessie had been there], and he had the receipt. And, like the next day, he got a call from his company that he was being transferred. That was one reason he remembered the date." On having the victims' bikes in the courtroom: "They didn't matter to me, but it was kind of an eerie thing, seeing them sitting there in the room with us." On the sticks prosecutors introduced as possible murder weapons: "I didn't pay them much mind, because they said they didn't know if this was the murder weapon or not, I thought, 'Then why are they here?'" On photos of the victims: "Some of us were looking at the photos of the little boys. They bothered me because they're pretty gruesome. There was a few of the ladies that just didn't want to look at them." On the unrecorded parts of Jessie's police interview: "There's a lot of times police will take you in for questioning that they don't know what they've got. To me that explains the time between the time they brought him in and time they started recording everything. [As to the gap between recorded parts,] I can't explain it. I don't understand it." On Stidham's argument that Jessie's statements were coerced: "I never considered that the police may have told him what to say. But, even listening to the tapes, you can hear where there were times when they said, 'Don't you mean...?'" On how Jessie changed the times when he said the murders occurred: "I didn't disregard that he got the time wrong, but I also took it that he was trying to put himself far away from it anyway, like he was watching it and not involved, because he knew it was wrong." On Jessie's mistakes about the boys' ligatures: "I remember looking at the shoestrings myself. I took them out of the bag and put them on the table. I just told myself that he was calling the shoestrings rope. And the shoestrings were dirty. They were underwater in mud, so they looked brown, of course." On what Jessie knew: "Everybody thought all three had been mutilated or castrated. But he knew it was just one. Even if he got the wrong one, that wasn't common knowledge to everybody. And he said he chased down one boy. That was important to me. His confession was the biggest thing, but there were those little things too." On the jury's votes: "When we took our first vote, it was seven to five 'guilty,' and then, before we went home that night, it was eight to four. We listened to the tapes two or three times in deliberation—hearing the tapes and following along on the transcripts. The hold-outs were mostly on the coercion factor. I felt like they were reading that into it. When we finally broke for the night, I went home and was thinking and thinking about it. That's why, the next morning, I asked them to not read and just listen. They agreed. So we pushed transcripts aside and listened to the tapes, like we were in the room with them. A few just closed their eyes. A few put their heads down on the table. Nobody made a sound. We just played the tapes, and we took a vote right after that. It was twelve to nothing." On why they acquitted Jessie of capital murder: "He helped, but he didn't do the actual killing." On Stidham's claim that while the jurors were deliberating, Burnett opened the door and asked if they wanted him to order lunch; that they 'said no, because they were about finished; that Burnett responded, "Well, you're going to have to come back for sentencing anyway, so I'm going to go ahead and order some food;" after which the foreman asked Burnett, "Well, what if we're going to vote not guilty?": Williams reported, "Yeah, I'm going to say that happened." On whether it affected the jury's vote: "Oh, no, no, no. I'm pretty sure we had already made up our minds by then." On how he felt afterwards: "I felt like a burden was lifted off my shoulders. You've got his life in your hands. It was a horrible thing to have to go through. I can't imagine what it was for those parents to go through. It was hard. I'll say this, from what I was shown as evidence, I got it right. We did what we thought was right, from what we had. All twelve of us did."

44 Ironically, the opportunity to present Jessie with the possibility of receiving a term of years, despite the jury's having sentenced him to life in prison, arose from a reading of Arkansas law intended to grant judges special powers of fairness, not for use by prosecutors seeking to negotiate for testimony in a future trial from a person who has already been sentenced. In arguing the fairness of Arkansas's process for administering the death penalty, Chief Justice John A. Fogleman wrote, in the pivotal 1977 Collins case, "The trial judge is not required to impose the death penalty in every case in which the jury verdict prescribes it." He then quoted the state statute that reads, "The court shall have power, in all cases of conviction, to reduce the extent or duration of the punishment assessed by a jury, if, in the opinion of the court, the conviction is proper and the punishment assessed is greater than under the circumstances of the case, ought to be inflicted."

45 Cureton said: "When they realized they didn't have any evidence, Davis called me and asked me if I had a file on Michael Carson. I said, 'I have a file on every kid who's walked through that back door.' He asked me to pull it and said, 'It would sure help if there's something in there about him and Jason playing cards.' I knew exactly what he was

saying. 'If it's not there, put it in.' I cannot remember any time those two were together. When I took it to his office and he looked at the file he slammed it on the desk and said, 'there's not a damn thing in here that can help us.'"

46   Arkansas's Second Judicial District, where Jason was about to go on trial, had a rich history of offering citizens stark—and often ugly—choices. The district lies in east Arkansas, alongside a large piece of the Mississippi River. Its soil is deep and fertile, and fortunes have been made from it. Yet this region, including Crittenden County, ranks among the poorest in the nation. About a fourth of the population lives below the poverty line, more than a third of all children do, and fewer than fifteen percent of adults have a college degree. For many, lives spent facing "impossible situations" have been the norm. Before the Civil War, vast plantations ran on the sweat of African slaves. But even after the slaves were freed, the social structure remained largely unchanged, with large farms in the delta operating on the sweat of freedmen who now worked as tenant farmers and sharecroppers. There were many of them—and they could vote. Within twenty years after passage of the fifteenth Amendment, black men in Crittenden County held the positions of judge, county clerk, assessor and representative in the state legislature. But the white ruling establishment put an end to that. In the February 7, 2008 issue of the *Arkansas Times*, writer Grif Stockley related Crittenden County historian Marion Woolfolk's account of African-American officials being rounded up and run out of the county: "A group of about eighty whites assembled at Marion about 10 a.m. July, 13, 1888, and marched to the courthouse where David Ferguson [the county clerk] was forced to resign at the muzzle of a Winchester rifle and afterwards was escorted to the 3:30 p.m. train." The other black office holders were similarly herded onto a boat to Memphis, where they were released. The office-holders' appeal to the governor of Arkansas was rejected, and for the next one hundred years, no blacks held public office

in Crittenden County. Poor whites in the region fared only marginally better than blacks. After the disastrous Mississippi River Flood of 1927, which was followed by a devastating drought and then the Great Depression, approximately two-thirds of Arkansas's independent farmers lost their farms and fell into tenancy, a form of lease arrangement whereby a tenant rents, for cash or a share of crops, farm property from a landowner. Many whites, including the parents of the late singer Johnny Cash, joined African-Americans working the fields of the wealthy. But tenancy was widely abused, forcing many workers into a condition of virtual servitude. The Southern Tenant Farmers Union, which was founded in eastern Arkansas in 1934, became one of the first integrated unions in the United States. Racial prejudice in the region remained strong, but the sharpest social divide was—and has remained—economic. Power was exercised with a vengeance, mainly against blacks, but also against poor whites. As late as December 7, 1936, Time magazine ran an article titled "Slavery in Arkansas." It described a private prison farm being run by a deputy sheriff in Crittenden County who used the forced labor of local black men who had been tried and convicted of "vagrancy." During that era, the Ku Klux Klan rode at night, terrorizing black citizens and sometimes lynching them. White people who defended blacks were threatened or run off. Justice ran on a double standard. Julian Fogleman, the father of the man about to take Damien and Jason to trial, was the city attorney in 1954, when the body of Isadore Banks, a relatively wealthy African-American man, was found tied to a tree and burned just outside Marion. Julian's brother John A. Fogleman, who later became chief justice of the Arkansas Supreme Court, was an assistant prosecuting attorney at the time, but Banks's murder was never investigated. Years later, when Julian Fogleman was asked about the lack of investigation, he responded vaguely, "There was some community discussion about who might've done it, but I never heard any suggestion of any name." When

asked how he felt about the murder going unsolved, Julian
Fogleman responded, "I don't know what I think." Nine years
after the murder of Banks, Julian Fogleman was an assistant
prosecuting attorney when a white woman drove down a
street in Marion crying for help and saying that she had seen
a Negro try to rape her eight-year-old daughter. According
to a July 19, 1963 Associate Press report, a mob of white
men, including six deputy sheriffs, assembled and chased a
young black man, Andrew Lee Anderson, into a soybean field.
While running, Anderson, who was unarmed, was shot in the
back of his leg. He died in the field two hours later from loss
of blood. A coroner's jury of nineteen white men took just
twenty minutes to rule that his death was justifiable homicide,
based on an Arkansas law that gave private citizens or officers
the right to attempt to capture a felon. When questioned
about the lack of investigation in that killing, Julian Fogleman
told a reporter, "We don't think the decision was wrong and
don't plan to go any further with it." The killings of Isadore
Banks and Andrew Lee Anderson are among one hundred
eight priority cases identified by the Federal Bureau of
Investigation's Civil Rights Cold Case Initiative, which was
established in 2006. When I began researching the region for
a book about the case, a veteran attorney in the district told
me, "If you're black, you have to pay dues to live here. If you're
white, you can do whatever you want"; "local police have
become an enormous political power in their own right;" that
"people who have money buy their freedom:" that "courage is
a high-priced commodity"; and "that's just the way it is."

47   The legality of the first samples was debated at a pretrial
hearing on Aug. 4, 1993. Jason's attorney, Robin Wadley,
argued that the samples taken upon Jason's arrest were
"illegally obtained," although he did not state the fault at issue.
Burnett ordered that new samples be taken after hearing
from Fogleman. Referring to Fogleman, the judge said,
"apparently he's telling me there is trace evidence that they
[the prosecutors] need to make comparisons on all of those

items." Burnett asked Fogleman, "Is that what you're telling the court?" Fogleman answered: "That's correct, your Honor."

48 The circumstances of Jessie's post-conviction statement of Feb. 17, 1994, (http://callahan.8k.com/wm3/img/j_misskelleyfeb.html) prompted Jessie's attorney, Dan Stidham, to file a motion asking that the prosecutors be held in contempt of court and punished accordingly. The motion, (http://callahan.8k.com/pdf/jm_motion_2_22_94.pdf) was denied.

49 Fogleman's opening statement: http://callahan.8k.com/wm3/ebtrial/stateope.html.

50 Cureton said that when video of Carson's testimony was shown on television at the detention center, "There were some black kids in there, and when Carson was on , they went ape. They said, 'He's a'lying, Ms. Joyce, he's a'lyin.' They said, 'Get him.' They would have torn him apart, had they [deputies] brought him back to the jail." She added that she understood Carson was "facing several years," but that after she took his file to Davis, "I never saw it again, and the prosecutor is the only person who can do away with a juvenile's file."

51 The comment remained unknown for years. It was not caught until the producers of Paradise Lost allowed supporters to post the entire audio files from both trials online. http://callahan.8k.com/wm3/audio/eb/html/eb_j_driver.html

52 Testimony of Det. Bryn Ridge, Mar. 7, 1994, http://callahan.8k.com/wm3/ebtrial/bridge_march7.html.

53 Griffis said he received his Ph.D. in 1984 from Columbia Pacific University, an unaccredited, nontraditional, distance-learning school that operated legally in California for twelve years. Griffis testified that he took no classes to obtain the degree. In a 1997 lawsuit to compel closure of the school, a California deputy attorney general called CPU "a consumer fraud" and "a complete scam." The California Supreme Court ordered CPU closed in 2000.

54 The proffered documents: http://callahan.8k.com/wm3/img/states_exhibit_300.html

55 Jason could have insisted that he be allowed to testify, but that would have required him to overrule his counsel—something he did not feel competent to do.

56 No record in the case of the West Memphis Three better illustrates the difficulty the state faced in articulating a coherent theory of the murders than Fogleman's closing argument. http://callahan.8k.com/wm3/ebtrial/closefogleman.html.

57 Grinnell acknowledged that at the time of the trial, her "nerves were really shot." She said she wanted to testify "about Jason being at home in bed that night," and that "Ford could have encouraged me to testify, but he discouraged me."

58 Cureton said that Ford asked her to testify as a character witness for Jason between the guilt and sentencing phases; that, on Friday night at the end of the trial, he asked if she would testify that Jason "caused no problems with any of the staff or the other kids;" that she'd responded that the question "put her in a spot;" that Ford said, "Because you're afraid of losing your job;" that she responded, "You said that;" that Ford's remark was, nevertheless, true because she had an invalid husband to support and she knew that the sheriff, her boss, did not want her to testify; that Ford could have avoided the problem if he'd subpoenaed her, but "he had not suggested it, and now it was too late"; that during the night, the sheriff became concerned that she might be called to testify and told her, "They're probably getting a subpoena right now;" that he told her, "I want you in that car and out of the county," and that she had obeyed.

59 There was at least one person in court that day who shared Jason's disbelief. Marie South was attending Arkansas State University in Jonesboro at the time of the trials. Her class schedule allowed her to attend only the sentencing phase of Jason and Damien's trial. In an email interview in 2011, she wrote: "I grew up in a small town much like West Memphis/Marion. My family was poor, like the families of the WM3, so I was able to put myself in their shoes, so to speak. I knew

how it felt to grow up in a small town and face some of the same ridicule for being different or dressing differently." By the time of the trials, she said, "I thought the Satanic panic was most unfortunate because no one cared to delve more deeply into it. Once the theory was accepted, it appeared that the police were no longer considering anything else about it."

60 The women with Cureton were Sue Weaver and Patty Burcham.

61 As a reporter, I have entered many prisons. Even knowing that I will be able to leave, entering is an unnerving experience. Metal bangs against metal. Concrete floors and concrete-block walls distort and exaggerate sounds. Except for wardens and secretaries, everyone wears a uniform. White-suited inmates move all around, working under close supervision. Posted rules and warnings substitute for art on the walls. Iron-barred gates click open at the sound of an electronic switch. Cameras relay images to control rooms. An impersonal, militaristic brusqueness seems the professional norm. Every gesture, structure and sound presents itself as necessitated by security— and yet, perhaps because security is so emphasized, the feeling conveyed is one more of fear than of control.

62 In a letter dated Dec. 10, 2001, Jason reported: "I never saw that guy again, but I learned how to handle guys like him, and I ran into many of them during my stay in prison. God watched out for me and nothing bad like that ever happened."

63 Caleb Smith, an associate professor of English at Yale University, writes eloquently about this concept in his book, *The Prison and the American Imagination* (Yale Studies in English), 2009. From the blurb on Amazon.com: "Exploring legal, political, and literary texts—including the works of Dickinson, Melville, and Emerson—Smith shows how alienation and self-reliance, social death and spiritual rebirth, torture and penitence came together in the prison, a scene for the portrayal of both gothic nightmares and romantic dreams. Demonstrating how the "cellular soul" has endured since the antebellum age, *The Prison and the American Imagination* offers a passionate and haunting critique of the very idea

of solitude in American life." http://www.amazon.com/
Prison-American-Imagination-Studies-English-ebook/dp/
B002RDDZXM/ref=sr_1_1?s=books&ie=UTF8&qid=139793
7057&sr=1-1&keywords=prison+american+imagination

64 The correspondence between the girl and Jason would
continue throughout his life in prison. He elected to exclude
details about that and other relationships with girlfriends
from the story told in this book.

65 The 1980 film is a fictionalized version of the 1969 book,
Accomplices to the Crime: The Arkansas Prison Scandal by
Tom Murton and Joe Hyams, detailing Murton's uncovering
of extortion and torture of inmates at Arkansas's two prison
farms, the Cummins and Tucker units.

66 A sally port is a secure, controlled entryway, usually at a
military fortification, courthouse or prison. The word *port*
is ultimately from the Latin word *porta* for door. The word
sally is derived from a defensive military maneuver. While
the term sally port has nautical references, on land the term
has described a door in a castle or city wall that allows secure
entrance and exit by the use of a series of two locked doors.
In modern court buildings, a sally port secures the prisoners
in a holding area or brings them directly from the jail area
separating them from the court, with entry through the sally
port controlled by the bailiff. In modern prisons, passages
between corridors are usually controlled by a sally port that is
operated electronically by a guard.

67 While Jason was working in the fields around Varner, I drove
to the prison where Arkansas's death row was housed for
my first interview with one of the convicted teens. ("Witch
on Death Row," *Arkansas Times*, June 23, 1994. http://www.
arktimes.com/arkansas/witch-on-death-row/Content?oid=1
886149&storyPage=7) Damien and I were separated by glass,
as is typical for visits with death row inmates. He told me
about his early life, his religious views, and that Jason was his
only close friend. About the police, prosecutors and jury, he
said: "They wanted a monster. It was such a horrible crime;

they couldn't imagine who could do a thing like that. They looked at us and they thought, 'These cold, heartless little creeps—they could have done it.' They wanted a monster, and they don't want to hear now that an innocent person has been sentenced to death."

68   A couple of years later, the Arkansas Legislature passed a law requiring inmates who lacked a high school diploma to work towards obtaining a GED.

69   In October 1994, five months after Jason's assignment to Varner, I drove to the West Memphis Police Department for my first look at files from the case. In November, after several days there, I wrote a column subtitled "Grasping for something solid." Obviously, I had not found it. "The trials were supposed to haul the crime into the sunshine of reason, where, presumably, its demonic nature would wither like a vampire," I wrote. "But the trials were themselves full of shadow, innuendos, and dark, unexplored corridors. They failed to either expose or explain the crime. Or so it seemed to me."

70   The Varner Unit was now headed by Warden Terry Campbell, who had been demoted and moved there from the state's Maximum Security Unit, where Damien Echols was held, after Campbell spoke out about corruption and lack of security at that unit. Campbell sued the Arkansas Department of Correction and, in August 1998, the U.S. Eighth Circuit Court of Appeal ruled in his favor. http://caselaw.findlaw.com/us-8th-circuit/1350268.html

71   Getting a disciplinary in prison is like getting charged with a crime. A formal charge is written and a hearing set. The person charged may call witnesses or enter other evidence. Only two pleas are allowed: guilty and not guilty. Appeals are allowed. If a guilty plea is made or sustained, punishments may include time in punitive detention, loss of privileges and reduction in class.

72   Contraband—that can range from glasses to cell phones and drugs—is common in prisons, despite the illusion of

security presented by concrete block buildings, chain link fences and razor-edged accordion wire. Years before I began writing about the West Memphis case, I broke a story about a death-row inmate, Mark Gardner, who had managed to get a faux leather recliner installed in his cell. The *Arkansas Times* published photos to support the account—photos that had been taken by another prisoner with a contraband Polaroid camera during a "party" that Gardner was hosting in his cell. The violations were possible because of bribes being paid to the warden, who had a gambling problem. When the warden did something that earned Gardner's displeasure, Gardner provided me with the photos, resulting in the warden's removal.

73   The politics of capital punishment were harsh and getting harsher when Damien entered death row. In 1994, President Clinton signed the Violent Crime Control and Law Enforcement Act that expanded the federal death penalty to some sixty crimes. Three of those—espionage, treason, and drug trafficking in large amounts—did not involve murder. Two years later, in response to the Oklahoma City Bombing, President Clinton signed the Anti-Terrorism and Effective Death Penalty Act of 1996. The Act, which affected both state and federal prisoners, restricted review in federal courts by establishing tighter filing deadlines, limiting the opportunity for evidentiary hearings, and ordinarily allowing only a single *habeas corpus* filing in federal court.

74   In the opinion delivered Dec. 23, 1996, Justice Robert Dudley wrote, "Baldwin argues that the occult evidence should not have been admitted because there was "little if any" evidence to link him to such activity, and the only reason for it to be admitted against him was to inflame the jury. Prior to trial, Baldwin filed a motion in limine to prevent the State from eliciting testimony that the crimes were occult-related without first conducting an *in camera* hearing to determine that there was a sufficient basis to find that he was involved in such activities and that the activities were a motive in the

homicides. The trial court granted the motion "until such time as the Court is convinced in an *in camera* proceeding that there is competent evidence that [Baldwin] was involved in occult and/or occultic type activities and/or that this crime is indicative of a ritualistic occult killing." The trial court subsequently found that Michael Carson's testimony that Baldwin told him he had dismembered one of the boys, sucked the blood from his penis and scrotum, and put the testicles in his mouth was evidence by which a jury could conclude that he was involved in occultic-type activities. From the *in camera* testimony of Dr. Dale Griffis, an expert on ritual killings, there was evidence by which a jury could find that the crimes were a ritual killing. Dr. Griffis stated that one of the facts that led him to believe that the killings were cult-related was that Christopher Byers was castrated and had had the blood sucked from his penis. Thus, there was sufficient evidence of Baldwin's participation in occult activities, and the trial court correctly allowed the evidence." Dudley, who is now retired, declined a request to be interviewed for this book. http://opinions.aoc.arkansas.gov/weblink8/0/doc/198989/Electronic.aspx

75 In July 1997, while Jason was at Varner, Wadley was reprimanded by the state Supreme Court. He was disbarred in 2001.

76 *Black's Law Dictionary* defines a petition as, "A written address, embodying an application or prayer from the person or persons preferring it, to the power, body, or person to whom it is presented, for the exercise of his or their authority in the redress of some wrong."

77 Asked later about the significance of Jason's Rule 37 petition, Stidham said that, had it not been submitted, "He wouldn't have had all the issues available to him that he ended up having. It would have been bad. Those procedural doors are hard to get through." He added, "I was there the day of or the day before the deadline. I said, 'Sign here,'" and he did. I'm not sure I would have done it, seeing Misskelley's lawyer

come through the door. But he signed. He didn't have anyone to talk to from a legal perspective. After meeting Jason, I became more concerned about him than about Jessie or Damien, because I knew that, one way or another, they would be represented."

78 Sauls became the group's unofficial spokesman, articulating the website's purpose and explaining intricacies of the case. Whatever people thought about the West Memphis case after seeing the documentary, few could understand why anyone would commit so much time, energy and money to the seemingly hopeless task of trying to free three convicted killers in Arkansas. For each of the four, the answer was personal. For example, Sauls explained that he had grown up in Florida. "While I was watching the film for the first time, I went from thinking that they must be guilty, and that there were likely things that hadn't been shown in the film that proved it, to thinking that they might have been victims of the witch-hunt mentality I grew up around—one of going to a Baptist Christian school and seeing how some of the ideas behind religion can be subverted in a way that justifies hatred." Even as a little kid," Sauls said, "I felt like I understood that people were taking these vague ideas from Bible verses and interpreting them however they wanted— sometimes in convoluted ways—just to make them feel righteous and 'correct' about whatever ignorant and hateful habits they had." Bakken, whose childhood was spent in Kentucky and Georgia, had a similar reaction. She saw in *Paradise Lost* a Southern-Gothic tale of "blood lust based on fear-based religion." She saw the prosecutors' use of Damien's interest in Wicca as both familiar and frightening. "For anyone who's artistic and trying to find their way, it's really hard, living in that kind of atmosphere." From what she saw in the film, the case against Damien "looked like a Christian-based persecution of someone who was not Christian. And then, also, there were all those little things, like 'where's the evidence?'" Sauls, who'd met Bakken in

Georgia, also viewed the prosecution as an unsupported attack on imagination, intellectual curiosity, and creativity. "I grew up in a family that encouraged creativity," he said, "but then when I stepped out of my home, the part of the Bible belt I lived in was suspicious of creativity and art and music. If they didn't immediately understand it, they used those religious terms to tear it all down. Music they didn't like became "devil music," and they were burning records at tent revivals. I believe the guy who originated the big record burnings of the 1970s and early '80s, Reverend [Charles] Boykin, was from Tallahassee where I grew up, so the idea that musicians were using music to 'possess' teenagers was a pretty big deal with a lot of people around that area." (Sauls provided this link, http://myq105.cbslocal. com/2011/12/06/rock-flashback-tallahassee-roasts-the-rolling-stones-1975/, to an article looking back at those times, which included the minister's claim that out of a thousand girls giving birth out of wedlock, nine hundred eighty-four were listening to rock music when they got pregnant, plus a video from 1967 of the Rolling Stones performing "Let's Spend the Night Together.") Like many who would become supporters of WM3.org, Sauls saw the prosecutions of all three teenagers as an abuse of something he deemed precious. "Despite all these claims that movies, music and art in general were tools of Satan to steal the souls of young people and turn them into Communists or Satanists," he said, "what confused me was how much I loved music, movies and art. I was in love with comic books and monster movies and science fiction and music—all those things that were allegedly leading me to Hell. I couldn't get past how amazing and inspiring and beautiful a lot of it was, and how good it made me feel to be in the presence of real creative genius." For example, "How could something as great as Led Zeppelin be the work of some magical entity who wanted my soul to burn for eternity in Hell? How could the great comic book artists like Steve

Ditko and Jack Kirby, whose work was so full of energy and fun, be a trick by Satan to lure me into taking drugs or worshipping Satan? It never made sense to me, especially considering the fact that my father was a brilliant artist who treasured art and music, too." Sauls said he realized "pretty young" that the zealots were "simply wrong." He and Bakken escaped that environment by moving across the country to Los Angeles. But in *Paradise Lost*, they saw kids who reminded them of themselves on trial for their lives. "It was pretty clear to me what kind of kids Damien and Jason were," Sauls later said. "Jessie wasn't quite as familiar to me, but it was pretty clear that he was the kind of kid who would be easy to coerce—someone that floundering police officers would probably be thrilled to question because he'd be so easy and agreeable. Damien and Jason, however, were a lot like the kids I hung around with in high school. We were all into art and drawing and music, as well as horror movies and Stephen King books." Seeing themselves in Jason and Damien made their trial—and Jessie's—personal. "These were kids who under different circumstances (and perhaps in a different part of the country) might have grown up to be artists or musicians or even life-long fans of movies and music and horror novels," Sauls said. "But because of the influence of these religious ideas that had been subverted into hatred protocols, they were being sent to prison. They were being used as scapegoats to compensate for inept police work and a shoddy investigation of a triple child homicide. The people they were being judged by were calling them 'devil worshippers' and 'Satanic,' without even really knowing what they meant by it." To him, however, "The truth was obvious: they were creative kids who enjoyed things that other people considered 'weird.' And in some areas, 'weird' is a bad and often dangerous word." Sauls, Pashley, Bakken and Fancher all made many trips to Arkansas, to attend hearings and to keep in touch with the men in prison. Fancher recalled, "It was a lot of fun going to the hearings and meeting supporters from all over the world." On the down-side, she remembered the difficulty of saying "goodbye" after visits to the prisons. Pashley took photographs that went onto the website and appeared around the world. For Fancher, the prisoners "became family" in a way. "Even at my broke-est," she said, "I just charged the plane fare and expenses to Arkansas on credit cards because it's only money—I had to show the courts that I was going to stand up for them no matter what kind of crap we knew Judge Burnett would throw our way." She wrote, "We were four or five (including Brent Turvey) and then we became thousands!"

79 The Tennessee dentist is Dr. Mark Cowart of Chattanooga; the Oklahoma woman, Jennifer Nickell of Norman; and the Danish man, Christian Hansen.

80 The tape-recorded, post-trial confession referred to here was one that Jessie made during questioning by Davis on the night of Feb. 17, 1994, after his own trial and shortly before Damien and Jason's trial, at which he had refused to testify. (http://callahan.8k.com/wm3/jmfeb.html) Jessie's attorney, Dan Stidham, who was not informed that his client was to be questioned, was furious when he learned of the interview. In a hearing on Feb. 22, Stidham argued that state officials had no right to remove Jessie from prison for any reason, much less to interrogate him in a prosecutor's office. He charged that the questioning constituted prosecutorial misconduct and insisted that the court investigate, but Judge Burnett refused.

81 "Two HBO Films Examine Darker Aspects of Mid-South," by Tom Walter, *The Commercial Appeal*, Jan. 22, 1996.

82 Driver stole more than a bag of chips and candy. In 2000, he pleaded no-contest to a charge of theft after a state audit revealed he'd written $27,400 in unauthorized checks on a county fund. In September 2000, Judge Burnett ordered Driver to repay the stolen money in monthly installments of $241. Driver, sixty by then, was not sentenced to time in jail. "Ex-Crittenden Official to Pay Up," by Bartholomew

Sullivan, *The Commercial Appeal*, Sept. 27, 2000. http://westmemphisthreediscussion.yuku.com/topic/2780#.UziBSxZCjR0

83 Though a number of drugs were identified in Melissa Byers' body, the Arkansas Medical Examiner's report listed both the cause and manner of her death "unknown." In 2012, the sheriff of Sharp County where she died denied my request to see the investigative reports on her death, claiming that an investigation into it remained "open."

84 Fogleman's claim that there was "no soul" in Damien has literary precedent. In his 1942 novel, *The Stranger*, Albert Camus described the murder trial of a man known only as Meursault. At one point, the prosecutor said he had peered into Meursault's soul "and found nothing." The prosecutor then urged that Meursault be beheaded on the grounds that such a person had no access to humanity or morality, and thus did not belong in society.

85 Governments have used private prisons for centuries, but the explosive growth of prison populations in the 1980s that resulted from the War on Drugs led many states, especially in the South and West, to turn to the private sector to build and operate prisons. Private prisons have since become a huge business in the U.S. By 2000, when Jason was in Grimes, corporations ran more than one hundred private correctional facilities in the country, holding more than one hundred thousand prisoners. In 2002, a Danish company bought Wackenhut, the company that operated Grimes, for five hundred seventy million.

86 I began writing to Jason in 1999, soon after his arrival at Grimes. By then, he had already spent five years in prison; my first book, *The Boys on the Tracks*, was about to be published; and I was preparing to write my next book, *Devil's Knot*, about the West Memphis case. All three of the convicted men accepted my requests to let me interview them. Jason did so by inviting me to visit at his "humble estate." During the years that followed, I wrote to and visited with Damien and

Jessie several times. But my most sustained communication developed with Jason. Early on, he wrote a few lines that I thought captured both his personality and his predicament. "In case you haven't noticed already," he wrote shortly after we'd met, "I am a very hopeful and optimistic person and I don't give up easily. Especially when my life is involved! It's been long and hard, and I still don't really have a strong sense or grasp on what it is actually that Damien, Jessie and I are up against . . ." I couldn't grasp that, either, which is why, while Jason coped with prison, I directed my liberty at trying to unravel the twists and turns of a legal case that had, on one hand, outraged so many non-lawyers while winning, on the other, unmitigated approval from my state's judiciary.

87   Val Price, Damien's trial lawyer, testified at the Rule 37 hearing that he and co-counsel Scott Davidson had contracted with HBO for three interviews at $2,500 each and that it was his view that HBO still owed them $2,500. *The Commercial Appeal* newspaper reported on June 11, 1998 that filmmaker Bruce Sinofsky "admitted he paid at least $37,000 to the families of the three murder victims and to three defendants." Though the exact amount paid was not mentioned during the Rule 37 hearing, the fact that money was paid was discussed. "It comes across like checkbook journalism, which is not the case," Sinofsky testified. "We did not buy their interviews." He said the money was not paid to gain access, but as a "humanitarian gesture."

88   In the U.S., indigent defendants are allowed a court-appointed attorney at trial, but not for appeals, except in death-penalty cases.

89   Jason's girlfriend reported this to me soon after it happened in a letter in which she also expressed concern for Jason's safety.

90   When I countered that Jason had grown up without good men around, he objected. "I did have a positive male role model. My grand-uncle Hubert. We'd have dinner with him. I'd cut his lawn. He was kind of crazy, but in a good way. He was fun. And my Uncle Allen, my mom's brother. He was

positive." He continued, "It's true that I didn't know my father well. But you can still find role models, even in popular culture, like on TV or in books. You can appreciate things as entertainment, but if you look closer, a lot of times you'll see that the authors are trying to convey things through their characters, things that are moral or inspirational." He said that growing up and even in prison, he'd found instruction and inspiration in G.I. Joe, ThunderCats, Ninja Turtles, Super Mario Bros., Gobots, Voltron, Smurfs and Transformers. "They're teaching you right from wrong and what to do in certain situations. Even if you're a latch-key kid, if you know where to look, you can find these guides. So pop culture is full of role models and stuff." But you had to use discernment, he said. "You wanted to be G.I. Joe, not Cobra."

91 The classes were offered in association with Arkansas State University at Jonesboro. Jason became good friends with the outside staff who came into the prison for both the high school and the college classes. Because he'd missed the higher-level math classes in high school, he started with algebra, followed by two accounting classes "just because they were being offered." He could have taken college-level correspondence courses, but, much as he wanted an education, he wanted only classes that were taught in person. After being burned by "Dr." Dale Griffis, the court-approved "expert" on the occult whose correspondence-school degree was thoroughly discredited, Jason said, "I didn't even want to approach that."

92 Like most judges in Arkansas, Burnett routinely denied Rule 37 petitions. Prisoners have the right to appeal those denials to the state Supreme Court. That court routinely affirms the lower court's rulings. But twice in 1999, the Arkansas Supreme Court reversed Burnett on Rule 37 petitions because he did not justify them with the required written "finding of facts." On September 16, 1999, the high court ruled in a cases titled Coleman v. State and Dulaney v. State that, while Burnett had presented some findings, they were "conclusory"

and did not reflect how the trial court applied the standard for ineffective assistance of counsel claims," as required by law. In denying Damien's Rule 37 petition, Burnett wrote simply that "The petitioner has failed to prove a valid claim of actual innocence or to demonstrate incompetence of counsel." He said that many of the issues raised by the new team of lawyers constituted nothing more than second-guessing Damien's trial lawyers' strategy.

93 Ware also wrote in her eight-page letter: "You were observed more than you know, because I was impressed with you and the way you didn't have as many opportunities as some of the other students, but you pulled yourself up and made yourself something good." Regarding Jessie Misskelley: "Jessie has claustrophobia. His Special Education teacher used to let him do his lessons in the doorway or outside. This was never written up because he was being accommodated for it. So this was never brought up in court either. Jessie would have confessed to anything to get out of the interrogation room. It is beyond me why anything he would say would be admissible in court." Regarding the murders: "You were in my class the day of the murders, during the time period Jessie first gave! And you were in my class the day after the murders." Regarding the man at the Bojangles' restaurant: "This is what I believe, and I'm giving you the account from facts I know about the case. On the night of the murders, a man went into the bathroom of the Bojangles' restaurant on Missouri Street. He was covered in mud and had blood on his face and arm. He was upset and the manager called the police. In the meantime, he left, and left mud and blood in the bathroom. The bodies of the three boys hadn't been found yet, and the police didn't see any reason to take samples from the bathroom. After the bodies were found the next day, the police went back to the restaurant and scraped samples of blood from the walls. But the sample was later lost. I never thought you'd be convicted. I was amazed and shocked. I thought the Bojangles' incident would be dealt with more

fully in court. I got a map of West Memphis and noticed that the bayou from Robin Hood Hills came out right behind the restaurant. It is interesting to note that the newspaper got the location of the bayou wrong. They showed it as the bayou that is much south of there, and doesn't connect to the restaurant. You know that bayou that runs near where Finishing Touch Frame Shop used to be, near Century 21 and the BBQ place on Missouri St. I don't know if the mistake was made by the police or the newspaper. If you were the police and had let a prime suspect in a murder case slip through your fingers, and on top of that, lost the evidence, wouldn't it be convenient if the information in the newspaper appeared insignificant? I drove to Bojangles' and looked behind it, but it [the bayou] was impressively close. The bayou from Robin Hood Hills comes out closest to this restaurant. Now, you know how many fast food places there are on Missouri St. Let's say you are a man upset, covered with mud and blood, and you've got to get to a restroom on Missouri St. If you are coming from the south, you would stop at one of the many fast food places south of Bojangles'. If you are coming from the west or the north, you are going to stop at MacDonald's or Krystal first. It wouldn't make any sense to cross a busy four-lane street or go further. That means the man had to have come from the east and the Robin Hood Hills area. Someone would have seen him if he had come from anyplace else. On the Sunday before the murders, it rained only .11 inch in the Memphis area. It didn't rain in Marion or West Memphis because I was at the art exhibit and remember. On Monday it didn't rain and on Tuesday it didn't rain. The bayou was the only place he could have gotten muddy that night. Here are the facts. You've got three little boys dead in a bayou, and you have a man with mud and blood on him, who obviously is too credible to be coincidental. It seems to me that an eight-year-old idiot could look at these facts and know the man had to be involved—if not the murderer, one of the murderers. I am amazed that this was not investigated further. Mistakes were made. I can't blame the judge or the prosecuting attorney. They are well-respected top-notch men and they were only doing their jobs." On Jason's situation: "You were railroaded. But I don't know what to do. I don't have any money or power either. I wish you could get a lawyer on the caliber of Johnny Cochran or F. Lee Bailey. But one would have to win the Powerball Lottery to be able to afford them." She concluded, "I believe that justice will come to light, and I believe that you will be released. But, like you, I just don't know when."

94   In March 2000, two reporters who had covered the West Memphis case extensively for *The Commercial Appeal* published their account of what happened under the title, *Blood of Innocents*. It was factually accurate, by and large, and seemed to share the official and widespread opinion that justice had been done. But aspects of the case struck me as absurd. I was troubled, for instance, by the courts' willingness to allow Jessie Misskelley to forfeit his right to have an attorney present when he was questioned by police—even though, at seventeen, he could not legally buy a pack of cigarettes, see an R-rated movie, or enter a legally binding contract without his parent's permission. As I wrote in the *Arkansas Times*, in an article about juvenile law, kids in Arkansas "cannot have their ears pierced without a parent present. Yet, if they get into trouble—trouble so serious that it could send them to prison for the rest of their lives—the protections disappear." After that article appeared, a reader forwarded to me the contents of an email exchange he'd had with an aide to Arkansas's governor, Mike Huckabee. My correspondent had asked the governor to "look into" the case of the West Memphis Three. Huckabee's liaison for criminal affairs had responded, "I do want to assure you that DNA testing was done, and that a match was found among the men convicted." The statement was patently false, but my calls to the governor's office for comment were not returned. In a similar vein, I often heard the case discussed in casual settings with great certainty. When I asked what evidence

anyone knew of that connected the three in prison to the murders, the responses became vague but no less confident. I heard endlessly, "There was evidence that the three were guilty that was never introduced at the trial." Those saying this were certain because someone in law, law enforcement, or politics had told them it was so. (No one seemed willing to question why evidence so crucial had not been introduced at the trials.) Meanwhile, Arkansas officials stood solid in their defense of the verdicts, dismissing those who criticized the police or the conduct of the trials, describing critics as out-of-staters who'd learned about the case from a movie and who "didn't know what really happened." That could not be said of Stidham, who continued to criticize the trials. Nor could it be said of Ron Lax, owner of Inquisitor, Inc., a private investigations company in Memphis, who had questioned the teenagers' arrests from the moment he'd learned of them in June 1993. Almost on the spot, Lax became the first person to volunteer to help the newly appointed defense teams, offering his services for free. The lawyers for Damien and Jessie had welcomed the help, but Jason's lawyers declined.

95 In that interview, which may be the only one Gitchell gave after leaving the department, he also said: "We treated Jessie and everyone else who was involved in this case as if they were our own kids. It's the law. You've got to. But we also knew the media was watching. We had to watch what we did because we knew we would be judged on it." "The fight to free the West Memphis 3" by Stephen Lemons, *Salon*, Aug. 10, 2000. http://www.salon.com/2000/08/10/echols/

96 In 2004, the PBS program Frontline reported that almost 95 percent of all cases resulting in felony convictions never reach a jury. They are settled through plea bargains in which the defendant agrees to plead guilty in exchanged for a reduced sentence. http://video.pbs.org/video/2216784391/

97 In the early 1990s, three Arkansas women formed a group called ARWAR—Arkansans Working Against Repression— as the first Arkansas base of support for the West Memphis

Three. Amanda Lamb, Wendy Crow and Mary Boley braved some hostility but mostly indifference to organize concerts, print information, and create a website calling attention to problems with the trials. Lannette Grate, a writing instructor at the University of Central Arkansas, subsequently became the first person I knew associated with a state institution who was willing to encourage her classes to critically examine the case.

98 *Hit List* magazine, April/May 2000.

99 That "crew" consisted of Danny Bland, the Supersuckers' manager, and Scott Parker, a Los Angeles record producer. Bland explained, "I personally have not committed an unselfish act in my life. Still, this has been about our own protection and everybody else's too. Look at the life I take for granted. I haven't done anything wrong, but if the police came to my house and started confiscating my books and music to be used against me in a trial, they would have a field day. Also, on a business level, most of the Supersuckers' audience is in their twenties to mid-thirties. You can't make a living selling music to kids and then turn your backs on them, and that's what I told these artists when I contacted them. I reminded them that these kids sitting in prison represent a lot of people. They support us. It's only right that we should give our support to them."

100 "Hear No Evil," *Arkansas Times*, April, 21, 2000.

101 John Doe observed, "The world is unfair, damn it, and we're here to try to keep it a little more fair in any small way we can. If there's anything you can do to stop that sort of injustice, you've got to be there. You've got to contribute."

102 Lycos Chat, May 15, 2000.

103 Bright and Philipsborn taught together at the annual California Death Penalty College. Burt, editor of the "California Death Penalty Manual," was one of the defense lawyers on the first Menendez brothers' case.

104 They recruited some from the San Francisco area: Tom Quinn to work on Jason's case and Nancy Pemberton

for Jessie. Theresa Gibbons would lead investigations for Damien. The lawyers asked Ron Lax in Memphis to rejoin the case, which he did.

105 In the preface to its book, *Strengthening Forensic Science in the United States: A Path Forward*, the National Academy of Sciences wrote in 2009, "The forensic science system, encompassing both research and practice, has serious problems that can only be addressed by a national commitment to overhaul the current structure that supports the forensic science community in this country." https://www.ncjrs.gov/pdffiles1/nij/grants/228091.pdf

106 Affidavit of Marc Scott Taylor, Nov. 6, 2000. http://callahan.8k.com/images/m_taylor/marc_taylor_1.jpg

107 The Yahoo announcement said: "Here's an intriguing site that details a controversial triple murder case in West Memphis, Arkansas. The site's creators contend that the men convicted of the gruesome crimes are the victims of an all-too-common hysteria known as 'Satanic Panic,' where the furor surrounding tragic events overcomes the judicial system's ability to keep things fair and square."

108 "Stars Crusade for Man on Death Row," *Cinema.com*, Sept. 11, 2000 http://cinema.com/news/item/333/stars-crusade-for-man-on-death-row.phtml

109 Documents obtained by the *Times* confirmed that, at about the time the inmates were contacting the paper about abuses, the Arkansas Department of Correction fined Wackenhut a total of seventeen thousand five hundred dollars for contract violations. The state's contract with Wackenhut required that at least eighteen critical security posts at the prison be staffed during the day, and sixteen at night. But guards said they'd run the prison with far fewer officers. "Tagliaboschi said he'd worked nights when only nine guards were on duty to supervise six hundred inmates." Haddigan's exposé presaged Arkansas's eventual decision to end the use of private prisons.

110 Jason laughed that, in trying to cheer him up, some people wrote things like, "Man, I thought I had it bad, but you've

really got it bad. You make me have to cheer up. Anyway, I hope you have a happy birthday."

111 The office of Arkansas Attorney General Mark Pryor argued against sending the case back to Burnett. Pryor, the son of a former governor and U.S. senator, would later himself become a U.S. senator.

112 This was at least the second time in less than two years that the state Supreme Court had chided Burnett for submitting orders that were "conclusory in nature," without providing reasons in support of his conclusions. In September 1999, the high court reversed and remanded a case from Burnett's court, noting that, "Unfortunately, the circuit court has failed to make sufficient written findings on the points raised in appellant's petition for post-conviction relief . . . We have held without exception that this rule is mandatory and requires written findings . . . We made it clear that the requirement of written findings of fact applies to any issue upon which a Rule 37 hearing is held."

113 Damien's attorneys had raised forty-six claims, or reasons, why the court should have granted a new trial on the basis of ineffective assistance of counsel. Burnett rejected each one. He wrote, for example, that Damien argued that his trial attorneys should have challenged Burnett's acceptance of Dale Griffis as an "expert" in the occult, in the belief that, had that happened, the court would have excluded that testimony. However, if that was Damien's belief, Burnett wrote, "He is mistaken. Indeed, whether such an objection could have succeeded at trial is doubtful at all, considering the Supreme Court's determination on direct appeal that the occult evidence went to show motive, which is broadly admissible."

114 By now Jason knew that the National Registry of Exonerations was tracking the number of people who were wrongly convicted of crimes and later cleared of all charges. http://www.law.umich.edu/special/exoneration/Pages/About-Us.aspx

115 Ulaby's report included an interview with the Supersuckers' Danny Bland, in which he explained why bands like his and L7 were part of "an increasingly high-profile movement" on behalf of the men in prison. "We all realize this could happen to any one of us," he said. "You know, if they rounded up half of the kids around here with black hair and who listen to Black Sabbath and wear black coats, you know, there'd be no one around here to work at Burger King." Ulaby noted that some stores refused to sell the benefit CD the Supersuckers produced "because of the controversial cause."

116 Supermax and Security Housing Unit (SHU) prisons are controversial. In 1996, a United Nations team assigned to investigate torture described SHU conditions as "inhuman and degrading." A 2011 New York Bar association comprehensive study http://www2.nycbar.org/pdf/report/uploads/20072165-TheBrutalityofSupermaxConfinement.pdf suggested that supermax prisons constitute "torture under international law" and "cruel and unusual punishment under the U.S. Constitution."

117 The Jaycee program has since been dropped from Arkansas prisons.

118 In 1977, when Jason was born, the U.S. had fewer than a half-million people in prison. By 2001, when he returned to Varner, the national population had quadrupled, to more than two million. Drug sentences accounted for most of that surge.

119 After having reported on the West Memphis case for years, I began writing *Devil's Knot* in 1998. I intended to focus it on the story of Damien and Lorri Davis, and received their written permission to do so. After the project was underway, they told me that their attorneys advised against their participation and that they wanted to be released from their commitments. I agreed and, deciding to write more in-depth about the case, I contacted Ron Lax, the private investigator who had amassed what I discovered were the best files then in existence. This was shortly after the Arkansas Supreme Court denied all three men's direct appeals, and no significant

legal work had begun on their behalf. Lax, who was highly offended by the way the men's cases were prosecuted, gave me access to his files in the hope that my reporting would cast more light on the story, expose conduct he considered disgraceful, and keep the case alive. When the book was released, a review in the *Toronto Globe* said *Devil's Knot* took readers inside a case that "has become a Gordian knot for U.S. justice and the nations' sense of its freedoms." Bartholomew Sullivan, who had co-authored *Blood of Innocents*, wrote in *The Commercial Appeal* that *Devil's Knot* now offered "the best blow-by-blow account available of the investigations and trials," a grace note if ever there was one. A reviewer for *Reason* magazine observed that *Devil's Knot* presented "a horrifying and infuriating look at how moral panics over youth culture can lead to the denial of justice," adding that the West Memphis case represented a "cautionary tale about the awesome and frequently careless power of law enforcement and the damage it can do when informed by ignorant moral panics and unchecked by rational individuals." The reviews were good, though some critics felt I had gone too far in pointing to John Mark Byers, the stepfather of Christopher Byers, as the prime suspect. Perhaps I did, but I remain convinced that police should have focused their attention, first and foremost, on him and the victims' other parents. Instead, the parents, step-parents, extended family members and neighbors were barely investigated at all. As I spoke about the case at bookstores around the state, I learned that many Arkansans who'd questioned the state's conduct of the trials had felt isolated in their opinions and overwhelmed by the certainty of those who supported the convictions. The manager of a bookstore in Jonesboro where I was once scheduled to appear told me that announcements of my book signing were taken down faster than staff could put them up. Supporter Marie South, who lived in Jonesboro and who had attended part of the second trial while in college, said she'd found it "unfortunate" that everyone she knew seemed to accept without question the state's theory of Satanism as a motive for the murders. Only after message boards and chat rooms appeared on the Internet did South learn that she was not alone. "When the three were convicted, I figured that was it," she told me. "I was stunned and touched when I found out that others were interested in the case."

120 This episode followed earlier investigations of area law enforcement, recounted in *Devil's Knot*, that were going on around the time of the murders. Martin Hill elucidated on those more thoroughly on his webisite: http://www.jivepuppi. com/west_memphis_confidential.html. Note that, according to news reports, Judge David Burnett was said to have been a recipient of the misappropriated evidence. Due to a decision at the time by prosecuting attorney Brent Davis, no one involved was charged with criminal activity.

121 As Sullivan explained, "The interstate turkey shoot has always been lucrative. Cops say that if you want to find drugs, stop the suspicious eastbound traffic. If you're looking for money, check for Texas or California plates heading home." He quoted narcotics detective James Sudbury's remark in his pre-termination interview with the mayor: "Our main objective has been to put money in the bank. And I was doing that as best I could." "Four accused of pocketing drug money," July 26, 2002 and "State wants drug inquiry wrapped up," July 27, 2002, Memphis *Commercial Appeal*.

122 The indictments named Barry A. Davis, a Crittenden County sheriff's deputy; Louis F. Pirani, a former deputy; E.A. 'Tony' Bradley, a former West Memphis police sergeant; and Joseph W. Applegate, who worked at times for both departments.

123 "The Real Story behind the Controversy," a research paper by Lindsey D. Fry, 2008.

124 At first, Hill was disturbed by discrepancies in the trials that he believed pointed to "the falsity of the evidence." For instance, he noted that, in Fogleman's summation of the case to the jury, the prosecutor claimed that wax on the victims' clothes matched wax that had been collected from Damien's

house. Yet Hill recalled that Fogleman had mentioned the alleged wax earlier in the trial, and that when Damien's lawyer challenged Fogleman to produce the crime lab analyst's report "—if there is one, regarding any candle wax," Fogleman had responded: "I don't know if there is one. She said that what she puts in her report is when there are matches. She claimed that didn't match anything."

125 "Identifying the source of critical details in confessions," *International Journal of Speech Language and the Law*, 10, no 1 (2003): The article's abstract reads: "Interrogations leading to confessions can elicit both an admission of guilt and details to help validate the confession. Using a novel means of analysis, the interrogation was treated as a series of dynamic informational exchanges and the source of key details was identified. Questions and answers were classified according to the degree to which they provided information. Using a test case, in two hundred twelve of three hundred forty questions the interrogators provided details to confirm or deny. In other questions, critical details were provided by the police without requesting confirmation. This pattern was reflected when the confession was divided into individual topics. None of the key, specific, verifiable details were provided by the confessor. This method of analysis is presented as a means of assessing the degree to which a confessor demonstrates guilty knowledge." https://www.equinoxpub.com/journals/index. php/IJSLL/article/view/563 Hill also noted that the few facts that Misskelley got correct—for example, that the boys had been severely beaten and that one's genitals were mutilated— had been reported as early as May 7 in both the Memphis and West Memphis newspapers and were common knowledge in the community. Other observations by Hill about the handling of Jessie's case can be found at: http://www.jivepuppi. com/case_for_innocence_misskelley.html

126 In the opinion delivered December 23, 1996, in which the Arkansas Supreme Court denied Damien's and Jason's direct appeals, Justice Robert H. Dudley wrote: "Both

Echols and Baldwin objected to the trial court giving the accomplice instruction. AMI Crim. 3d 401 (Accomplice). They contend that there was no testimony that placed them together on the day of the crime, and, since the jury was instructed to consider the evidence against each defendant separately, an accomplice instruction was precluded. The trial court correctly gave the instruction because there was evidence from which the jury could reasonably find that both defendants said they killed the children; fibers from clothing found in both defendants' homes were similar to fibers found on the victims' clothing; the description of the person identified as Domini Teer, who was seen with Echols the night of the murders, also fit the description of Baldwin, who was also very thin and had long hair; Echols and Baldwin were best friends and spent two or three hours together a day; a knife similar to one Echols had owned was found near Baldwin's residence; sticks similar to the ones both had been seen carrying previously were found at the scene; two different types of knots were used to tie the victims; there were three victims, and there was sufficient evidence from which a jury could have concluded that the murders were not committed by one person. We have said that if there is some evidence to support an instruction, it is appropriate for a trial court to give it. Mitchell v. State, 306 Ark. 464, 862 S.W.2d 254 (1993)." http://web.archive.org/web/20000824033616/http://courts.state.ar.us/opinions/1996a/961223sc/cr94-928.html

127 Many of the men's supporters have questioned why the state opposed new forensic tests if the state did not have to pay for them. The answer touches a sensitive area of law. Prosecutors, including attorneys general, who are the top prosecutors in a state, properly consider it their duty to represent the state's interests, much as private attorneys represent people who hire them. That duty blurs, however, when one asks, "in situations like this, what are the interests of the state?" The American Bar Association has established what it calls "standards" for

prosecuting attorneys. One of those standards states, "The prosecutor is an administrator of justice, an advocate, and an officer of the court." That is a widely held view of the job, though many states, like Arkansas, have not adopted the ABA standards. A more problematic standard is one that says that, as an officer of the court, it is a prosecutor's "duty to seek justice, not merely to convict." In the West Memphis case, like many others, Arkansas's attorneys general have seen their role as advocates for the state, bound to uphold the state's convictions, more than as officers of the court with a "duty to seek justice." Thus, the attorney general opposed any testing that might produce evidence that could erode those convictions. In part, because of this case, this limited stance is encountering increasing public resistance, particularly in light of another ABA standard which maintains, "It is an important function of the prosecutor to seek to reform and improve the administration of criminal justice. When inadequacies or injustices in the substantive or procedural law come to the prosecutor's attention, he or she should stimulate efforts for remedial action." Some groups believe that is not happening. For example, the Center for Prosecutor Integrity, http://www.prosecutorintegrity.org, was formed to combat ethical complaints against prosecutors, including what Chief Judge Alex Kozinski of the U.S. 9th Circuit Court of Appeals called an "epidemic" of prosecutor misconduct.

128 The Arkansas State Crime Laboratory's record of Fogleman's call: http://callahan.8k.com/pdf/bm_rule37_pet/bm_rule37_pet_exh77.pdf

129 By the time the memo was written, the crime lab had examined the knife that John Mark Byers had given to a member of the HBO film crew. Had he been asked, Peretti presumably could have said that the weapon in question referred to that knife. The most troubling issue concerning the reference to a "transparency" was that no report of it was provided to the defense, thus precluding them from questioning what "weapon" was at issue.

130 Caryn Coleman and her husband, Sean Bonner, hosted the exhibit, titled "Cruel and Unusual: An Exhibition to Benefit the West Memphis Three," at their gallery, sixspace. Coleman said later that the event raised more than twenty thousand dollars.

131 The student bar association at the University of Arkansas's Bowen School of Law in Little Rock had first invited me to speak about *Devil's Knot*. I explained why people around the country—and, by then, around the world—had begun questioning the verdicts in the case. If the evidence was strong enough to sentence a person to death and two others to life in prison, I asked, shouldn't it have been apparent to the filmmakers who attended and recorded both trials and to me in researching my book? What were we to make of the apparent disconnect between ordinary people who could not make sense of the case and the state's Supreme Court's position that both trials were without error? I suggested that, if I had indeed missed key details or misrepresented facts in my book, critics by then had had two years since its publication to refute them, but no such criticisms had arisen—at least not publicly. After that appearance, the school invited Fogleman to speak.

132 Unfortunately, this inaccuracy also made it into the film of *Devil's Knot*. But I was not the only person confused about what oral exams were given—or not given—to Jason on the night of his arrest. In 2013, Jason told me that, while it is true that no x-rays were taken, he'd believed going into his trial—and for several years thereafter—that "an impression" had been taken of his teeth while he was at Crittenden County Hospital. "They gave me something like a wafer and told me to bite down on it," he said. In hindsight, particularly after dental impressions of all three prisoners were made following claims that wounds on the face of Stevie Branch appeared to be human bite marks, Jason reflected that the material put in his mouth on the night of his arrest may have been intended not for a dental impression but to absorb saliva.

133 In a letter dated April 6, 2007, Fogleman responded to a letter from a man in California who asked for his views on the case. That correspondent later sent me a copy of Fogleman's letter, which I posted on my website in 2012. http://maraleveritt. com/2012/04/2007-fogleman-letter-panned-devils-knot/

134 "The Architect and the Inmate," *Arkansas Times*, Jan. 9, 2004. http://www.arktimes.com/arkansas/the-damien-i-know- the-architect-and-the-inmate/Content?oid=964930. In that piece, as in most of what I wrote about the case by this time, I acknowledged my personal involvement with many of its participants. I'd befriended Lorri and grown fond of Jason. I admired the supporters, especially in Arkansas, who had the courage to speak out on behalf of men who were mostly reviled. Like the HBO filmmakers, who, when asked, made their film of the trials available to the defense teams. I also provided some of my records upon request to attorneys representing Damien. During the two years after *Devil's Knot* came out, I announced that, while I would continue to report on the case, I was now personally involved and would publicly advocate for new trials.

135 Order for DNA Testing, http://callahan.8k.com/wm3/ motions/de_jb_order_dna_testing.html.

136 The book's title referred to part of a grimoire, or textbook of magic, that was believed to have been written during the Italian Renaissance. Editors Brett Alexander Savory and M.W. Anderson explained, "The Seventh and last Pentacle of the Sun from the Key of Solomon is for freeing those unjustly imprisoned: 'If any be by chance imprisoned or detained in fetters of iron, at the presence of this Pentacle, which should be engraved in gold on the day and hour of the sun, he will be immediately delivered and set at liberty.'" My contribution was a piece intended to challenge writers Dean Koontz, Ann Rice, and Stephen King about why not one of them had commented on the real-life horror story of Damien and Jason's trial, in which prosecutors had exploited the fact that Damien read their books. I had been

impressed by the response of musicians, who'd opposed the prosecutors' persecutions built partly on two of the defendants' tastes in music. At a fairly desperate time in the men's incarceration, I wished that at least one of these three famous authors would use his or her celebrity to press for a closer look. It never happened.

137 "Complete fabrication" by Tim Hackler, *Arkansas Times*, Oct. 7, 2004. http://www.arktimes.com/arkansas/complete-fabrication/Content?oid=1886107

138 "'They messed with my words'" ibid. http://www.arktimes.com/arkansas/they-messed-with-my-words/Content?oid=964537 In the article, Hackler reported on the incident before the arrests, when Hutcheson decided to "play detective" by inviting Damien to her house. Police obtained her permission for them to install a listening device under her bed, with the microphone attached to a lamp in the living room. She described the device as "a fancy one with several reels of tape, so that one would begin when the other was filled." Hutcheson said she turned the recorder on when Damien showed up a few days later, that she told him she wanted to become a witch, and that he'd laughed at that. She said she'd heard that he liked to suck blood. According to the article, "Damien said he encouraged such stories as a 'mechanism' to keep people from prying into his life. 'What's a mechanism?' she'd asked. She says Damien replied, 'It means leave me the fuck alone.'" Hackler also interviewed Hutcheson's son Aaron, who was now eighteen, but who'd been eight at the time of the murders. He also repudiated statements he'd made to police. Aaron told Hackler that police "tricked" him and led him to say things that were not true. Aaron's voice had been heard only at Jessie's trial—and then, only on a tape-recording that Gitchell played that allowed jurors to hear the boy saying, "Nobody knows what happened but me." (Fogleman later told me he had not called the child himself to testify because he was not "comfortable" with the roles Vicki and Aaron

had played in the investigation. Nevertheless, interviews police conducted with Aaron helped shape both their investigation and the prosecutors' claim that the slayings had arisen from the occult.

139 The hiring of Riordan and Horgan represents another of the many points where media impacted this saga. After publication of *Devil's Knot*, the USA network optioned it and hired Anna Hamilton Phelan, who'd written the Oscar-nominated script for Gorillas in the Mist, to write a screenplay for the book. I later sued the network in federal court over a payment issue. That dispute was settled out of court, and the project was dropped. But while Phelan was working on the screenplay, I had introduced her to Lorri Davis, and Phelan, in turn, had referred Davis to her friend, Dennis Riordan.

140 Kent Arnold, the jury foreman, has disputed the general accuracy of this claim. https://web.archive.org/web/20050505030756/http://www.kark.com/news/default.asp?mode=shownews&id=4434

141 Petitioner's Motion to Recall the Mandate and to Reinvest Jurisdiction in the Trial Court to Consider Petition for Writ of Error *Coram Nobis* or for Other Extraordinary Relief, filed with the Arkansas Supreme Court. http://callahan.8k.com/wm3/motion_to_recall_mandate.html

142 Blackstone, William. *Commentaries on the Laws of England: A Facsimile of the First Edition of 1765—1769*. Chicago: University of Chicago Press, 1979. http://press-pubs.uchicago.edu/founders/documents/a1_9_2s4.html

143 Petition for a Writ of *Habeas Corpus* by a Person in State Custody, filed in U.S. District Court, http://callahan.8k.com/pdf/echols_usdc/Habeas_Petition_Echols.pdf

144 Motion to Dismiss Petition for Writ of *Habeas Corpus* for Non-Exhaustion, Mar. 2, 2005. http://callahan.8k.com/pdf/echols_usdc/Motion_to_Dismiss_Echols.pdf

145 Less than a month before Beebe filed his argument in federal court, Damien, Jason and Jessie each signed documents

giving up their right to have crucial evidence in their cases preserved. The waiver was ironic, considering how hard the men's lawyers had worked to assure that the evidence was preserved. But now it was necessary, because the tests that they wanted conducted might destroy some of that evidence. (State officials had been required to sign similar waivers, which explained part of their hesitation during negotiations.) The men's decisions were not made lightly. At the time of their trials, in 1994, most of the technologies that were about to be used did not exist. What if using the current technologies produced nothing of value and, at the same time, destroyed the irreplaceable evidence, putting it out of reach of any science that might be developed in the future that might be able to probe it more deeply? It was a risk the men felt had to be taken. Each signed a document that acknowledged that he had been informed by his lawyers that, should the proposed testing go forward, "it is likely that a number of hairs which were obtained as part of the investigation of my case will be completely destroyed . . . and that there are no similar hairs that could be used for further testing" if the results were unsatisfactory. Each agreed that, with this waiver, he was "freely, knowingly, and voluntarily" consenting to the use of "destructive DNA testing. "Petitioner Jason Baldwin's Acknowledgment of information on Destructive DNA Testing Waiver of Statutory Rights to Retain Specific Biological Evidence for Retesting," filed Feb. 8, 2005. http://callahan.8k.com/wm3/motions/img/jb_waiver.html. Damien Echols's petition, filed the same date, http://callahan.8k.com/wm3/motions/de_waiver.html;

146 By the time of Wilson's ruling, Riordan and Horgan had been working on Damien's case for more than a year. During that time, they'd had to get up to speed on eleven years of prior events and work to prevent the erosion of Damien's legal position, especially by preserving his right to seek federal *habeas corpus* relief. Had they not acted

when they did, provisions of the federal "Anti-Terrorism and Effective Death Penalty Act" might have made a federal appeal impossible for having been filed too late. That law, which had a tremendous—and many say detrimental— effect on the ability of federal judges to grant *habeas corpus* petitions was enacted by Congress and signed into law by President Bill Clinton in 1996, in response to the bombings of the World Trade Center in 1993 and the federal building in Oklahoma City two years later.

147 "Miscellaneous Essays and Interviews" by David Jauss. http://www.davidjauss.com/miscellaneous_essays_and_ interviews_51285.htm

148 Burk Sauls, a co-founder of WM3.org, wrote in the book's preface, "The state of Arkansas wants very badly to execute Damien, but even a cursory look at his case tells the rational among us that he, along with Jason Baldwin and Jessie Misskelley, are innocent of the crime they've been locked up for. The three of them have come to be known as the West Memphis Three, and their cause has been embraced by people all over the world who see it for what it is—an example of how ordinary people can become victims of a system that is supposed to protect and serve us."

149 "Murder case draws musicians to cause," by Stephen Koch and Max Brantley, *Arkansas Times* Arkansas Blog, July 21, 2005

150 "West Memphis Free: Global event for convicted metalheads," by Mike Miliard, *Boston Phoenix*, July 22, 2005 http://www. bostonphoenix.com/boston/news_features/this_just_in/ documents/04838477.asp

151 *I No Longer Face the Storm Alone*, 21/31 Productions, 2005. http://www.2131-productions.com/publicitypress/

152 The 1980 movie *Brubaker* was based on these incidents. *The Encyclopedia of Arkansas History and Culture*: http://www. encyclopediaofarkansas.net/encyclopedia/entry-detail. aspx?search=1&entryID=4923

153 In Arkansas and some other states, all appeals return to the original judge. This means that appellants must attempt to get

a trial judge to find error in a trial where he or she officiated. Success is rare.

154 *Major Payne*, starring Daymon Wayans, Universal Pictures, 1995.

155 From an email to Lorri Davis dated Feb. 27, 2006, which Davis forwarded to me two days later. Philipsborn also wrote, "In closing, let me clarify something that I have communicated with you about, Lorri, but which our supporters may not have yet had explained to them. As was the case when I was the one making decisions on all of these matters, when only Pearl Jam, Henry Rollins, and private donation monies were available, one has to be very careful about thinking of Damien, Jessie and Jason as one entity—and as a group who will all rise and fall together. The harsh reality is that this may not be the case. That is why there is a legal requirement that each defendant in a serious case has her/his own lawyer. At this point, it seems that the most logical approach is to be fully cooperative—but we do so in the knowledge that any number of scenarios could actually have occurred here. Each of the legal teams has to concentrate on one client, but the effort, at this point, can logically be joined, and joint. However, in some areas, it cannot be—and that has led, and will continue to lead, to extra expenses. Not all matters can be investigated by one firm." In the months and years ahead, the issue of money would become an increasingly sore spot between Philipsborn and Davis.

156 Dr. Martin Hill, email interview, Jan. 21, 2011.

157 Lanette Grate, an instructor at the University of Central Arkansas, organized the event.

158 The knives were delivered to Stidham after *Devil's Knot* was published and optioned for film.

159 "Dimension ties *Knot*, *Variety.com*, May 7, 2006.

160 In addition, a question has been raised as to why Lax never obtained records of Damien's phone calls from the night of the murders—records that purportedly could have corroborated his claim that he'd been talking with girls in

Memphis. Lax recalled that one of his investigators had attempted to get those records but was told that they were not available because, though West Memphis and Memphis were located in different states, calls between the two cities were not billed as "long distance," so calls, times, numbers and duration were not documented.

161 Investigator Sandra C. Siligato found that Hobbs had had several encounters with Tennessee police and courts in the years after the murders. The most serious occurred on Nov. 11, 1994, eight months after the trials, when Hobbs shot Pam's brother-in-law in the abdomen during a fight. Jackie Hicks, Jr., was admitted to a Memphis hospital in critical condition. Terry Hobbs was charged with simple assault and given a six-month, suspended sentence (Jan. 12, 1995. Shelby County Criminal Court, charge of aggravated assault, Indictment Number 95-07669). On Feb. 20, 1996, the charge was amended to simple assault and he received six months in jail, all time suspended, and was placed on eleven to twenty-nine months of probation. While that incident was widely reported, future police run-ins were not. According to another complaint, Pam Hobbs called police to the couple's house, in August 2003, claiming that "she was afraid to go home alone because she had recently reported her husband to DHS [Department of Human Services] for physical and sexual abuse of their fourteen-year-old daughter." When officers entered the house they found "a plastic bag of marijuana under the mattress in the defendant's bedroom which the daughter, Amanda Hobbs, pointed out to the police." Police arrested Hobbs again. Three months later, he was found guilty of possession of a controlled substance and fined three hundred and fifty dollars. (Shelby County General Sessions Criminal Court, Booking No. 0312345). At that time, Amanda was fifteen, her half-brother Stevie was dead, and her family was coming apart. When Pam and Terry divorced in 2004, Terry was living in Memphis, Tennessee, and Pam in Blytheville, Arkansas. At Amanda's request, the court awarded

custody of Amanda to her father. But within months, Terry Hobbs called police to report that Amanda had run away at around one o'clock in the morning. Police noted that Hobbs "stated the victim (Amanda) had been having a hard time emotionally, so they were up until midnight talking, at which time, she took a shower and he went to bed. Complainant thinks victim then left out of her bedroom window." The incident report said that Terry Hobbs wanted Amanda "transported to juvenile court if found," (Memphis Police Department/Shelby County Sheriff's Department – Central Records, Incident Report No. 0412000361ME). A few weeks later, on Christmas Eve, Hobbs reported that Amanda had run away again. This time he told officers that he had given Amanda one hundred dollars to go Christmas shopping and that, after she'd left the house, she'd called him to say she was not coming home (Ibid. Incident Report No. 0412010222ME).

162 Personal correspondence.

163 "The Court of Public Opinion: Examining Pretrial Coverage of the West Memphis Three," A Donaghey Scholars Final Project, Dec. 12, 2006.

164 Some opponents of the War on Drugs, including me, see prisons as the best illustration of how doomed that effort is. If prisons, where inmates are guarded and monitored and where everyone entering is searched, cannot eliminate illegal drugs—or weapons, for that matter—what hope does such an initiative have in an environment that's supposed to be free?

165 A howl went up among some supporters when I reported Jason's arrest and detention. Some wrote that I was being disloyal to the men's claim of innocence, or even intent on harming Jason.

166 Hobbs offered an account of his actions on the night Stevie and his friends disappeared, starting between three and four P.M., when he believed he arrived home from his job at the Memphis Ice Cream Company, where he was a route deliveryman. He described dropping Pam off at work at 4:30 and then beginning to look for Stevie, who was supposed

to have been home by then. According to the report, Hobbs said he searched that evening with his friend and co-worker David Jacoby, as well as with Pam's father, Jackie Hicks, Sr. "He stated that they did search in the Robin Hood Hills area, and this was the first time he had heard of Robin Hood Hills. When people told him that he needed to search in Robin Hood Hills, Terry did not even know where or what that was. "He specifically recalled that they walked from behind the Blue Beacon [truck wash] through a trail and then at some point, he had walked down the trail towards where the boys were found, but not all the way to the ditch. He stated that after he began walking down this trail, the 'hairs on my arms stood up,' so he immediately turned around and walked back to where David and Jackie were. He told David and Jackie, 'There's somethin' down there,' but none of them proceeded to walk back down the trail." After discovery of the bodies the next day, Hobbs said neither he nor Pam was informed about how the victims were killed. All they knew was that Stevie had been hit in the face, he said, "because they could see that at the funeral." Geiser's report continued, "Terry talked about seventy items of evidence that were sealed' and wondered what the state was waiting for to introduce this evidence. We have no knowledge of this and told Terry that we did not." Terry mentioned to the investigators, however, that he had "recently had lunch with Gitchell" in Memphis. Geiser wrote, "It is Terry's opinion that the crime occurred late in the afternoon or early in the evening. He said he felt it was much earlier than the state tried to prove, but he could not explain the various 'sightings' of the three boys up until 6:30 P.M."

167 "Charlie Frago, "Prison officials confirm staff firings, demotion," *Arkansas Democrat-Gazette*, April 3, 2007.

168 I was one of that event's organizers, and I spoke at it. "Our message to the courts is that we wanted justice when the children were murdered, not scapegoats," I said. "To the extent that the West Memphis Three have been wronged, we have all been wronged. We want justice, and you have not

delivered it. Mistakes, as they say, have been made." In a spirit of acknowledgement, I admitted mistakes I'd made in *Devil's Knot*, including mistakes regarding the heritage of prosecutor John Fogleman, whose office was around the corner from where we all stood. I said I did not think admitting those mistakes weakened my book, rather that I believed the book's integrity was strengthened by their acknowledgement. "That is all we ask today of this state's justice officials," I said, "from this courthouse and judicial district to the offices of the state Supreme Court. Act responsibly and review what was done in this case . . . We know that attorneys for the convicted men are meeting with court officials, seeking a re-examination of this case. We stand outside the court, demanding the same thing." KAIT, a Jonesboro television station that covered the event, led its report with the voice of Kelly Duda, a Little Rock documentary filmmaker, telling the crowd, "Now, when people all over the world hear the words 'West Memphis,' they think of the murders of three little boys and the wrongful convictions of three other boys." Two days later, organizer Amanda Lamb wrote to participants, "Standing for justice is something many of us try to do every day. It is not, however, a daily occurrence that we have such an opportunity to publicly stand in solidarity with so many stouthearted individuals, and visibly demonstrate our devotion to this single concept. Dr. Martin Luther King defined justice as 'love correcting everything that stands against love.' Although the West Memphis Three case is the epitome of horrible injustice, it has encouraged positive action by human beings towards other human beings. Above all other definitions, I do believe that justice IS a work of love."

169 Hobb's first wife, Angela Castleberry, lived in Arkansas. According to Geiser's report, Castleberry had met Hobbs when she was fifteen years old and both of their fathers were Pentecostal ministers. She knew him for about four years before they were married in the late 1970s. When she became pregnant, Castleberry said, Hobbs stopped going

to church and began having affairs, drinking alcohol and smoking marijuana. He also began beating her, mostly slapping, sometimes punching. After their son Bryan was born, Castleberry said, Hobbs began partying with college-aged adults. She said she found marijuana and various pills underneath the seat of their car. During this time, Geiser reported, Hobbs was still physically abusing his wife "and on one occasion he beat her and strangled her, causing her to lose consciousness. When she awoke, Bryan, who was not even two years old, was over her, crying and trying to wake her. She noticed that she was extremely bloody, so cleaned herself up, and she and Bryan left the apartment." Castleberry then filed for divorce and was granted custody of Bryan, but she said that Hobbs often failed to pay child support. "It was interesting," Geiser wrote, "because Angela would sometimes make statements such as 'he beat me,' and 'he did not take care of our son,' but then would later state that he was a good father." Elsewhere in the report, Geiser noted Castleberry's remarks that, as an adult, her son Bryan had become "very controlling, like Terry"; that, "she had heard that Terry had also abused Pam"; and that "there is no way that Terry could ever harm a child." Also Castleberry mentioned that, while they were married, Hobbs had broken into a woman's house and assaulted her and that Castleberry believed he'd done this "because this woman had tried to help Angela during a previous altercation between Angela and Terry." Geiser found the 1982 arrest report from the police department in Hot Springs, Arkansas. It stated, "Subject admitted entering the complainant's residence and putting his arms around her as she came out of the shower. Subject was issued misdemeanor citation." The report indicated that the case was dismissed as Hobbs had agreed to counseling. Geiser then interviewed Mildred French, the woman who had filed the complaint. French reported that she had caught Hobbs "on several occasions looking in through her windows and additionally had caught him looking in the windows of another neighbor, a young female who was a nurse. On the day of the assault, French stated "that she had come home and specifically recalled locking her front door as she was already fearful of Terry, since he had been peeking in her windows. She had gone upstairs to take a shower and when she came out of the shower, Terry was in her bathroom and grabbed her from behind with his hands on her breasts. She immediately screamed, at which time Terry stated to her, 'Shhh, one of your cats got out and is on the street and is dead.' Mildred yelled at Terry to get out of her house, at which time he immediately ran down the stairs, out her door and into his house next door." The report continued: "Mildred, of course, described Terry as a 'pervert.' She also stated that prior to this she had heard approximately three substantial arguments go on in the Hobbs household. In these arguments Terry was always yelling at and slapping Angela. In one of the arguments, she heard Terry yelling and slapping Angela and also heard the baby crying. The baby abruptly stopped crying, which concerned Mildred, so she went next door to make sure the baby was okay. Angela eventually answered the door and told Mildred that everything was fine, but this seemed to aggravate Terry. She believed he had come into her house on this date because she had earlier intervened on behalf of Angela and the baby."

170 A transcription of the entire interview can be found at: http://callahan.8k.com/pdf/pam_hobbs_interview.pdf.

171 As the interview was ending, Mitchell asked Hobbs if there was anything he could add that might help police "follow up on this investigation." Hobbs answered that he wasn't sure it meant anything, but that he'd seen a picture of Damien Echols sitting on his couch at his house with Chris and Mike and Stevie. He asked the lieutenant, "Have you seen that?" Mitchell said he had not and asked Hobbs where he'd seen that picture. Terry said he thought Gary Gitchell had it, though he added that he didn't know how Damien "got with our couch and that picture got done." A bit later,

Hobbs told the officer that he and Pam had sold their rights for "a Hollywood movie." When Mitchell asked, "You said they bought your rights?" Hobbs said, "I think I made a big mistake." A transcript of the entire interview can be found at: http://callahan.8k.com/pdf/t_hobbs_interview.pdf.

172 "Death Penalty Debate : How to Treat Youngsters Who Murder," by Barry Siegel, *Los Angeles Times*, Nov. 3, 1985. http://articles.latimes.com/1985-11-03/news/mn-3894_1_ death-penalty-debate.

Made in the USA
Charleston, SC
06 March 2015